Organizations and Activism

Series Editors: **Daniel King**, Nottingham Trent University and **Martin Parker**, University of Bristol

Organizations and Activism publishes books that explore how politics happens within and because of organizations, how activism is organized, and how activists change organizations.

Forthcoming in the series:

Organizing Food, Faith and Freedom:
Imagining Alternatives
By **Ozan Alakavuklar**

Out now in the series:

Food Politics, Activism and Alternative Consumer Cooperatives
By **Beyza Oba** and **Zeynep Özsoy**

Co-operation and Co-operatives in 21st Century Europe
Edited by **Julian Manley, Anthony Webster and Olga Kuznetsova**

Reimagining Academic Activism:
Learning from Feminist Anti-Violence Activists
By **Ruth Weatherall**

Anarchist Cybernetics:
Control and Communication in Radical Politics
By **Thomas Swann**

Guerrilla Democracy:
Mobile Power and Revolution in the 21st Century
By **Peter Bloom, Owain Smolović Jones** and **Jamie Woodcock**

Find out more at

bristoluniversitypress.co.uk/organizations–and–activism

Organizations and Activism

Series Editors: **Daniel King**, Nottingham Trent University and **Martin Parker**, University of Bristol

Find out more at
bristoluniversitypress.co.uk/organizations-and-activism

ORGANISING FOR CHANGE

Social Change Makers and Social Change Organisations

Silke Roth and Clare Saunders

BRISTOL
UNIVERSITY
PRESS

First published in Great Britain in 2024 by

Bristol University Press
University of Bristol
1–9 Old Park Hill
Bristol
BS2 8BB
UK
t: +44 (0)117 374 6645
e: bup-info@bristol.ac.uk

Details of international sales and distribution partners are available at bristoluniversitypress.co.uk

British Library Cataloguing in Publication Data
A catalogue record for this book is available from the British Library

ISBN 978-1-5292-3600-2 hardcover
ISBN 978-1-5292-3602-6 ePub
ISBN 978-1-5292-3603-3 ePdf

Cover design: blu inc
Front cover image: Silke Roth
Bristol University Press use environmentally responsible print partners.
Printed and bound in Great Britain by CPI Group (UK) Ltd, Croydon, CR0 4YY

FSC
www.fsc.org
MIX
Paper | Supporting
responsible forestry
FSC® C013604

To the social change makers who are
fighting for progressive change, and to our
students and teachers

Contents

Series Editors' Preface

Daniel King and Martin Parker

Organising is politics made durable. From co-operatives to corporations, Occupy to Meta, states and non-governmental organisations (NGOs), organisations shape our lives. They shape the possible futures of governance, policy making and social change, and hence are central to understanding how human beings can deal with the challenges that face us, whether that be pandemics, populism or climate change. This book series publishes work that explores how politics happens within and because of organisations and organising. We want to explore how activism is organised and how activists change organisations. We are also interested in the forms of resistance to activism, in the ways that powerful interests contest and reframe demands for change. These are questions of huge relevance to scholars in sociology, politics, geography, management and beyond, and are becoming ever more important as demands for impact and engagement change the way that academics imagine their work. They are also important to anyone who wants to understand more about the theory and practice of organising, not just the abstracted ideologies of capitalism taught in business schools.

Our books offer critical examinations of organisations as sites of or targets for activism; and we will also assume that our authors, and hopefully our readers, are themselves agents of change. Titles may focus on specific industries or fields, or they may be arranged around particular themes or challenges. Our topics might include the alternative economy; surveillance, whistleblowing and human rights; digital politics; religious groups; social movements; NGOs; feminism and anarchist organisation; action research and co-production; activism and the neo-liberal university, and any other subjects that are relevant and topical.

'Organisations and Activism' is also a multidisciplinary series. Contributions from all and any relevant academic fields will be welcomed. The series is international in outlook, and proposals from outside the English-speaking global north are particularly welcome.

This book, the fourth in our series so far, speaks directly to a concern with how 'social change organisations' and 'social change makers' can incubate and solidify new forms of social relations. The authors generously define social change organisations as a 'broad range of organisations that work to bring about or resist social change through any combination of service provision, advocacy and protest.' They also suggest that 'social change makers' cover a wide variety of roles, and include many people who would not necessarily define themselves as activists. Silke Roth and Clare Saunders want us to see 'activism' as only one element of social change, in part because it is a word that tends to dramatise moments of protest rather than focussing on the patient and time-consuming process of building networks and institutions. Change happens not only because of visible demonstrations and actions but also behind the scenes in people's daily lives, and through the workings of a ramified network of people, groups and organisations.

Adopting a broad conception of social change that includes political, cultural, economic and cultural transformations, the authors insist that we should not assume to know what 'small' or 'large' effects are produced by particular forms of organising. In other words, a noisy street protest could be spectacular but not lead to discernible long-term effects, but an invisible consciousness raising group could impact on the trajectories of many lives. This multi-layered social interactionism informs an approach that stresses the historically situated relations between people and organisations, not assuming that larger organisations are more important than small ones or that organisations that provide services (in a rape crisis centre for example) are somehow not part of a struggle for social change. (On this in particular, see Ruth Weatherall's book in this series.)

The historical and sociological perspective that this book provides allows us a different way of understanding the relation between 'reformist' and 'radical' strategies. Condemnations of the former tend to be associated with accusations of co-optation, of being captured by the state or market, but Roth and Saunders show that understanding social change means moving beyond such simplistic dichotomies. Vanguardist projects always grow from, and produce, networks of people and organisations that embed social changes in durable ways. When Erik Olin Wright wrote about the differences between 'ruptural', 'interstital' and 'symbiotic' strategies for social change he could be understood as dramatising the differences between revolution, prefiguration and entryism. This book suggests that all of these moments matter, perhaps simultaneously, and maybe that they are not really 'choices' at all.

The authors want their readers to understand that their argument is practically important too because it can encourage those involved in such struggles to build coalitions, rather than finding differences which produce factionalism. This is also important in terms of identities, recognising that people move between organisations and different forms of activism, and it is hence important not to fetishise one particular form as being 'purer' than others. Theirs is an inclusive approach, one that celebrates all elements of a struggle towards a different future, whether that be working in a co-op or engaging in the formal political process. Roth and Saunders have written a realistic yet optimistic book that should encourage all its readers to engage with social change organisations in whatever way they can. As they say, 'activism is hard to do, but rewarding in unexpected ways', and this should 'help people to gain a sense of political efficacy by reducing feelings of helplessness'. Being part of a struggle, in whatever way you can, is itself a form of affirmation which can itself produce quiet collective activism.

We hope you enjoy this book. If you want to discuss a proposal yourself, then email the series editors. We look forward to hearing from you.

List of Figures and Tables

Figures

Tables

Acknowledgements

We wrote this book during the COVID-19 pandemic, alongside our other responsibilities and with the help of modern technologies. In fact, except for a three-day writing retreat spent in Silke's house and Clare's parents' kitchen, we worked remotely on this joint project using various platforms and technologies. Aside from technology, friendship and humour were great resources. We thank Paul Stevens, Ellen Pearce and their colleagues at Bristol University Press and the series editors Daniel King and Martin Parker for their enthusiasm, good communication and support. Many thanks to the anonymous reviewers for their perceptive suggestions. We also benefited from useful comments when we presented the ideas that underpin this manuscript at the 'Activists and Activism' session of the American Sociological Association, in 2021, and at the Voluntary Sector and Research Conference panel on 'Advances in Theory and Methods', in 2022. When finalising this manuscript Silke had a research semester. She thanks her colleagues at the University of Southampton for giving her the space to complete this project. Since May 2021, Clare has worked on the manuscript alongside her Head of Humanities and Social Sciences, Cornwall Department duties, and gives thanks to Alexa Skilton for helping her organise her diary to carve out space to work on this project.

We give special thanks to all of our research participants across the decades, as well as to the broader population of social change makers who are working on social change projects. You have contributed to social change in multiple ways that we hope our work gives you credit for. We also thank our students for asking perceptive questions.

Silke thanks her friends and her mother, Liese Roth, for their love, support, and nourishing conversations. Clare would like to give special thanks to her husband, Matty, for being a loving partner and patient source of support. She would also like to thank her late friend, Ian (also known as 'Spud'), who sadly passed away as we were finalising this book. The inspiration from his music will live on in the memories held by his family, friends, and audiences. We thank Sophia Unger for her hard work on the copy-editing of the manuscript and the index. We are grateful to Alexandra Gregory for assisting with the cover design.

Introduction

The first two decades of the 21st century have been shaped by multiple intersecting financial, health, and environmental crises, and rapid social change. The financial crisis of 2008 generated economic and fiscal consequences that resulted in unemployment and austerity measures. The COVID-19 pandemic, which began at the end of 2019, reshaped our societies dramatically and revealed the challenges of dealing with a pandemic within national health systems already under strain. The ongoing environmental and climate crises threaten the homes and livelihoods of many, particularly in the Global South, but also in the Global North, and have huge ramifications on how societies across the world organise their economies and citizens live their lives. These crises have intensified global economic, racial, and gender inequalities and thus must be analysed from an intersectional perspective (Crenshaw, 1991). Together, these intersecting crises have resulted in a wide range of mobilisations, from large-scale protests on the streets to self-help and DIY (do it yourself) mobilisations, which are less visible. This book is about the organisations and people that are responding to crises and seeking to bring about as well as resist social change. We call these organisations *social change organisations* (SCOs) and the people engaged in them *social change makers* (SCMs).

We argue that focusing on SCOs and SCMs in a historical perspective contributes to the development of a theory of social change that takes into account structure and agency. SCOs and SCMs are constrained by the contexts in which they are active, but at the same time they are contributing to the transformation of these contexts – more often incrementally than rapidly. Our approach goes beyond models of social change that focus on the dynamics between incumbents and challengers (McAdam et al, 2001; Fligstein and McAdam, 2012). We argue that it is important to broaden the perspective on efforts to bring about change beyond contentious politics (various forms of violent or non-violent protest) by paying more attention to insider activism and prefigurative politics. *Insider activism* refers to social change making that seeks to pressure institutions to change (or resist change) in more formal contexts than contentious politics (Pettinicchio, 2012). *Outsider activism* does not only comprise protest and other forms of contentious politics but also prefigurative politics or the creation of alternative institutions and forms of decision-making (Yates, 2015). We use the term *prefigurative politics* to refer to forms of social change making that provide self-help, community help, or services for others. This might be a direct response to institutional change or a response to the need for action due to a lack of institutional change and support. As we will demonstrate throughout our book, our approach goes beyond established perspectives on social change making, and allows us to more fruitfully examine 'awkward movements' (Polletta, 2006). Such movements are 'uncomfortably close to something else that is not a movement' but may be self-help groups interest groups or denominational groups (Polletta, 2006: 475). We agree with Polletta (2006) that conceptual boundaries between different types of organisations reflect the development and idiosyncrasies of subfields, rather than the phenomena themselves. We are introducing a new research direction on studying organisations that are seeking to bring about or prevent social change, and we are thus addressing calls for a more inclusive concept than social movement organisations (SMOs) (Walker and Martin, 2018).

As scholars of social movements, NGOs, and not-for-profit organisations[1] we are aware – not withstanding some important exceptions – that scholarship on social movements still tends to pay more attention to protest (a form of contentious action) than other important forms of social change making that take place in community spaces, NGOs, and institutions. We also note that scholarship focusing on NGOs and other not-for-profit organisations rarely makes use of concepts developed for the analysis of organisations and campaigns involved in protest and contentious action, despite similarities in the goals and organisational practices of the units studied. Organisations providing services for, receiving funding from, and cooperating with, governments and other institutions are (sometimes too) easily accused of co-optation, elite capture, and NGOisation, that is processes of professionalisation and bureaucratisation, which we will discuss in more detail later. Scholars have, hitherto, missed an opportunity to interweave the very effective and useful conceptual toolboxes developed by the respective fields of research.

Organising for Change looks beyond narrowly conceived strategies and concepts and instead encourages scholars and activists working on and within varieties of SCO to engage in fruitful dialogue. Throughout the book, we demonstrate the contributions that a range of strategically differentiated, but sometimes overlapping SCOs can make *to social change* and *to each other* in synergy through sets of interactions and reactions. Thus, we highlight that efforts to bring about social change are not necessarily contentious; they might be collaborative or cooperative. To do so, we draw on and constructively interweave different and unconnected bodies of scholarship that so far tend to ignore each other. We argue that social change is brought about by these SCOs and the individual SCMs involved in them.

In this introduction, we introduce our key concepts, give an overview of the core ideas of our book, and explain why they matter. We briefly introduce our data and methods, and provide a synopsis of each chapter of our book. We end our introduction with a statement on our positionalities and how they have shaped our work. First, let us illustrate the importance of looking beyond protest, and of examining *social change organisations* acting in synergy in sets of actions and reactions, by starting with an outline of social change in the area of gender equality.

Beyond protest to actions and interactions

Efforts to promote women's rights and gender equality illustrate our approach well. They show that protest is only one way to bring about change and that SCOs and SCMs often employ different strategies and tactics simultaneously or successively. Although we are primarily examining SCMs who work in or for SCOs, we also use the term SCMs to refer to people who pursue social change outside of SCOs but in relation to their causes. As we discuss later, some SCMs pursue the 'march through the institutions' (Schelsky, 1974) and change mainstream organisations from within. They may also have conflicting values that contribute to contentious chains of interactions and reactions. It is important, therefore, to first note that speaking about SCOs that pursue 'women's' interests raises many questions. To begin, we might ask what SCOs and SCMs mean by 'women' given contention over whether the term is a way to categorise by sex at birth or by gender as a social construction. There is enormous diversity of women's experiences, positionalities, and interests reflected in whether they are cis-, trans or gender fluid[2], and according to their nationality, class, race, ethnicity, sexuality, and other markers of inequality. Famously, Sojourner Truth[3] asked 'Ain't I a Woman?' challenging notions of femininity, as well as demonstrating that the US suffrage movement excluded African American women from its demands. Second, we need to stress that neither are all feminists women, nor are all women feminists – in other words, some men might be feminists while some women might not be. Third, it is important to keep in mind that gender equality does not only concern women but also men and those who do not identify with binary gender categories. Acknowledging the complexity of and contradictions between gender equality, women's, and feminist interests has consequences for the conceptualisation of SCOs promoting 'women's interests' – they might be feminist or not and they might be (trans)-inclusive or not. In addition, men might benefit from some feminist demands securing their own rights (for example, paternity leave). Thus, throughout the book, depending on the context and what is most appropriate we refer to 'women's SCOs', 'feminist SCOs', or 'gender equality SCOs'.

Having established the difficulty of talking about 'women's interests' it is quite obvious to us that, despite significant progress towards gender equality in many countries, it is impossible to present the achievement of SCMs and SCOs pursuing 'women's rights' as a simple or straightforward success story. Generations of women and their allies have fought tirelessly for the vote, for reproductive choice and justice, for better equality in the workplace, and for the sharing of domestic chores and childcare responsibilities (Roseneil et al, 2012; Berry and Lake, 2021). Significant progress has been made, in Western democracies and beyond, but it is important to keep in mind that these rights vary by women's positionality and experience. In many countries, voting rights for women are taken for granted, men no longer assume that women are ill-equipped to vote, and more women than ever now take up higher education. However, the gender pay gap is persistent (although slowly shrinking); moreover, women still carry out the majority of unpaid care-work, and hard-won reproductive rights are under attack (Fillieule and Broqua, 2020; Allotey et al, 2021).

Not all women have the same opportunities, even when they have the same rights. We would like to give two examples. First, they might not be able to access reproductive health services equally, depending on access to economic resources or location. A woman's reproductive rights are thus affected by where she lives. She may not have access to a local healthcare provider who offers reproductive choice or have the means to travel to receive it. Second, depending on electoral voting protocols, women (and of course this applies not only to women) might need a photo ID in order to participate in elections or travel to polling stations. This might make voting harder and exclude groups of (not only) women. Because the experiences, interests, and demands of women, feminists, and those who are fighting for gender equality (categories that can be overlapping as well as mutually exclusive) are highly diverse, even those who share some common demands might disagree about how to achieve them. On the one hand, there are controversies among feminists – for example, whether feminists should mobilise independently from the state and other institutions, which are deemed inherently patriarchal and impossible to reform, or whether they should join these institutions and try to change them from within (Ferree, 2012; Mackay 2023; Littler, 2023). On the other hand, we see conflicts between feminists that seek to challenge gender inequality and stereotypical assumptions about the gender division of labour, and people who defend 'family values' such as the hetero-patriarchal family, which relegates women to caregiving (Pavan 2020). Other controversies concern the conflicts around abortion rights, the failed struggle for the *Equal Rights Amendment* (Mansbridge, 1986) in the US, or the current gender-critical movement and its attacks on abortion rights, LGBTQ+ rights, and trans-people's lives and rights (Verloo and Paternotte, 2018; Graff and Korolczuk, 2021).

Struggles around gender equality or sexual politics are just one example of the many ways in which social change does not happen as a linear process, but through complex sets of actions, interactions, and reactions between and among people, organisations, and institutions (Jasper, 2015). It happens not only in the visible protests and actions that are recorded in popular media and remembered for their audacity. It also happens behind the scenes in people's daily lives, through the complex inner workings of groups and organisations, and is also contributed to by less visible individuals and organisations offering, not dramatic protest events, but more run-of-the-mill services (Bassel and Emejulu, 2017; Jupp, 2022; Kavada, 2023). Rape crisis centres are one area of women's activism, for example, that sit behind the scenes of visible protest, but which are equally a part of a struggle for progressive social change (Maier, 2008; Weatherall, 2022). They exist as a reaction to abuse against women but are also politically aware entities wishing and sometimes overtly demanding that the root causes of the problem be vanquished.

Not only are there visible and less visible forms of pressure that encourage social change, it is also important to note that social change processes are also resisted and facilitated by other sets of people and organisations. A progressive turn can result in backlash, as we have seen with attempts to restrict women's rights to an abortion. At the time of writing, the Roe v Wade ruling had recently been overturned in the US, allowing US states to set their own abortion policy, with severe potential ramifications for women's rights to have control over their own bodies. Similarly, abortion rights are under attack in other countries. This illustrates how, at times, social change processes hit brick walls, rebound, regather energy, fizzle away, pop up somewhere else or gain new momentum.

Moreover, even individuals and organisations that wish for similar outcomes disagree on the best methods through which to push for change. Throughout history, some women have been content with step-by-step reform through moderate activism, whereas others have wanted radical reform and declared it through confrontation and violence (Ferree and Hess, 2004; Kantola and Squires, 2012; Newman, 2012; Mackay, 2015; Grosser and McCarthy, 2019; Littler, 2023). Reformist women learn a lot from the actions and demands of their more radical counterparts, and vice versa. Furthermore, individuals and organisations themselves change as they learn more about the affordances of different approaches to social change. In this ever-interacting model, previous social change activism and volunteering impact what happens next. New organisations emerge because existing organisations succeeded, failed, were ignored, or failed to situate themselves in relation to social change and existing or newly emerging grievances. Of course, existing organisations also undergo transformations due to changed constituencies or changed contexts.

Our key concepts

In this book, we make novel use of a set of concepts for understanding these complex processes. We draw heavily on social movement theory but expand it in multiple ways. First, we take note of the ways in which broader historical processes and interactions among different causes intersect (Tilly, 2006; Fligstein and McAdam, 2012). That means we are putting *social change* and historical developments at the centre of our analysis. Social change includes political, cultural, economic, and technological changes that are often initiated, or responded to, by SCOs. Any attempt to understand social change necessitates a historical perspective (Tilly, 2006). After all, historical change results in changes of norms, institutions, and rights, which have been, or may yet be, fought for or against by SCOs. To date, social movement scholarship's engagement with historical perspectives is somewhat limited and would benefit from reorientation (McAdam and Sewell, 2001; Gould, 2005; Tilly and Goodwin, 2006; Cox and Nilsen, 2014). We call the broader environment that often changes gradually, but sometimes rapidly, *historically variable contexts* (see Chapter 2).

Much existing literature on social movements tends to either be deterministic – over-egging the case that structure determines movement form – or has focussed disproportionately on visible protests and succumbed to short-termism (see critiques of, Goodwin and Jasper, 1999; Saunders, 2009a). Thus, common approaches to the study of social movements can suggest, or at least imply through their focus on particular types of social change making, that popular large-scale movements are the most important trigger for social change processes. Such an understanding risks overlooking more modest but equally important precursors to social change, as well as the range of important activities that generate, sustain, and resist social change outside of protest arenas (Armstrong and Bernstein, 2008; Rojas and King, 2018). We draw attention to social transformations and social change as outcomes of social change processes that stem from interactions among economic, technical, social, and cultural forces, with which SCOs are inextricably intertwined. These processes allow once radical thoughts and actions to slowly become accepted (or unthinkable!) and then institutionalised (or formally eschewed!) over time. Institutions then embed those societal changes, as individuals and organisations push for further change, which may become accepted and institutionalised (or, conversely rejected and suppressed), and another set of actions and chain reactions ensues (see Wessels, 2014; and Chapter 2). However, gains with respect to gender equality, de-criminalisation of homosexuality, and sometimes even democracy itself, are also countered by backlash. In this sense, societies act within, and react to, the social world provided to them by those who paved a way before them. The result of processes of social change over time are significant shifts in the ways society functions (Abrams, 1959).

Second, we introduce the concept *social change organisations* as a way to refer to varieties of organisations that mobilise protest events, engage in advocacy and provide services. Only a small handful of studies take up the challenge of considering the analytical and normative advantages of analysing how a range of organisations that work for social change relate to one another – whether they cooperate, ignore each other, or are in conflict with one another (Clemens and Minkoff, 2007; Saunders, 2009a; Blee, 2012; Newman, 2012; Diani, 2015). We thus contribute to the terminological debate to find a more inclusive term for organisations that seek to bring about or resist social change (Walker and Martin, 2018). We will examine these relationships later in this book; here we only want to point out that even if organisations do not interact with one another, they impact on one another, and it is therefore important to analyse them together. Analytically, it is important to note that the different approaches and disciplines that are employed to understand these types of organisations can inform one another and provide deeper knowledge of how social change happens. Normatively, existing theoretical work stresses the advantages and disadvantages of different strategies to achieve social change. Looking at varieties of SCO together helps us to see where a fruitful division of labour between these organisations might emerge, as well as explain conflicts between factions that, although pursuing similar goals, differ with respect to the strategies and the level of their willingness to make compromises to achieve them.

It is important to stress, once more, that social change processes are complex and involve a variety of actors at multiple levels. The premise of this book is that SCOs have been, and continue to be, key agents in bringing about or resisting societal change. To be clear, we use the term *social change organisations (SCOs)* to refer to the broad range of organisations that work *to bring about or resist societal change through any form or combination of service provision, advocacy, and protest.* As we show throughout this book, we find the term SCOs useful because it allows us to use our interactionist and constructivist approach to interweave literatures that focus on SMOs, third sector organisations (TSOs) (which in the US are known as NPOs – not-for-profit organisations), NGOs and other related types of non-commercial organisations that work to bring about social change directly or indirectly. Drawing on the insights of these literatures, our book identifies the core characteristics, affordances, and issues associated with these organisations. More importantly, it considers how they act and react in complex processes of social change. We provide a fuller discussion of these organisations in Chapter 1.

Finally, we introduce the concept SCMs to refer to the individual activists, volunteers and staff members who participate in the more and less visible actions that drive social change processes. Individuals are central to all organised efforts. People's lives intersect with social change processes as well as, directly or indirectly, with their participation in SCOs in fascinating ways. Individuals are central to the frictions that take place within organisational settings and for the sustainment or demise of such efforts, just as SCOs are important in shaping who people are and who they become. We refer to SCMs rather than activists, volunteers, or protesters to highlight the enormous varieties of roles that can be undertaken in, for, and in relation to the causes supported by SCOs – sporadically or continuously, paid or unpaid, simultaneously or consecutively (more fully discussed in Chapter 1 and Chapter 5). Furthermore, the term acknowledges that those involved in SCOs do not necessarily identify as 'activists'.

We proceed with our introduction to *Organising for Change* by introducing the core ideas of this book. We then explain the importance of our arguments and provide a short synopsis of what follows in the following chapters.

Organising for change

Our book is about the complex set of actions, reactions and interactions that organisations and individuals encounter and generate as they attempt to bring about social change and 'make the world a better place'. We need to stress that SCOs' and SCMs' interpretations of 'making the world a better place' can differ widely and might include efforts that are more or less altruistic or self-serving. Although we primarily examine progressive SCOs, we also include in our analysis conservative and reactionary organisations that seek to maintain or restore 'tradition' and existing power relations. Environmental mobilisations, for example, often seek to prevent the building of unwanted and polluting infrastructure developments. Moreover, reactionary mobilisations can be reactions to the perceived gains of progressive SCOs and seek to defend privilege. Likewise, the emergence of reactionary movements in turn can constitute an impetus for progressive SCOs to emerge or act in new ways. This means, that we see SCOs in constant interaction (Roth, 2003; Saunders, 2013; Jasper and Duyvendak, 2015; Roth, 2018) as we have illustrated earlier with respect to organising for gender equality. We acknowledge that the work of SCOs is never complete, it is an ongoing struggle with temporary gains and setbacks, as for example Meer (2022) has recently argued with respect to the on-going need to mobilise for racial justice, and Emejulu (2022) has explored concerning the liberation of Black women. If successful, SCOs get issues on the agenda, but further attempts to engender social change require the adoption and implementation of the achieved gains and the defence against attacks.

Our approach is much deeper and wider than standard accounts of the causes of social change. Our work is deeper because we consider SCOs within a broader historical context to show how they are simultaneously responding to and seeking to bring about social change. We reveal the back-story and the dynamism of socio-cultural currents, which have profound impacts on what SCOs do and what they are able to achieve. We show how social and political structures politically enable or constrain social change. Our work is wider because of the variety of organisations we include in our analysis. Our interactionist approach clearly illustrates how previous social change and social change making efforts underpin what happens next – though not in a deterministic sense – and why it is that new SCOs form to fill perceived gaps. We also zoom in on the processes that take place within SCOs, which are all part of the cycles of actions, interactions, and reactions that are at the centre of our approach.

Organising for Change contributes to the development of a theory of social change that puts change-making organisations and individuals at the centre of its analysis. Our emphasis on organisations and individuals within the broader context of sweeping social changes over long periods of times, necessitates that we take seriously both structure and agency. The relationship between micro-levels (individual) and macro-levels (political, social and cultural) of social life is a core concern of sociology. Indeed, it is a major task for social scientists to understand whether social action is rational or interpretative, and whether social order is negotiated between individuals or imposed by collective or emergent forces (Alexander and Giesen, 1987; Fligstein and McAdam, 2012). We resolve this by taking a social interactionist (Mead 1977) approach to what Giddens (1984) calls structuration, and we draw on Bourdieu's examination of structure and agency (Bourdieu and Wacquant, 1992). Put simply, we are interested in how structure and agency are mutually constituted through the work of SCOs and SCMs. In such an approach, the constitution and transformation of intersectional inequalities such as race, class, and gender, evolves in interaction and negotiation (Gerson and Peiss, 1985; West and Zimmerman, 1987) at multiple levels inside and outside of SCOs. In our view, symbolic interactionism and social constructivism provide us with a framework to examine the interlocking nature of systems of domination and the varieties of consciousness in which they result, and thus are important contributors to the study of collective action (Morris, 1992; Fligstein and McAdam, 2012; Jasper, 2015; Fillieule and Broqua, 2020).

Social change, then, can be seen as a set of processes involving creative action differentiation, in which there is contestation for ascendency among different SCOs (working in collaboration, competition and conflict, see Chapter 6) for ascertaining the intersubjective validity of norms (Joas, 1990). In this sense, we can think of SCOs as intertwined in a set of processes at the macro-, meso-, and micro-levels. At the macro level, they respond to the state, the economy, culture, and technological regimes; at the meso-level, SCOs with similar and different values interact, influence each other or otherwise rub against each other. Service delivery organisations mediate the meso and individual level, providing services for communities, families and individuals. At the micro level, individuals work on the best strategies for their organisations and preferences for social change mobilisation befitting the stage of their life course.

We share Cox and Nilsen's (2014) perspective on social movements as being constituted by, and constituting, practice, and being involved in the making and unmaking of structures and processes in which collective action is taking place but extend it to SCOs more broadly. Cox and Nilsen (2014) reclaim Marxism as social movement theory but build on it by including other critical approaches such as feminism, queer theory, postcolonialism, and critical race theory. Gould (2005) noted that the social movements of the 1960s and 1970s started out with a class-based analysis but, frustrated with its limitations in addressing complex inequalities, turned to other aspects of inequality. Although we acknowledge the benefits a Marxist perspective can bring through its emphasis on 'people making their own history', we are wary of focusing too narrowly on class-inequality.

We share Jasper's (2015) emphasis on strategic interaction of players in arenas, but it is important to us to broaden the analysis beyond protest and acknowledge the change making that is also going on in everyday politics (Armstrong and Bernstein, 2008; Bassel and Emejulu, 2017; Rojas and King, 2018; Jupp, 2022; Kavada, 2023). The ongoing conflicts among pro-choice and pro-life advocates, which are shaped by action in the legislature (for example, *Roe v Wade*) and which intersect with (sometimes) illegal abortion clinics and rape or battering services, provide a clear example of the sorts of multi-level interactions we expose in this book, including consideration of how social change and individuals' lives intersect. SCO participation changes people's lives in multiple ways. Service delivery, for example, encourages individuals to understand and seek to redress the root causes of the problems whose symptoms they seek to reduce (Jupp, 2022).

We tackle these issues by drawing on research we have conducted over the past 30 years on a range of projects that connect the interrelated fields of volunteering, NGOs, and social movements. Our topic-specific expertise is on volunteering across the life course, coalitions of labour and women's organisations, environmentalism, people working in humanitarianism, and global justice mobilisations. These causes have been salient for the past three decades and remain of utmost importance today. Communities increasingly rely on volunteering for their functionality (Jupp, 2022), gender issues remain salient, trade unions are crucial in times of rising living costs, many nations have declared climate emergencies, and humanitarian and global justice SCOs continue to seek to redress increasing inequalities. We also draw attention to the way the issues of social justice, equality and diversity, and environmentalism intersect. The long view we have of volunteering, NGOs, and social movements has afforded us a wide lens through which to observe attempts to achieve social change, and how to situate them within a broader field of literature on a range of different types of SCOs. In the research projects on which this book is based, we have employed a mixture of quantitative (for example, surveys) and qualitative (participant observation and life history interviews) methodologies, which provide insights on interactions between and among the state, organisations and individuals. Please see the appendix for more information on our previous projects and how they have informed this book.

Why our book matters

We argue that our book is important and timely for four key reasons. First, we believe that, despite the growing importance of Information and Communication Technologies (ICT) and social media, SCOs play a central role in contemporary societies. ICT and social media do not replace SCOs, rather they transform aspects of the work of SCOs. Moreover, social media are contributing to polarisation and undermine democracy; this makes SCOs – intermediary organisations – particularly relevant. Second, we recognise that there is no single silver-bullet solution to the world's problems. The ways in which we merge insights from different literatures helps us to illustrate the importance of a multi-pronged attempt to bring about (and resist) social change. Third, our book is shaping the field by a reorientation of approaches, across a broad range of disciplines, that examines the structures and strategies of SCOs. Finally, our work is useful for SCMs and SCOs by highlighting the need for compromise, the existence of overlap between different forms of activism, and by pointing towards an effective division of labour between different SCOs. We acknowledge that progressive SCOs strengthen democracy, whereas reactionary SCOs undermine democracy. We believe that we need to understand the full range of SCOs to bolster democracy and social justice. Let us explain the usefulness of our intervention more fully.

ICT, crises, and the persisting importance of SCOs

Given the central role that ICT play for connecting, coordinating and informing people – especially during periods of lockdown to contain COVID-19 – the astute observer might ask whether organisations still matter for social change (Shirky, 2008). We argue that SCOs matter as much as they always did in bringing about and reacting to social change (Earl, 2018). SCOs are ever transforming and evolving with respect to their aims, strategies and use of ICT. They have also been shaped by the COVID-19 pandemic. Work by SCOs always involved the use of information and communication technologies including letters, telegrams, newsletters, radio, and television, which are increasingly replaced by digital communication (Brescia, 2020). Each of these technologies has different affordances (Tufekci, 2017). But without at least some form of organisation, online campaigns for or against social change would be almost impossible. Thus, SCOs are not replaced or made obsolete by ICT and social media, instead SCOs develop new and hybrid forms that combine online and offline action (Bennett and Segerberg, 2012; Pavan, 2014). Moreover, it is important to understand *how* SCOs make use of ICT and social media. Throughout the book, we reflect on the affordances of ICT: as tools for macro social change, strategies, resources (as well as means through which resources can be garnered), and as means to recruit and sustain individual participation. ICT also foster links between SCOs, and facilitate SCO outcomes.

ICT, social media, and online communication have initially been welcomed as means to widen democracy; however, more recently it has become clear that ICT benefit conspiracy theorists and undermine democratic processes through polarisation. In fact, conservative politics and politicians appear to gain more from the use of social media than progressive politics (Schradie, 2019). We argue that SCOs play a crucial role, both for the defence of and attacks on democracy and other crises. In fact, given the threats to democracy related to social media (polarisation, echo chambers, radicalisation) we believe that the interactions between different types of SCOs strengthen democracy by allowing for dialogues and develop relationships across differences.

The role of ICT and SCOs becomes clear when we are turning to some recent crises. We note that various crises – democratic, financial, economic, environmental – are intertwined, gendered, and racialised. In just a few short months, the COVID-19 pandemic resulted in outcomes for which environmental groups, disability activists, and scholars who need visas to participate in international conferences have fought for many decades: a shift to hold virtual conferences that make it possible to work remotely together across the world and thus a contribution to the massive reduction of air travel. Another significant change has been an acceleration from face-to-face to online communication that has sat alongside intensified interaction with neighbours and brought more attention to local communities. In high-income countries in the Global North, the pandemic has affected people from Black and other ethnic minority (BAME) backgrounds more adversely than the White majority populations (Cheshmehzangi, 2021). BAME citizens represent a high proportion of key workers in health and other care work, delivery and transport, and retail where they are exposed and have close contact to other people increasing their risk of infection. In May 2020, the killing of George Floyd by police officers in Minneapolis, in the US, drew – again – attention to cases of police brutality and stop and search powers that disproportionately affect BAME people. The protests responding to police brutality sparked a wave of contention around the world underpinned by social media, which mobilised people to the streets. The words 'Black Lives Matter (BLM)' appeared on Facebook in 2013 in response to the acquittal of the police officer George Zimmerman who had been on trial for the murder of the teenager Trayvon Martin (Ince et al, 2017). Further police killings of unarmed African Americans (in particular the killing of Michael Brown in Ferguson, Ohio, on 11 August 2014) (Ince et al, 2017: 1819) contributed to the ubiquity of the slogan Black Lives Matter first in public discourse in the US and later in the UK and other countries. The BLM movement has many allies throughout society, but it also provides a good example of online activism and of the internet as a tool to mobilise offline protests (Bennett and Segerberg, 2012; Pavan, 2014; Tufekci, 2017). For BLM, social media platforms played a central role in disseminating videos of police brutality and the defiance of activists. Social media have also provided a crucial infrastructure for groups that organised mutual aid within communities during the COVID-19 pandemic, as well as organising protests of anti-vaxxers or spreading disinformation and conspiracy theories. Moreover, social media can provide safe spaces, but at the same time also are sites of attacks on political opponents, migrants and other groups.

We thus argue that, in the age of social media, SCOs remain highly relevant but are to some extent transformed through the availability of ICT. SCOs are responding to crises and negotiating the survival of democracy. They are crucial for bringing about – and trying to prevent – social change. We now explain in more detail why we think a more holistic approach to SCOs is important for understanding social change.

Multi-pronged approaches to social change

To explain how SCOs with different remits are interrelated and important in different ways, we first cast your attention back to the refugee crisis in Europe that occurred from spring 2015 onwards. In our view, this was foremost a crisis for the one million or so people who fled persecution and war, mainly from Syria, Afghanistan, and Iraq. The war in Ukraine, which started in 2022 and is ongoing at the time of writing, demonstrates yet again how refugees are racialised and that depending on the country or region of origin, refugees find more or less support. In many countries, the refugee crisis was framed as problematic for existing citizens and used as a tool to bolster support for right-wing parties and resulted in new anti-immigrant movements. As we saw in dramatic media coverage, many refugees drowned at sea and others lost their lives in refrigeration trucks. Some made a long and exhausting journey by foot to finally find refuge in Italy, Greece, Austria, Germany, and other European countries. In some places, refugees were greeted by volunteers from the Red Cross and other humanitarian networks welcoming them with essential items for survival – food, clothes, medicines, and temporary shelters. In addition, diasporic networks matter for the support of refugees and other victims of disasters as the devastating earthquake in Turkey and Syria in February 2023 demonstrates.

Let us have a think about how academics from different disciplines characterise the migrant support networks that emerged. For scholars of social movements, the work of volunteers is obviously politically motivated and movement oriented. In contrast, research on humanitarianism often focuses on the needs of beneficiaries. The volunteers' intentions were not always politically overt (Feischmidt and Zakariás, 2019). Instead of being directly political, their voluntary efforts were characterised as 'humanitarian: they were giving shelter, food, clothes, advices [sic], language classes and children's entertainment in an attempt to cater for immediate, urgent needs' (Vandevoordt and Verschraegen, 2019: 103). And yet it is wrong to call them apolitical because the actions were oftentimes directly counterposed to authorities' preferences to exclude migrants.

Vandevoordt and Verschraegen (2019) argue that there is an overlooked space in between the political approach of scholars of movements and apolitical stance of those who study humanitarianism. They consequently conceptualise the work of migrant support networks as 'subversive humanitarianism'. Similarly, our interactionist approach recognises that servicing crises is incredibly important as a response to social and political conditions. Some recent studies of minority and White women's everyday activism in the UK (Bassel and Emejulu, 2017; Jupp, 2022) demonstrate that mutual aid and resistance against austerity are deeply intertwined. The biographical approach we advocate (discussed in Chapters 1, 5 and 7) highlights how being involved in the front-line provision of essential services wakes people up to the political roots of social problems. Volunteers sometimes begin to realise that, while 'sticking plasters' on problems (Jupp, 2022) can perpetuate the problems themselves, the act of sticking on plasters is also deeply necessary. The provision of services that are otherwise unavailable, inaccessible or forbidden – regardless of the issue area – may well sometimes be ambiguously political, but we argue that such services are always a direct interjection into social change processes. But perhaps most fundamentally, our work highlights the need to see providing services, engaging in advocacy, and protesting as closely interrelated and interdependent activities taking place as part of social change processes. Eliasoph (2013), similarly, points to relationships between 'volunteering' and 'political activism' noting that both can do harm as well as good.

In much of the existing literature about different types of SCOs we can see a pattern of constructive criticisms being levelled at the different types of SCOs. But the oft-repeated failure to see them *together* as living interactive bodies, means that the advantages of a multi-pronged approach are often overlooked. We know, for example, that SMOs might try – but sometimes fail – to prefigure democratic norms (della Porta, 2009). But it is sometimes also the case that large SCOS may perform better in their internal democratic practices than their smaller and grassroots counterparts (Freeman, 1972; Saunders, 2009b). We can also learn from existing literature that large and well-established NGOs are sometimes considered to be fake public proxies that stifle systemic critique (Lang, 2013; Stroup and Wong, 2017), that small advocacy organisations are oftentimes considered ineffectual (Fisher, 2006; Blee, 2012), and that certain types of volunteering might distract SCMs from the need for structural change (Eliasoph, 2013; Coule et al, 2022). Indeed, some forms of participation – such as outsourced fundraising rather than grass-roots mobilisation – are seen as relatively meaningless (Fisher, 2006). And yet raising funds, or other useful resources, are part-and-parcel of the work of all SCOs. Different resource choices have different implications, but few can be made without confronting difficult moral or ethical arguments (see Chapter 3).

One important debate concerning the relationship between democracy and SCOs concerns 'NGOisation' (Lang, 2013) a term used to refer to the professionalisation of NGOs. Lang (2013) distinguishes different forms of advocacy: public advocacy, which involves unruly practices; and the mobilising and organisation of citizens and institutional advocacy or lobbying with a restricted public voice. She argues that the NGOisation of civil society results in some damage to democracy by institutionalising advocacy and so allowing NGOs to serve as proxy publics, which provide legitimacy for local government while silencing critique. NGOs and local government are therefore seen to represent a co-dependency among unequals. Similarly, Stroup and Wong (2017) describe the 'authority trap' in which 'leading NGOs' – large, influential NGOs like Greenpeace – pursue incremental demands and mild strategies, which result in limited 'vanilla victories'. Thus, it is commonplace to view large-scale NGOs in collaboration with the state as restrictive on NGOs' activities, and muzzling of critique.

We sympathise with the notions that incremental change can be disappointing, that structural change is necessary, that volunteering and fundraising can be depoliticising and disengaging for volunteers and that sticking plasters on wounds, through service delivery and mutual aid, cannot solve systemic problems. Yet at the same time we seek to reorient scholarly literature to more overtly to recognise (a) how incremental changes can cumulate, (b) how the compromises of large-scale NGOs provide fertile ground for the emergence of more critical SCOs that are able to push forward the terms of a debate and (c) the ways in which service provision and mutual aid intersect with other political efforts to secure social change, sometimes as a direct route into social change making. Thus, we believe that more radical and more diplomatic forms of organising for change are equally important, which we will illustrate throughout the book. The silver bullet might not exist, but living and interacting varieties of SCO and SCMs consciously differentiated to maximise social change might be better placed to win battles (Jasper, 2015) than SCOs and SCMs that pitch themselves against each other. Moreover, it is important to keep in mind that the dynamics of social change making go beyond the relations between incumbents and challengers (McAdam et al, 2001; Fligstein and McAdam, 2012), also including insider activism and prefigurative politics (Armstrong and Bernstein, 2008, Rojas and King, 2010).

The on-going relevance of our argument

Much of the recent scholarship on SCOs that we outlined previously has important precedents in the social sciences literature that spans more than the past 100 years. The 'iron rule of oligarchy' (Michels, 1911), similarly to Lang's (2013) and Stroup and Wong's (2017) work we introduced earlier, argued that large political organisations lose touch with the grassroots and tend to become undemocratic in their organisational processes as consequence. In 1997, Jordan and Maloney's powerful critique of *The Protest Business* pointed the finger at large NGOs for being more corporate than activist-focused, similar to critiques from Fisher (2006) who examined the consequences of outsourcing fundraising activities rather than building community networks.

It may always be possible to juxtapose large-scale and relatively powerful NGOs against 'other NGOs' (Stroup and Wong, 2017), thought to be smaller and weaker. Many accounts of grassroots activists' groups find that – although such groups are more easily able to condemn the state than large moderate NGOs – they are considered as politically non-salient and therefore go unheard of by decision-makers. This argument was as relevant for Gamson back in 1975 in his famous *The Strategy of Social Protest* as it remains today. He suggested that such small organisations lack 'acceptance'. Along the same lines, Blee (2012) found that smaller scale activist groups 'were also unfocused and their progress was halting at best' (p 134). Staggenborg (2020) similarly reported that grassroots environmental organisations often falter due to issues related to their low capacity to achieve their aspirations.

In *Organising for Change* we view small grassroots organisations and large bureaucratised NGOs as partners in social change processes and therefore as more influential together than separately. If big NGOs are too compromising and small activist groups are inconsequential, how would social change ever happen? We argue that it is because of the dynamic interactions between and among different SCOs and SCMs, which will continue to take place through dynamic processes over time, into the foreseeable future. We reflect on the processes that have led to significant societal change as well as smaller processes that have the potential to aggregate into more significant changes in the future. In relation to macro societal changes, we situate our dynamic argument first within the context of colonialism, which underpinned the emergence of racialised capitalism (Virdee 2019), which then spurred anti-capitalist resistance in the form of socialism, environmentalism, and humanitarianism. In some countries, anti-communist racialised capitalism turned into fascism. We also discuss independence from colonial rule, the emergence and retrenchment of welfare states, the end of state socialism, as well as responses to terrorism and the global financial crisis in Chapter 2. The emergence, consolidation, resistance to and (in some cases) downfall of each of these regimes were to some extent brought about by SCOs or affected the work of SCOs. The conditions that enable and constrain social forces facilitating social change processes are known as political opportunity structures in the literature on social movements (Tarrow, 1994; Meyer and Minkoff, 2004) and more recently in the literature on NGOs (Saunders and Roth, 2019). In line with Jasper's (2015) discussion of social movements, we reorient the notion of political opportunity structures by emphasising the dynamic interaction of SCOs and SCMs in different arenas (see Chapter 2) using the concept of *historically variable contexts*. Over time, regime changes included different waves of democratisation that gave citizenship rights to men, women, ethnic minorities, and de-criminalised sexual minorities. The processes of social change, however, do not always result in such dramatic and large-scale regime change. Sometimes they result in much smaller changes to policy or baby steps towards changing social and cultural norms. These little alterations to the practices of a service or commercial sector and gestures that help individuals and communities in need may seem insignificant; but we argue that they are all part of complex processes of social change that aggregate and accumulate into significant shifts over time.

Even Blee's (2012) pessimism finds some scope for optimism by suggesting that the relatively ineffectual activist groups she studies can remain on the front foot by ensuring that they do not foreclose opportunities open to them. Her argument talks to the relevance of examining social change over long periods, which is central to our approach, rather than single organisations or protests. We can quite confidently predict that SCOs and SCMs will continue to influence each other and to affect and be affected by social change as they have done so for time immemorial.

Relevance for social change makers

We are sensitive to how critiques of SCOs may affect the people who have worked tirelessly to make them function well. We can anticipate that scholars' tendency to focus on the negative parts of action for social change must be disempowering for people who care. Constructive critiques can, also, of course, help big NGOs to improve their accountability and transparency. But we believe that our more nuanced argument about social change as processes of interaction have three major benefits for activists. First, it can help them to realise that it is important to make compromises to work together for the greater good. This can help in the generation of (albeit sometimes uneasy) coalitions rather than factions. Second, we argue that an account that recognises the overlap between different forms of activism can help people to accept why it is that they feel the need to shift from one form of organising for change to another, or not to worry about simply taking a break before resuming their engagement. There need not be an identity crisis, a feeling of letting the side down, or of bailing out. Finally, our approach helps SCMs by illustrating that all actions oriented towards social change might be helpful – to a greater or lesser extent. Providing someone with something they need is of immense importance and social value, just as is advocating for significant structural change. Even a good attempt that goes wrong is an important lesson in the quest for social change. Knowing that activism is hard to do, but rewarding in unexpected ways, can only help people to gain a sense of political efficacy by reducing feelings of helplessness.

Overview of the book

In the next chapter (Chapter 1), we develop our key concepts – *social change organisations* and *social change makers*. In the first part of the chapter, we focus on SCMs and explain that a biographical perspective is needed to understand their involvement in SCOs. In the second part, we review the ways SMOs, NGOs and service providing organisations have been conceptualised in the existing literature. We make the case for SCOs as a more useful concept and distinguish varieties of SCO that traverse strategies, targets, and audiences. We situate our argument vis-à-vis existing scholarship. How have others defined SCOs? And how have different SCOs been analysed? We then loosely conceptualise different forms of SCMs involvement in SCOs.

In Chapter 2, we set out the macro-level components of our argument by introducing the concept *historically variable contexts* and examining key projects of social change. We suggest a refinement of political opportunity structure theory, from social movement research, that explains the effect of the political environment on SCOs' emergence, consolidation and success (or not), and examines how SCOs engage dynamically with the state and seize on opportunities, or lose out from foreclosures of opportunities, made by others. In this process, SCOs shape the state and the state shapes them. Drawing on Cox and Nilsen (2014), we also demonstrate how a Marxist approach to social movements illuminates ways in which 'people make their own history', bringing about social change through revolutions and reform movements, while being shaped by social and political structures.

We distinguish different relationships between SCOs and the state, which are shaped by legislative frameworks and discuss the interaction between different modernisation processes. Given that historical processes are deeply intertwined, rather than following a strict chronological order we pursue three historical sequences of social change. First, we turn to colonisation processes, which underpinned the emergence of racialised capitalism, were intertwined with the development of humanitarianism, and led to independence struggles. The exploitation of Indigenous people and knowledge in the context of racial capitalism also has significant consequences for environmental destruction and climate change (Sultana, 2022). We acknowledge that not only settler colonialism, but also Western NGO's demands to create 'nature reservations' have had significant negative impact on Indigenous peoples. Next, we turn to the emergence of socialism as a response to capitalism and discuss the mixed economy of welfare involving charities, self-help groups, and the state. The development of these structures is not only shaped by class differences and gendered but also characterised by racial stratification and thus requires an intersectional approach. Last, we address the rise of fascism in the first half of the 20th century and discuss contemporary populist movements. We distinguish between right-wing and left-wing populism. Right-wing populism can be understood as a 'politics of losing' (McVeigh and Estep, 2019) and involves the defence of a wide range of privileges (White, male, heterosexual, and so on). We demonstrate that different regime types give rise to different types of SCOs and, conversely, that different types of SCOs can contribute to the emergence of different regime types.

In Chapter 3 we look more specifically at the ways in which SCOs go about contributing to social change and turn to the repertoires, strategies, and tactics that they use in order to do so. We recognise that the combination of activities used by SCOs depends on the historically variable context in which they exist. We also recognise that the activities of SCOs are rooted in the values of their leaders and members and are related to their goals, which are both closely interrelated. We illustrate how the actions of SCOs are a set of processes stemming from how they react to each other and the historically variable contexts in which they are active. In other words, they shape and are shaped by historically variable contexts. Furthermore, technologies play a crucial role for the sustainability and transformation of repertoires of SCOs. The chapter explores the key tactics of SCOs through the lens of a selection of causes. This includes violent uprisings that we illustrate through struggles for the end of colonial rule. We also discuss non-violent protest and routine demonstrations, illustrated through various causes, including environmentalism. We then turn to advocacy drawing on examples of humanitarian organisations. This is followed by a discussion of service provision by feminist organisations. Our approach might seem counter-intuitive – humanitarian organisations are primarily associated with providing support for people in need, while feminist organisations are well known for advocating for gender equality. Thus, we highlight the perhaps lesser-known activities of these SCOs when providing examples for different tactics. We show how the different causes attract varieties of tactics, even though we use each cause to primarily illustrate a different tactic. We also note that the more everyday focused SCOs, which provide services, help guarantee continuity in social change struggles through times of reduced activity and visibility. In other words, they serve as submerged networks (Melucci, 1989) and abeyance structures (Taylor, 1989), which keep people interested in the causes and sustain activists who are confronted with slow progress, behind the scenes. As such, service providing SCOs represent important infrastructures for the people who participate in a variety of tactics and SCOs.

To carry out their work, SCOs need to mobilise a variety of resources, which we discuss in Chapter 4. We consider different types of resources that SCOs require that are related to the tactics they perform and their organisational structures. We illustrate how all resource choices have a cost-benefit balance, which – true to our interactionist approach – leads to further sets of actions and reactions among SCOs. We demonstrate that every resourcing choice involves compromises and that none can ever be perfect. This chapter has three sections, first, we consider how resource demands are related to the strategies and tactics of SCOs. Organisations with different primary functions, goals and specialisms require different combinations of material and non-material resources. Second, we discuss the sources from which SCOs obtain resources and how this relates to their goals and values. Third, we focus on the consequences of resource choices, including organisational pathways and technological change. How do organisations that seek upward accountability (towards donors) above all else fare – are they more at risk of organisational demise? And do SCOs that side-step downward accountability (towards communities) risk distancing themselves from their supporters?

In Chapter 5 we turn to the undoubtedly most important resource of SCOs: SCMs, the people who found, run, and participate in SCOs. It is important to acknowledge that participation in SCOs is embedded in everyday life and matters for the recruitment as well as for the sustainability of SCO involvement throughout the life course of SCMs. The chapter discusses recruitment and participation in SCOs as well as professionalisation processes. We also address what motivates SCMs and how preventing burnout can contribute to the sustainability of social change making. SCMs might stay in the same SCO for many decades, but they also might engage in multiple SCOs across different causes and tactics over their lifetime. These 'patterns of participation' (Corrigall-Brown, 2012) also contribute to the interaction between SCOs to which we turn in the following chapter.

Chapter 6 examines the relations between SCOs in more depth by discussing the collaboration, coalitions, conflict, and competition among SCOs and the circumstances under which they occur. It focuses on the core idea of our book, that we cannot understand the emergence, activity, and impact of SCOs in isolation. Interactions among SCOs have important ramifications as they influence each other to a greater or lesser extent when they come into, or purposefully avoid, contact with one another. We illustrate the dynamism of contact between SCOs, as actions and reactions that come to shape whether trust-benefit relations can be built. This chapter is informed by debates about intersectionality, coalition-building, and counter-movements. We show how competition can result in institutional isomorphism as well as differentiation. Our emphasis on SCOs more broadly allows us to examine the circumstances under which organisations collaborate or compete. Collaboration between SCOs is important because it might cancel out the risks of NGOisation: we argue that it is the synergy of SCOs that results in social change. We acknowledge the importance of radical uncompromising critique as well as pragmatic – and diplomatic – compromise. Lastly, we also examine conflict between SCOs in the context of counter-movements.

In the beginning of this book, we demonstrated that SCOs are co-producers of social change that are simultaneously creating and responding to social change and continue to be involved in historical, political, and social transformations. After having surveyed strategies, resource mobilisation and the relationships between SCOs, we return in Chapter 7 to the outcomes of SCOs. Drawing on a wide range of empirical studies, we examine four broad categories of SCO 'outcomes'. We start out with political and legislative outcomes, which include institutional transformation. Then we turn to discuss mobilisation outcomes with respect to networking and diffusion processes. This is followed by socio-cultural outcomes. Finally, we look at the effects on individuals involved in social change making (internal individual outcomes) as well as individuals who benefit (or not) from the material/well-being services provided by SCOs (external individual outcomes). The different outcomes reflect the goals and strategies of SCOs as well as the context in which they operate. We note that the different types of outcomes of SCOs can be related to one another and that SCOs often achieve more than one outcome. Nevertheless, it is important to analytically distinguish between different types of outcomes and how they are (or are not) related.

In our conclusion we return to our argument that a focus on SCOs contributes to a theory of social change that acknowledges both structure and agency. We highlight that analysing different types of SCOs synergistically and historically allows us to recognise their important role in generating social change. Our holistic understanding of SCOs is made possible through, and contributes to, the integration of social movement studies, third sector studies, and the study of NGOs. Our examination of SCMs' biographies and the coalition-building between different types of SCOs requires a holistic view of literatures while integration of literature enhances analysis of SCOs.

A note on our positionalities

While we aim to discuss SCMs and SCOs in a global and intersectional perspective, we are aware of our biases and thus include a short statement on our positionalities. We are aware of our privileges as White, straight cis-women who won scholarships for their PhDs and are now full professors at research intensive Russell Group universities in the UK. One of us, Silke, is an EU migrant who grew up in West Germany where she commenced her studies in Sociology in the 1980s. She considered herself a feminist since she was a teenager but always found a narrow conception of 'women' and 'gender' limiting and exclusionary. Since her youth, she attended demonstrations on various causes, initially against environmental pollution and the stationing of cruise missiles. After moving to West Berlin, she supported various organisations including the women's cooperative *WeiberWirtschaft* (discussed later). She completed her PhD in the US in the late 1990s where she also worked before starting a permanent position in the UK where she continues to occasionally attend demonstrations addressing a variety of causes. She supports a range of organisations financially, and is involved in a conservation group.

The other one of us, Clare, grew up in the UK in a working-class family. When she was at primary school, most of her friends thought she did not have a father because he worked 12-hour shifts at the local factory to earn enough money for the family to have a reasonable standard of living. She commenced her studies in Human Geography and History in the 1990s, graduating with a PhD in Environmental Sociology in the mid-2000s. She has pursued her entire academic career in the South of England. She has extensive experiences conducting international and comparative research with European partners. She has always been committed to environmental causes and has been a Friends of the Earth local group co-ordinator and participant in Camps for Climate Action. Clare also donates to a range of environmental and humanitarian causes.

Both of us have adopted a pro-environmental lifestyle. Except for small pilot projects that both of us have carried out in Tanzania and South Africa, we have conducted the bulk of our research in the UK, US, Germany and other European countries. Due to our training and linguistic limitations, we are primarily drawing on Anglo-Saxon literature which dominates academic writing, including social movement (MacSheoin, 2016) and voluntary sector research and, to a lesser extent, non-governmental organisations (NGOs), and thus neglecting not only the franco- and lusophone literature, but also literature published in other languages. We look forward to future collaborations that allow us to better capture the intersectional approach we desire to encapsulate.

1

What Are Social Change Makers and Social Change Organisations?

Let us start with a couple of examples of SCOs and SCMs. Members of the Coalition of Labour Union Women (CLUW), an organisation that was founded in Chicago 1974 and which bridges the US women's and labour movements (Roth, 2003), have been involved in a range of social movements simultaneously and successively. Some of the 'founding mothers' who were born in the 1920s and 1930s were long-standing trade unionists who were also involved in the civil rights movement marching with Martin Luther King and supporting the women's movement and the struggle for the Equal Rights amendment. In contrast, some of the 'rebellious daughters', who were born in the 1940s and 1950s, had been involved in the farmworkers' movement, supported the Black Panthers, and were involved in various feminist organisations including a feminist healthcare collective that provided abortions. The 'political animals', were involved in community organisations and the Democratic Party, and became union members after starting to work in the public sector. Finally, the 'fighting victims' became politicised after they had received support through their union at the workplace. While each of these four types came to CLUW on a different trajectory, what was important to all was to frame 'women's issues' as 'workers' issues' and vice versa while also fighting for racial justice. Many felt that supporting the Democratic Party was an important strategy in addition to participating in strike action and engaging in lobbying at the local, state, and national levels.

Our second example is based on our knowledge of environmentalists, derived from our in-depth interviews with environmental activists and participant observation in environmental organisations. Jo thinks of their self an environmentalist. For the past 15 months they have worked as a conservation volunteer with a county-wide branch of a national conservation organisation in the UK. They spend one weekday every week (outside of the school holidays) working with a small group of other conservation volunteers removing invasive species, planting trees, opening up spaces to allow cattle to graze, and managing ponds. Jo has always been a nature lover, but since volunteering began to appreciate the gravity of the environmental and climate crises through their communications with others. They now attend annual climate change marches, and have, more recently, joined a network that engages in civil disobedience to raise the profile of the climate crisis. At the previous annual climate change march, they encountered a counterdemonstration. The activists on the counterdemonstration were chanting 'the scientists are liars' and claimed that anthropogenic climate change was an elaborate hoax to support climate researchers' careers. This motivated Jo to also engage in climate change communication and education of the masses through social media. Jo has a non-binary gender identity, uses the pro-nouns 'they/them', and engages in a monthly transgender support meeting. Jo would like to form a transgender environmentalist network that better represents their gender *and* environmentalist identities.

The members of CLUW and Jo are what we term *social change makers* (SCMs), individuals engaged – often in multiple ways – usually with at least one *social change organisation* (SCO). Jo's case in particular illustrates how participation in a seemingly non-political organisation – a conservation volunteering group – can have very significant political ramifications, leading to engagement in protest marches and direct action. To recap, we discussed a similar example of a seemingly apolitical service provision organisation for immigrants leading to significant political consequences for volunteers in the Introduction to our book. This is a process that Vandevoordt and Verschraegen (2019) called 'subversive humanitarianism'. We use this vignette to illustrate that, just as there is 'subversive humanitarianism', there is also 'subversive conservationism', a process through which the apolitical becomes directly political. We anticipate similar happenings across multiple causes. This illustrates the fine line between apolitical and political activities, which both address social problems. As we show in this chapter, service providing organisations are one type of organisation bringing about social change by addressing needs. Care work, in particular 'caring for the civic body', can expand our understanding of political participation (Kavada, 2023). In this sense, service-providing organisations are engaging in 'prefigurative action' (Yates, 2015), they sustain SCMs and are also drawing attention to causes.

Both vignettes illustrate how the identities of SCMs can influence the shape of SCOs moving forwards. In the first case, bridging women's and worker's issues, and in the second case towards establishing a transgender corner of environmentalism, sensitive to some of the assumptions implicit in eco-feminism (do women necessarily have an ethic of care because of their gender?) (Buckingham, 2004). Moreover, the vignette describing Jo included an anti-science of climate change counter-movement, which has repercussions on the SCOs and SCMs engaged in the protest march that was being countered.

We proceed with this chapter by developing two of our core concepts – *social change makers* and *social change organisations*. (We discuss social change itself in the next chapter, Chapter 2.) In the first part of this chapter, we argue that a biographical approach is useful to understand the role participation in SCOs plays in the lives of SCMs. Later on in the book (Chapter 5), we examine how SCMs are recruited into SCOs and how they sustain their involvement over the life course, as well as what impact this has on SCMs (Chapter 7). In the second part of this chapter, we loosely distinguish varieties of SCO, while also recognising significant overlaps among these organisational varieties. We end this chapter with a brief discussion of different forms of participation of SCMs in SCOs.

Introducing social change makers

As noted in the introduction, we introduce the concept SCMs to refer to the individual activists, volunteers, and staff members who participate in the more and less visible actions that drive social change processes. We refer to SCMs rather than activists, volunteers, staff, or protesters to highlight the enormous varieties of roles that can be taken on in SCOs – sporadically or continuously, paid or unpaid, simultaneously or consecutively. Furthermore, the term acknowledges that those involved in SCOs do not necessarily identify as 'activists' (discussed in more detail in Chapter 5). We argue that the participation of SCMs is shaped by social and political contexts, stages in the life course and a 'taste for tactics' (Jasper, 1999), that is the commitment to values and causes and preferences for specific tactics (for example, service provision, advocacy, protest) (we will discuss these strategies in Chapter 3), which has different material and personal consequences (see Chapter 7).

We argue that a biographical/life course approach to understanding the participation of SCMs is important (della Porta, 1992; Roth, 2000; Miethe and Roth, 2005; Fillieule and Neveu, 2019). SCMs' work for SCOs varies from unpaid to paid with good salaries, and from roles that require non-skilled labour through to highly specialised skills. However, pay and skill are not correlated: neither the type of skills nor the amount of time devoted to participation in SCOs is necessarily related to being paid. In general, pay in the third sector and NGOs tends to be lower than in the private and public sectors and the employment status of workers is usually more precarious (Eltanini, 2016; Taylor and Roth, 2019). In SCOs, the boundary between paid employment and unpaid volunteering is not always clear. Moreover, many SCMs – like the women in CLUW and the character 'Jo' in our opening vignettes – are boundary-crossers (Lewis 2008; Roth 2015; 2016) and bridge-builders (Robnett, 1996; Rose, 2000; Roth, 2003) who move and connect SCOs – from NGOs engaged in service provision to SMOs but not necessarily in that order. Voluntary and full-time social-political commitment can be exercised simultaneously or successively, which is reflected in a variety of careers and participation trajectories. For example, a voluntary commitment in the workplace can lead to a staff position in advocacy work, or vice versa (see also Taylor, 2004; Newman, 2012), while various forms of volunteering, including 'voluntourism' (Vrasti, 2013) – volunteering overseas – enhance the career opportunities of university graduates (Harflett, 2015; Hoskins et al, 2020).

A biographical perspective allows us to see how SCMs are involved in different SCOs simultaneously and successively. We will examine different patterns of participation, which include dropping out, being temporarily not involved, switching between tactics and causes, and resuming participation later in the book (Chapter 5). A biographical approach allows us to see that not only do the political and historical context matter for the recruitment and participation of people in SCOs, but the life stages and life spheres of SCMs do as well. We argue that it is important to recognise that SCO participation is embedded in everyday life and matters for the recruitment as well as for the sustainability of SCO involvement throughout the life course of members and leaders (Roth and Saunders, 2022; forthcoming). Involvement in SCOs often goes hand-in-hand with other aspects of SCMs lifestyles, such as parenting and employment (Wilson, 2000). Such milestones in the life course can provide people with ties and obligations, necessitating a biographical approach (della Porta, 1992; Miethe and Roth, 2005; Valocchi, 2013) to understanding how the lives of SCMs interact with SCOs. As we now turn attention to SCOs, we would like to remind our readers that SCOs comprise individuals whose own political participation, life courses and choices shape the organisations in which they participate (see Whittier, 1995; Roth, 2003).

Introducing social change organisations

While an SCO is a single entity, central to our argument are the actions, interactions and reactions that SCOs have with social change as a historical and ongoing process, with each other and with SCMs. In this book, we introduce the concept *social change organisations (SCOs)* to refer to the broad range of organisations that work *to bring about or resist societal change through any form and combination of service provision, advocacy and protest.* This definition covers organisations that, in various literatures, are examined as SMOs, third sector/voluntary sector/not-for-profit organisations (TSOs/VSOs/NfPOs), NGOs and other related varieties of non-commercial organisations that work to directly or indirectly bring about social change. This novel concept allows us to fruitfully merge a range of hitherto relatively unconnected literatures. This is important in order to more fruitfully analyse conceptually 'awkward' movements (Polletta, 2006). By crossing conceptual boundaries in the study of different types of organisations, we are contributing to – and aim to resolve – the terminological debate regarding the need for a more inclusive concept (Edwards and Martin, 2018).

Scholars have begun to merge literatures, but so far not very comprehensively. Recently, della Porta (2020: 938), identified how a 'toolkit of concepts and theory' from social movement research can usefully contribute to the sub-fields of voluntarism and the third sector. Like Lewis (2015) and della Porta (2020) we find it puzzling that there has not been more cross-fertilisation of ideas, given that social movements, civil society, voluntarism, and the third sector all represent forms of collective action that are oriented towards, as we put it in our Introduction, 'trying to make the world a better place' (even if different SCOs and SCMs have different notions of what constitutes 'a better place'). Rightly, della Porta (2020) challenges accounts that caricature social movements as disruptive, confrontational, and informal, and third sector organisations as civil, co-opted, and formal. She argues that these depictions do not reflect the multi-faceted nature of many entities known as social movements and third sector organisations. We agree with della Porta (2020), and purposively develop the concept of SCOs to move beyond fake juxtapositions.

In fact, the scope for cross-fertilisation of knowledge is immense. Some organisations that are called SMOs have matured, professionalised, and institutionalised, and the civil society and voluntary sector literature can very fruitfully be deployed to interpret their strategies and actions. Similarly, some voluntary organisations like Oxfam have increasingly turned to advocacy and protest (Rootes and Saunders, 2007). They have also entered into coalitional arrangements, especially in challenging political environments – an organisational form usually thought of as more common in social movements than the voluntary sector. The difficulties of organising during COVID-19 lockdowns has arguably made SCOs more service oriented and encouraged them to engage with new forms of voluntarism; just as environments that criminalise (for example, rescuing migrants from drowning) – or otherwise discourage – service provision encourage politicisation.

For these reasons, we question dominant approaches that tend to treat these varieties of organisations – SMOs, NGOs, TSOs, interest groups – separately and note that the same organisations are oftentimes classified differently depending on the sub-discipline of the scholar writing about them. The famous environmental organisation Greenpeace, for example, has been variously referred to as a SMO (Shaiko, 1993), an NGO (Stafford and Polonsky, 2000), a not-for-profit-organisation (Molloy, 2009) and an interest group (Dickson and McCulloch, 1996). There is obviously a lot one could write about an organisation as fascinating as Greenpeace, but there is a danger that forcing SCOs into one category or another serves mostly to cut interrelated scholarly interests off from one another.

Let us now consider how varieties of SCO have been treated in the literature and introduce a very loose way of differentiating varieties of SCO, which we find more helpful than strict categorisations. Given the many overlaps among varieties of SCO, what we delineate are tendencies to understand and define SCOs rather than sets of hard and fast rules.

We are not the first ones to use the term SCOs, but we are developing the concept to make it much more inclusive than others have done. Some scholars (for example, Ospina and Foldy, 2010) use the term SCOs, but exclude from their conceptualisation organisations that function professionally, those that are well financially resourced, and/or those that are in the mainstream. Other scholars (for example, Ostrander, 2010) exclude organisations with a primary function of service provision directed at individuals. Others still (for example, Chetkovich and Kunreuther, 2006) focus only on grassroots organisations. In contrast to these approaches, we include in our conceptualisation professionalised SCOs, organisations that contribute to small and individual level changes, as well as grassroots organisations. This matters, as we are seeking to explore the affordances of varieties of SCO and how they complement each other.

Varieties of SCO

In order to introduce our conceptualisation of varieties of SCO, we now provide a brief overview of existing literature on NGOs, TSOs, and SMOs, all of which we conceive as SCOs. We wish to emphasise similarities as much as differences between varieties of SCO, and so, instead of pigeon holing, we identify – in line with the chapters that follow – SCOs' interactions and reactions to broader historically variable contexts, their strategies and their resources, the roles of SCMs within them, SCOs' relationships with other SCOs, and the diverse outcomes of organising for change. We draw on the rich variety of work undertaken to date on SCOs to show how (and why) scholars from different sub-fields have defined NGOs, TSOs, SMOs, and VSOs in the ways in which they have. We show how the delineation of (sub)disciplinary boundaries has constrained the ways in which scholars conceive of varieties of SCO. We demonstrate that there are overlaps, but also some areas of distinction, among supposedly different organisational types. We use this work as a basis for devising our own way of grouping varieties of SCO. Our approach is more fluid than most others and provides grist to our argument that SCOs must be analysed together as interacting agents that shape and are shaped by social change, by one another, and by SCMs.

Non-governmental organisations

The term non-governmental organisation is best thought of as a heuristic device, differentiated on an 'inclusive' and 'exclusive' continuum (Saunders and Andretta, 2009). In short, the 'inclusive' approach has few criteria for inclusion in the category of NGO – simply being non-governmental is enough. For example, for Mansbach and Rafferty (2008: 393) 'NGOs are organizations whose members are individuals who do not represent the government of any state.' However, even this belies the fact that organisations that are referred to as NGOs have a variety of relationships with the state that might be conflictual, competitive, cooperative, or even co-opted (Saunders, 2009a; Stroup, 2019). As we will see in this book, there are tensions between achieving incremental reforms and seeking structural change. NGOs are often considered to be organisations that have professionalised. The processes of professionalisation and NGOisation are presumably associated with selling out. For some scholars, particularly those in critical development studies (for example, Petras, 1999; Lang, 2013; Stroup and Wong, 2017), the term NGOs is thus used in a critical sense. It captures organisations that seemingly lack a democratic mandate, and which have presumably cumbersome hierarchies, a bureaucratic nature, support for the neo-liberal state and therefore allegedly (and sometimes actually) purport inappropriate 'solutions' to development issues. Much scholarly work on NGOs focuses on humanitarian organisations (for example, Duben, 1994; Salamon and Anheier, 1996: 12–13; Edwards, 1997; Aal et al, 2000; Mitlin et al, 2007). 'Exclusive' approaches are a lot pickier about what is and is not an NGO. In this sense of the term, they are characterised by a formal organisational structure with professional staff (Howes 1997), a budget (Griffiths and O'Callaghan, 2002), insider status (Reese et al, 2006) and/or a relationship with the United Nations (UN) system (Heater and Berridge, 2001).

We consider the organisations typically described as NGOs as one variety of SCO that engages primarily in service provision and advocacy. Occasionally, NGOs might engage in protest (Saunders and Roth, 2019). What matters to us is to highlight that NGOs contribute to bringing about social change, whereas they are often depicted as sell-outs. In the following chapters, we critically engage with the notion of NGOisation and show what consequences it has on SCOs as sets of interacting agents.

Third sector organisations

Scholars that write about third sector or not-for-profit organisations classify them as a distinct type of SCO. What is a third sector organisation? The term 'third sector' is commonplace in the European literature and denotes a sector distinct from 'market' and 'state', although it draws resources from both of these two other sectors. US scholars might be more familiar with the similar terms of 'not-for-profit sector' or voluntary sector.

The development of the third (or voluntary) sector has resulted in a proliferation of not-for-profit associations and organisations that primarily deliver quasi-public services. Oftentimes, the term third sector is used interchangeably with other terms such as the civil society, social enterprise, non-profit and voluntary sectors (Teasdale, 2010). Third sector organisations are *private* insomuch as they exist outside of government control; they have a *public purpose* that sees them serving the broader community rather than generating profit; and – in theory – they have *free choice* insofar as they work without compulsion (Salamon and Sokolowskiu, 2016). The point about *free choice* should not deny that some people who volunteer in the third sector feel compelled to do so in order to gain requisite work experience in a challenging job market (Eliasoph, 2013; Taylor and Roth, 2019). Salamon and Sokolowskiu (2016) identify four clusters of the third sector: (1) not-for-profit organisations; (2) cooperatives and mutuals (see for example Knutsen, 2016); (3) social enterprises – that mix commercial and social objectives; and (4) individual activities, where they meet the definition of volunteering in the ILO *Manual on the Measurement of Voluntary Work*, including most forms of political participation – even demonstrations – and other activities that benefit the wider community beyond the volunteer's household or family (Salamon et al, 2011).

Salamon and Sokolowskiu (2016) point out that only not-for-profits are unquestionably part of the third sector. Not-for-profit organisations are distinguishable on the basis that it is established in their legal constitutions that their owners and directors are not permitted to take financial surpluses. The other three spheres overlap with the governmental sphere, for-profit businesses, and the private (household) sphere, such that only parts of them can be considered part of the third sector. In a recent review, Coule et al (2022) noted that non-profit studies only engage to a very limited extent with critical approaches including feminism and global justice. Our SCO approach links non-profit organisations to analyses and practices that challenge inequality and power relations.

Social movement organisations

Another variety of SCOs is typically referred to as SMOs, which can be defined as 'associations of persons making idealistic and moralistic claims about how human personal or group life ought to be organized that, at the time of their claims-making, are marginal to or excluded from mainstream society – the then dominant constructions of what is realistic, reasonable, and moral' (Lofland, 1996: 2-3). SMOs are not standalone organisations, they work with others (Diani, 1992). They engage in conflict – with the state or other targets, in their actions or rhetoric – and they represent a broader issue area through shared identity. In this sense, an SMO is a player within an arena (Jasper, 2015). According to Diani's (1992) understanding, (a) single organisations that work alone in the absence of a broader common goal; and (b) non-conflictual organisations are ruled out. Moreover, a tremendous diversity of more or less hierarchical SMOs exists (Clemens and Minkoff, 2004).

Thus, in the existing scholarship SMOs are usually distinguished from other SCOs in two main ways, both of which pertain only to the conflictual element of Diani's (1992) and Lofland's (1996) definitions. These are, first, the extent to which the organisation is institutionalised (Wilson, 1990); and, second, whether the balance of work of the organisations sways towards service and advocacy, or towards protest. In line with the second point, our own argument is that SMOs engage more in protest than advocacy, even though they may oftentimes do both simultaneously (Saunders and Roth, 2019).

Although it is typically argued that SMOs exhibit some form of contention whether that be in terms of their demands or their actions, we are clear that they are not restricted only to contentious forms of action. Take feminist organisations as an example. Feminist organisations have contentious claims and engage in some protest, but they also provide services, for example providing abortion when abortion was illegal (Kaplan, 1997), women's healthcare centres – when women's medical issues were and are still ignored – women's magazines, book shops and so on (see Ferree and Martin, 1995). That means they are not only advocating for change, but they are also responding to a lack of change and creating change through the services they are providing. Of course, that does not only apply to feminist movements, but also to gay rights and many others; ACT/UP was simultaneously engaged in service provision for people with HIV/AIDs, advocacy, and direct action (B. Roth, 2017). Trade unions are a form of SCO engaged in a range of different activities that include disruptive action (strike action, participation in demonstrations for political causes, for example anti-apartheid), negotiation with employers to improve working conditions, lobbying regarding labour legislation and service provision, for example legal support and case-work, for union members. We thus highlight that challenging and attempting to change the status quo can take many forms – it might involve protest and advocacy, but also service provision. Some organisations are engaged in all three of these varieties of activities, while others are only employing one or two of them.

Understanding the intersections of different SCOs

Remember that our argument is that the strategies and aims of varieties of SCO need to be analysed in historical context and in relation to each other as well as to SCMs that engage with them. This holistic approach is, we believe, the best way to understand SCOs as contributing to social change. While they might not necessarily collaborate and engage in a division of labour, they at least relate to each other indirectly, or in competition or conflict (see Chapter 6). A historical perspective allows us to consider change over time: at the macro- or societal level, at the meso- or organisational level, and at the micro- or individual level. SCOs and SCMs change over time. For example, some SCOs go through the process of NGOisation and others radicalise, and the involvement of SCMs changes over the life course.

Thus, you will have noted that, so far, we have not mentioned political parties. We are aware that political parties when in opposition often form coalitions with SCOs. This process is known as 'social movement partyism', where campaigns for electoral success merge with causes and adopt protest repertoires (Almeida, 2009). These forms of activism have become common during anti-austerity struggles in Greece, Spain, Italy, the UK, and the US (della Porta, 2017). It is also important to mention that SCOs can sometimes transition into political parties. Green parties, which still engage in protest repertoires in some countries, have become partners in governing coalitions (Poguntke, 2002). Some political parties such as the Women's Equality Party, which was founded in the UK in 2015 (Evans and Kenny, 2020), and right-wing parties in various countries, have retained the character of movement actors. Established political parties, whether forming a government or not, may distance themselves from extremist parties that are perceived as a threat to democracy such as populist parties, which criticise elites and perceive themselves as the voice of 'the people'. Despite their interactions with SCOs (which could be close or distanced), we do not include political parties, and for-profit entities as SCOs. This is because they, overall, represent more institutionalised forms of social change making and seek inclusion in parliaments and governments. But we do not dismiss political parties and for-profits entirely in our analysis: we recognise that they are part of the broader *historically variable context* with which SCOs interact (Hutter et al, 2018). Indeed, social movement partyism can result in new electoral coalitions that succeed in taking office. For a full discussion of the relationship between political parties and social movements see Tarrow (2021).

Our definitional scoping work reveals that SCOs are usually distinguished from each other on the basis of their strategies (protest, advocacy/lobbying, and services) and relationship to the state (conflictual, competitive, cooperative, complementary, or co-opted), their resources (organisational structures, budgets, and degree of professionalisation), their relationship with people (for example, with their volunteers, staff, and beneficiaries), the area in which they work (for example, rights, welfare, and humanitarianism) and their situation within an organisational field (networked or not). In Table 1.1, we illustrate the variety of shapes and forms of SCOs, without forcing them into a typology that would do injustice to the ways in which varieties of SCO are differentially theorised and empirically researched – even,

Table 1.1: Primary functions of social change organisations and their characteristics

Primary functions	Relationship to the state	Resources	Relationship with people	Field of work	Situation in organisational field
			[Applies to all three tactics]		
Protest	Conflictual Competitive	Professional or non-professional staff and volunteers, small or large budget	Accountable to beneficiaries, donors, and members	Rights, welfare, humanitarian action, and more	Can work alone or with others
Advocacy/ lobbying	Conflictual Competitive Cooperative				
Service delivery	Conflictual Complementary Cooperative Co-opted				

sometimes, within the same class of SCO. Although the vertical axis of our table is structured by primary function, we wish to emphasise that many organisations combine these functions, which further emphasises the need to refrain from pigeonholing SCOs into categories.

Our table suggests that SCOs who engage in protest – or contentious politics – have the most antagonistic relationship with the state, whereas SCOs engaged in advocacy, lobbying, and in particular those that provide services, have the most multi-faceted relationships with the state. They might gain government funding or shape the agenda and legislative change, but they are also at risk of being co-opted or finding their aims watered down. However, they might also have a more contentious relationship with the state. In the case of advocacy and lobbying groups, we consider the relationship conflictual when SCOs openly criticise the state. We consider service providers as engaging in a critical relationship, when they provide services that are illegal, for example providing access to information, education, and healthcare in the case of reproductive justice. A complementary relationship exists, when services are legal, for example alternative healthcare provision that goes beyond the services that are provided by the National Health Service (NHS) in the UK and other mainstream healthcare providers.

Different SCOs provide different opportunities for volunteer and staff involvement. Some large membership organisations – for example, Oxfam or Amnesty International – combine staff-led professionalised national offices with volunteer-run shops, groups, and projects at the local level. Hensby et al (2012) refer to this involvement as bureaucratic activism because these organisations offer limited and bureaucratised forms of activism for volunteers. The diverse array of opportunities that SCOs provide for SCMs make it necessary to distinguish between different forms of SCO involvement.

Varieties of involvement in social change organisations

We started the chapter with two vignettes that described different types of involvement in SCOs and after having defined SCMs and SCOs, we now return to varieties of involvement. Not just do the activities of different SCOs vary, the involvement of SCMs in these organisations varies as well. SCMs might be involved in causes and activities that contribute to their own well-being and improvement of their situation and can be considered beneficiary constituents (McCarthy and Zald, 1977). They might act in solidarity with other groups but (presumably) do not benefit themselves, as so-called conscience constituents (McCarty and Zald, 1977). We find the distinction between beneficiary and conscience constituents problematic because volunteering is associated not only with the causes supported, but also with volunteer well-being and thus has both conscience and beneficiary motivations (we elaborate on this in Chapter 7).

Among constituents, we can distinguish further subgroups. Some SCMs only participate sporadically, others are active for intense periods only for a short time, and others are active for many years as volunteers either in one SCO or moving between SCOs (Roth et al, 2023). Some SCMs take on leadership and other key roles as well as staff positions in SCOs. Of the roles that SCMs take, leaders and leadership roles have probably found most attention in the study of SCOs (Morris and Staggenborg, 2007; Reger, 2007). SCOs that employ collectivist decision-making can be considered as leaderless or leaderful (Costanza-Chock, 2012; Leach, 2013). Leaders and key figures of SCOs can take many different roles including 'the organiser, the strategist, the motivator and the representative' (Rucht, 2013). A further key figure, the broker, is involved in bridge-building between different organisations and arenas (Roth, 2016). Brokers are familiar with diverse political arenas and mediate between grassroots organisations, local government, international NGOs, and intergovernmental organisations. They can provide contacts and contribute to the diffusion of ideas (Keck and Sikkink, 1998; Woodward, 2003). Brokers have gained experience and knowledge through volunteer work and paid employment in SCOs and created networks. They connect SCMs and SCOs in different spheres who either do not know about one another or have difficulties collaborating and interacting with one another. The broker is constantly facing the contradictions and tensions between insider and outsider activism, co-optation, and transformation due to their border-crossing activities (Lewis 2008; Newman in 2012, especially Chapter 7). They are required to navigate the space between reform and radical critique. To understand SCMs' patterns of involvement, we find a life course and biographical perspective particularly useful.

We want to highlight two key points: First, involvement in one SCO is not mutually exclusive with participating in other SCOs; SCMs are frequently involved in boundary-crossing and bridge-building and thus contribute to diffusion processes among SCOs (Meyer and Whittier, 1994; Roth, 2003; Saunders, 2014; Roth, 2016). The range of involvement in varieties of SCO is a fundamental building block in our argument about actions and reactions at the individual and organisational levels. Second, different opportunities for involvement require different skills and commitments. SCOs that are involved in advocacy need to mobilise knowledge and broker connections with policy makers and the media. Some of these tasks are performed by paid staff. Advocacy focused SCOs also require SCMs to engage in fundraising and dissemination roles that can be taken on by volunteers or paid staff, who are taking this on sporadically or on an ongoing basis. SCOs that provide specialist services need committed SCMs who are regularly involved – either paid or unpaid. Depending on the services that are provided, they might need to be more or less skilled and trained. Finally, SCOs that engage in protest events need SCMs who are able to plan and manage such events, which are time-consuming activities. On the other hand, they need to mobilise a large number of SCMs who attend protest events, often for only a few hours. An individual SCM might be a paid staff member in an SCO focusing on human rights, and in their leisure time participate as unpaid volunteer in an SCO providing aid to refugees, and occasionally attend protest events of SCOs that challenge the immigration policy of a country.

Conclusions

The varieties of SCMs and SCOs that we introduced in this chapter are both shaped by and are shaping the social worlds in which they are active. SCOs are shaped by regulations that allow or limit protest and government resources that make service provision necessary or possible. As we noted earlier in this chapter, the work of some SCOs can be understood as 'prefigurative' action, for example the efforts of mutual societies which represent a basis of insurance systems, which we will discuss in the following chapter. Because SCOs are simultaneously shaping the historically variable contexts that enable and constrain their actions, it is imperative to examine them in a historical perspective. In the next chapter we therefore describe in more depth how SCOs have contributed to and are shaped by modernisation processes.

2

The Big Picture: Social Change Makers and Social Change Organisations in Historically Variable Contexts

The end of the Cold War, symbolised by the fall of the Berlin wall in November 1989, and the end of state socialism in Central and Eastern Europe (CEE) between 1989 and 1991, had far-reaching consequences for SCOs around the world. In Europe, these developments encompassed the enlargement of the European Union (EU) to include CEE countries such as Poland, Hungary and Slovenia, among others, as new member states. The consequences for SCOs, including those addressing gender equality in CEE countries, were significant.

A historical look at European women's movements (Roth, 2017) illustrates the ways in which various political and gender regimes enable and constrain the work of SCOs. As we noted in the Introduction to our book, gender equality movements around the world have been able to achieve significant gains with respect to political, economic, and social rights. Nevertheless, gender equality has still not been achieved at the beginning of the 21st century. Neo-liberalism, as well as the end of socialism, changed the context in which SCMs addressing gender equality in the CEE countries could mobilise. Their activism was shaped by several factors. First, the end of state socialism ended repression and surveillance. This enabled groups that previously met in a clandestine manner around kitchen tables, like the participants of the East German women's peace movement (Miethe, 1999; 2000) to, instead, organise openly. Second, people in the former socialist countries were confronted with high unemployment and a massive dismantling of the socialist welfare state. Third, CEE countries that, during the Cold War, had provided assistance to countries in Asia, Africa, and Latin America then became recipients of 'aid' focused on strengthening and restoring democracy and civil society. We are putting 'aid' in inverted commas to draw attention to the deeply unequal relations between those who deliver and those who receive aid (see Roth et al, 2024). That means that aid is not necessarily oriented at the needs of aid recipients. We discuss humanitarian assistance further later and in the following chapters. Much of this 'aid' was delivered by Western SCOs, notably women's NGOs and political foundations that supported the projects of their CEE partners (Wedel, 2001; Roth, 2007). The process of EU Enlargement, which forced CEE countries to align their legislation with EU regulation (the *acquis communautaire*), provided women's organisations in candidate countries with some leverage to demand the adoption of gender equality legislation (Roth, 2008). However, the perspective of SCMs in CEE countries on this process was ambivalent. They were concerned that the reforms were introduced top-down and that gender equality legislation imported from the West did not address the concerns of women in the new EU member states (Ghodsee, 2004; 2005; Kakucs and Pető, 2000). Furthermore, concerns were raised that access to funding resulted in the NGOisation of SCOs in CEE (Lang, 2013). Moreover, it was observed that after EU accession had taken place, adopted gender equality legislation was not implemented and gender equality offices were dismantled. However, it is important to note that the adoption and implementation of gender equality and LGBTQIA+ legislation in CEE EU member states still varies (Ayoub, 2016). In addition, gains with respect to gender legislation have also resulted in populist counter-movements, which seek to defend family values and attack 'gender ideology' (Pavan, 2020; Graff and Korolczuk, 2021).

This vignette illustrates that SCOs are both shaping and shaped by broader political and historical processes. As we are arguing throughout this book, we consider SCOs and SCMs as co-creators of social change and thus partially responsible for bringing about social change. In this chapter, we focus on the *historically variable contexts* in which SCOs and SCMs are active. Scholars have adopted different ways of referring to this broader context in which SCOs perform. These conceptions range on a continuum from relatively fixed settings known as political opportunity structures (for example, Tarrow, 1994) to more dynamic entities known as arenas (Jasper, 2021). Similar to other scholars (for example, Armstrong and Bernstein, 2008; Fligstein and McAdam, 2012; Ancelovici, 2021), we propose an approach midway between these extremes. However, we conceptualise context in a more holistic and interactive way than the relatively two-dimensional continuums of structure and contingency, and politics and culture that have preoccupied many contemporary debates on the context of social change making. Our approach takes into account how changes at the macro- (state and cultural norms), meso- (organisational), and micro- (individual) levels bounce off each other. In our view, social change processes are not only influenced by sources of power (for example, states, powerful corporations, and entrenched cultural norms) but also outcomes of SCOs and SCMs. Even the most benign and the most progressive SCOs engage in activities that kick-start new approaches or help new issues emerge onto the public agenda. We purposively use the term *historically variable context* to understand context as a sum of historical and contemporary processes taking place at multiple levels, while acknowledging the ways in which the context sometimes has some stability and inertia, often changing slowly in response to pressures for social change, but sometimes surprising us with more rapid changes. A historical perspective is central to our approach because SCOs respond to and influence legal frameworks and regimes, which change over time. SCOs also influence one another, and SCMs respond to other SCOs and other SCMs. Interactions at all of these levels shape *historically variable contexts*. This means that our approach emphasises agency – the impact that SCMs and SCOs have on society – but we acknowledge that they are constrained by structures that are the outcomes of earlier interactions.

After introducing our theoretical approach, we chart the relationship between SCOs working in a variety of local, national, and transnational historically variable contexts and outline major processes of social change through three historical threads. We use threads rather than a chronology to guide our narrative to illustrate the deep intertwinement of historical processes. We recognise that modernity and modernisation are deeply problematic concepts which are Eurocentric and racialised (Gilroy, 1993; Bhambra, 2014). In fact, we demonstrate how different and intersecting systems of inequality and privilege – including capitalism, patriarchy and racial hierarchies – have been challenged, transformed, and maintained through SCOs. Our first thread concerns colonisation processes, which underpin the emergence of racialised capitalism, humanitarianism, and counter-movements such as independence struggles, and fights for environmental rights. Second, we turn to socialism, which was a response to the inequalities caused by capitalism. Varieties of socialism encompass state socialism as well as the mixed economy of welfare involving charities, self-help groups and the (welfare) state in capitalist societies. Third, we discuss the rise of fascism in the first half of the 20th century and contemporary populist movements. We demonstrate that different regime types give rise to different types of SCOs and vice versa. While describing SCOs in a comparative, historical, and global perspective, we focus primarily on modernising, modern, and post-modern societies from the 19th through to the 21st century. We understand fascism, socialism, and social democratic welfare states both as outcomes of SCOs as well as having huge impacts on social change efforts in relation to freedom of speech and assembly, civil rights, housing, education, healthcare and many more rights.

This chapter sets the scene for the rest of our book by beginning to illustrate how historically variable contexts shape the structure, strategies, and access

Figure 2.1: Social change organisations in historically variable context

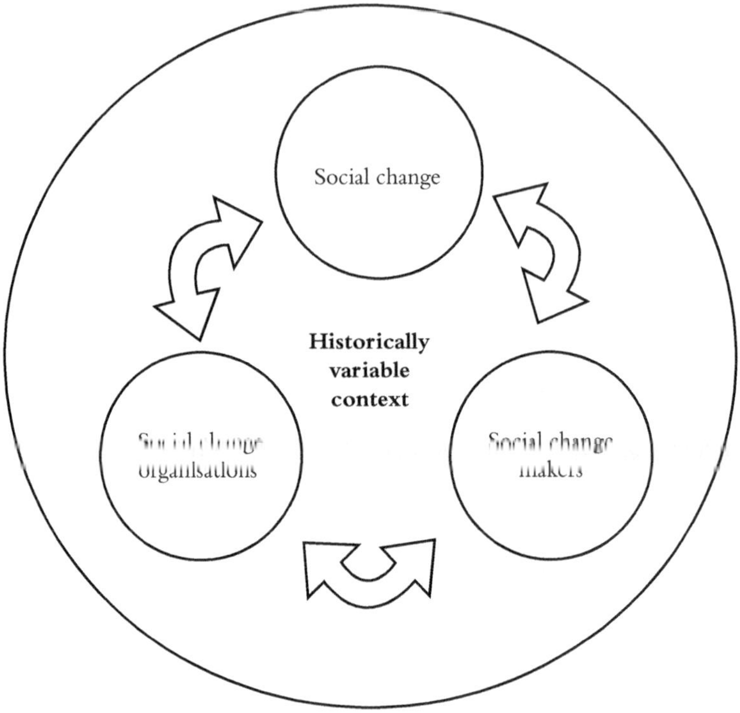

to resources of SCOs, just as the structure, strategies, and access to resources shape historically variable contexts. Figure 2.1 provides a schematic overview of the argument we present in this chapter. We emphasise that SCOs are co-creators of social (political, social, economic, cultural, and technological) change, but they are also affected by social change. Historically variable contexts shape both social change and SCOs, just as social change and SCOs can come to shape historical contexts.

In future chapters we will go in depth into different aspects that we are only touching on in this chapter (strategies in the following chapter – Chapter 3 – and resources in Chapter 4). We return to the outcomes of SCOs in Chapter 7. Let us first explain how we have built the notion of historically variable contexts before we explore the three threads sketched earlier.

Historically variable contexts

We use the term *historically variable contexts* to refer to the sometimes stable, often slowly changing and rarely rapidly altering background conditions that affect (and are affected by) organising for change. To build this concept, we draw on three bodies of literature on contingent political opportunity (structures) (Tarrow, 1994/2022; Saunders, 2009a); arenas (Jasper, 2021); and socio-technological transitions (Geels, 2019). We argue that the political opportunity structures literature is useful for understanding the more enduring and slowly changing aspects of historically variable contexts. In contrast, the concept of arenas captures the more rapidly changing aspects. The notion of socio-technological transition, usually applied to sustainability challenges, points to the ways in which multiple niche innovations eventually disrupt and alter incumbent systems. As such, it is a useful way to capture how contextual conditions for SMOs change in sets of actions and interactions among SCOs and the broader context, resulting in historically variable contexts.

There are multiple conceptions of political opportunity structure, but one of the most popular syntheses (Tarrow, 2022) suggests that it refers to three key factors. These are the presence or absence of state (or political system) allies, tolerance of the polity to protest (or, in our current rendition not just to protest but the actions of SCOs more broadly conceived), and repression or facilitation by the state (or political system). The central thesis of political opportunity structure is that these factors provide opportunities (or not) for movements to emerge, develop and succeed. In an open political system, which has state allies, tolerance to protest and facilitation, protests are permitted to develop. But in an extremely open polity, there may be no need to protest because channels are so open to challengers that they can cooperate instead of protest. In contrast, in a closed political system, which has no allies, no tolerance to protest and repression, protest movements may go 'underground' or result in insurgency.

Our description of political opportunity structures so far makes the approach sound much more coherent than it really is. Scholars often add new variables such that the approach has famously been recognised as being 'in danger of becoming a sponge that soaks up every aspect of the social movement environment' (Gamson and Meyer, 1996: 274). Apart from the complaint that political opportunity structure encompasses too many variables to be useful, there are two long-standing points of critiques of political opportunity structure theory. These are that it is too static and too state-centric (Goodwin and Jasper, 1999). Key advocates of the approach have sought to make it more dynamic by including more 'volatile variables', purposefully dropping the word 'structures' from the end of the name (Tarrow, 1998), and in rebranding the approach as a 'political process model' (McAdam, 1982). There has also been an attempt to consider cultural (Hallgrimsdottir and Benoit, 2007) and discursive (Koopmans, 1999; Ferree et al, 2002) opportunity structures.

More recently, scholarship has sought to decentre further the state as the locus of power by using the concepts of multi-institutional politics (Armstrong and Bernstein, 2008), fields (Ray, 1999; Fligstein and

McAdam, 2012) and field opportunity structures (Ancelovici, 2021). Each of these approaches are useful for recognising that SCOs and SCMs direct their energies not only at states but also at other institutions that hold power (for example, healthcare systems, businesses, and schools), as well as at sets of cultural norms that come to hold their own power. These approaches are useful for understanding the emergence and strategies of varieties of SCO, notwithstanding the difficulties of understanding what constitutes a field (for they are at the same time consensual and contentious, overlapping and distant, strategically oriented and cultural, inclusive of social movements and challenged by social movements, settled and changing and cultural).

A particularly useful advance of Armstrong and Bernstein (2008) is their insistence that politics and culture are multi-constitutive. This allows their approach to understanding the 'opportunities' for SCO emergence to account for contentious action, insider activism, and prefigurative politics. So far so good, this is very much in tune with our own argument. However, these existing approaches still focus on seemingly potent sources, and certainly very visible sources, of political or cultural power as if they are all that matters. Our own interactionist and constructivist approach invites a focus on the obvious sources of power to which other scholars refer, but also draws attention to the less likely places from which power emerges by taking a more holistic look at the sets of actions, reactions, and interactions that take place at the macro- (for example, states and institutional systems), meso- (organisational), and micro- (individual) levels. For example, as we explained in the Introduction to our book, service provision in response to a disaster is often political, even if inadvertently so, triggering new opportunities for SCMs and other SCOs, and contributing to social change processes. Despite weaknesses of the concept of political opportunities, even of its modern variants, we still find it useful as a building block in assembling the concept of historically varying contexts. Let us explain why.

Although we distance ourselves from the classic political opportunity *structure* approach, we take from it the basic premise that democracy, including the existence of a civil society or public sphere in which citizens have the right to assemble and discuss their opinions, is an important precondition (as well as outcome!) for the formation of many varieties of SCO. In autocratic or authoritarian regimes, civil rights are severely limited if not totally absent. This either prevents the formation of overtly challenging SCOs or forces dissident and insurgent groups under the radar (Johnston, 2015). This is not to suggest, however, that SCOs are entirely absent in authoritarian regimes. However, they represent a form of high-risk activism as the example of a group of German anti-fascist students around the siblings Hans and Sophie Scholl, the Weisse Rose (White Rose), who were executed in 1942 after distributing leaflets (Rickard, 2010), demonstrates. Furthermore, Owen (2020) deploys the concept of 'participatory authoritarianism' to capture the forms of active citizenship encouraged in China and Russia. These forms of participation are situated within illiberal contexts, channelling civil engagement in ways that do not threaten the regimes. Whether such forms of 'participatory authoritarianism' absorb or neutralise contentious action or underpin resistance and contribute to ending authoritarian regimes is an empirical question. Regardless of where a regime is positioned on a continuum between authoritarian and democratic, the regime type – a relatively stable structure – has a significant impact on the emergence, shape, and form of SCOs.

Of course, it is not only in the case of authoritarianism that there is an obvious link between background conditions and organising for change. Beyond this basic premise, there is a wealth of scholarly literature on protest-focused SCOs that reflects on how historically variable contexts influence social change efforts in cycles of actions, interactions, and reactions. Among other things, scholars have examined how labour movements react to economic and labour conditions (Barker et al, 2013; Cox and Nilsen, 2014), just as right-wing movements respond to a swing to the left (Diamond, 1995; Roth, 2018; McVeigh and Estep, 2019). Identity-based movements push for the rights of groups marginalised by cultural and political currents (Larana et al, 1994; Kriesi et al, 1995), and reactionary movements oppose their gains (Pavan, 2020; Parker, 2021; Graff and Korolczuk, 2021). To add to the abundant literature on contentious politics, we believe the question of how context shapes the emergence, transformation, and activities of professionalised NGOs engaged in advocacy and service-provision deserves more attention. SCOs that provide services and are engaged in advocacy are shaped by legislation and regulation that concern, for example, eligibility for grants, requirements for service-delivery, taxation, and – crucially – the right (or lack thereof) to take an openly political stance. Such questions are usually addressed in the literature that compares welfare states, and examines welfare state expansion and contraction as well as humanitarianism. Service-providing SCOs include domestic charities as well as internationally operating SCOs.

Our understanding of historically variable contexts takes heed of the notion of political opportunities being more than 'just structural' (Saunders, 2009a), recognising the varieties of SCO taking interactive roles in bringing about and resisting social change. We do this by pointing out that how one SCO or one SCM views the context in which they exist can vary drastically from how others do. For example, even in democratic regimes, civil rights have been and sometimes still are unequally distributed by race, class, gender, and other markers of inequality (Kollman and Waites, 2009). The criminalisation of homosexuality (at the time of writing still in 69 countries, nearly half of them in the Commonwealth, [Human Dignity Trust, 2023])[1] prevents LGBT[2] people from publicly forming and joining organisations representing their interests. The de-criminalisation of homosexuality is an outcome of successful mobilisation and in turn widens the political rights and participation of LGBTQ+ people (Ayoub, 2016). Furthermore, SCMs generate their own narratives of opportunities based on wider processes within their networks that allow them to construct stories about how they might be able to affect the political environment. For example, different generations of SCMs mobilising against climate change constructed very contrasting narratives about the opportunities they faced, based not on any objective measure of structural openness, but rather on their prior experiences (de Moor and Wahlstrom, 2019).

Political opportunities, then, are not fixed based on regime type or government policies. Saunders (2009a) distinguishes different relationships that SCOs have with the state – cooperative, contingent (depending on the issue or approach the SCO is taking), ambivalent, absent, or negative – which can also be applied to relations with transnational authorities (Bursens, 1997; Hooghe, 2008) as well as more localised decision-making entities (Garland et al, 2023), corporations, and other sources of more and less visible power. If, as Meyer (2003: 19) states, the national opportunity structure, therefore, is 'nested in a larger international environment that constrains or promotes particular kinds of opportunities for dissidents within a state, so, too, is the local state nested in the national'. Furthermore, 'boomerang effects' (Keck and Sikkink, 1998) enable local and national actors to use leverage from international actors as well as impact on them, causing what have been termed 'ping-pong effects' (Zippel, 2004).

Decision-makers are perhaps most likely to have positive relationships with professionalised NGOs with consultative status or with service-delivery organisations that deliver contracts for them. Ambivalent relations take place when the decision-makers do not seek the advice of SCOs but are not averse to it when it is offered. Advocacy work probably best fits this scenario. Contingent relations are common for SCOs that vary their tactics, such as Friends of the Earth England, Wales, and Northern Ireland, which has sat on government advisory committees in the UK but has also staged media stunts outside Westminster. Negative relations between decision-makers and SCOs are perhaps most likely among radical or law-breaking SCOs, like Just Stop Oil, or those that seek to overturn the state, like the Socialist Workers Party in the UK. An absence of relations with decision-makers is the common situation for nascent SCOs of any variety as well as self- and mutual-help SCOs. In a nutshell, a radical protest focused SCO will be less well received by any decision-makers compared to a more moderate one, just as a state that is relatively closed to an SCO that focuses on protest might be very open to a service-providing voluntary organisation (Lang, 2013; Stroup and Wong, 2017).

Instead of conceiving of the backdrop of social change-making as a structure, or set of structures, the arenas approach follows our own emphasis on sets of actions, reactions, and interactions. SCMs are viewed as 'players' who dip in and out of different types of SCOs and issues that are themselves fluidly conceived 'arenas' that exist in dynamic multi-directional cultural and political flows (Jasper, 2015). The advantage of this approach is not only the emphasis on fluidity but also the ways in which it moves beyond the state-centric bent of political opportunities, allowing for a full consideration of the cultural turn in movements. Armstrong and Bernstein (2008) highlight the overlap between culture and politics; an important part of social movement activity recognised since the 1970s. The new social movements of the 1970s were not so much about changing political systems as they were about changing cultural practices (Melucci, 1996). However, they also brought important legislative changes with respect to racial, gender, and sexual equality, for example in the form of affirmative action and anti-discrimination legislation. Duyvendak and Fillieule (2015) similarly adopt a fluid approach but, like us, emphasise the importance of historical processes. While we also understand social change as something dynamic and always in flux, and something that is political and cultural as well as economic, technical, and social, it is our view that some aspects of the context in which SCOs sit are a lot more stable than the arenas approach suggests. Take, for instance, authoritarian regimes that are much less in constant flux than their democratic counterparts. Cox and Nilsen's (2014) Marxist approach also takes a step away from fluidity, encouraging us to consider enduring structures of power and inequality, which are far from fluid and – in some ways – structure what SCMs and SCOs are able to attain. Not all SCOs and SCMs have equal power and access to resources because of structural factors.

We argue, then, that there are relatively stable elements of the historically varying context in which SCOs exist that change slowly and are shaped by power relations and inequality. We liken this to the notion of an incumbent regime in socio-transitions literature (Geels, 2019). Yes, relatively stable elements do change, sometimes slowly, sometimes quickly. In socio-economic transitions just as in social change making, new political, cultural, economic and social ways of doing things can emerge into a new regime (or, in our words, a new historical context) through a range of niche innovations. These innovations, in our sense of the transitions' literature, encourage and facilitate new ways of being in society. Some of these innovations will stabilise and gain credence, some will bounce off one another, or encourage other innovations, and they may eventually result in something new. In a nutshell, the triad of structure, contingency, and agency at multiple interacting levels is crucial to understanding historically variable contexts.

Historically variable contexts matter for all varieties of SCO. For example, as we will discuss later, SCOs have been involved in the delivery of welfare prior to the emergence of welfare states, during the golden age of the welfare state, and in the age of neo-liberalism (Young, 2000; Harris and Bridgen, 2007; Billis, 2010; Clemens and Guthrie, 2011). In fact, voluntary organisations and self-help groups can be understood as pre-figuring the welfare state (see Skocpol, 1992). Furthermore, the increasing budgets of SCOs engaged in service delivery go hand-in-hand with the neo-liberalist shift from the state to sub-contracted third sector organisations. This also applies to humanitarian organisations that emerged in the 19th century, and that grew especially since the end of the Cold War (Barnett, 2011).

SCOs in historical perspective: three threads

Informed by our interactionist approach we are now examining the central role that SCOs play in transnational and national modernisation processes, industrialisation, and colonial and imperialist endeavours, which are inextricably intertwined (Go, 2013; Steinmetz, 2013; Bhambra, 2014). As we mentioned in the introduction to this chapter, we disentangle these deeply intertwined processes by pursuing three threads. The starting point of the first of these three threads are colonisation processes and their consequences, which we follow to the contemporary BLM movement. We then turn to varieties of socialism in the second thread, which ends with contemporary neo-liberalism. The third thread focuses on fascist and right-wing movements that can be understood as an effort to respond to neo-liberalism as well as to defend White privilege.

Thread one: from colonisation to Black Lives Matter

The development of a civil sphere during the enlightenment is an important aspect of democracy, though civil and political rights were initially limited to those benefiting from White and male privilege. However, aristocratic women participated in the salons and secret societies – early SCOs of the privileged (Burke, 1989). Unravelling this thread allows us to examine the role of SCOs in humanitarianism, environmentalism, independence movements, and movements for racial justice. While some progress with respect to racial justice has been made, contemporary societies are still characterised by legacies of (settler) colonialism and racial stratification. In pursuing this thread, we demonstrate that ostensible benevolent humanitarian and conservation organisations are shaped by and perpetuate racial stratification, historically as well as today.

Now, in this first thread, we focus on SCOs that were entangled in contributing to, perpetuating, and resisting racial stratification and the displacement of Indigenous peoples. We note that SCOs worked alongside colonial administrators with the mission to 'civilise' people who were othered and constructed as 'less enlightened', 'savages' or 'barbarians'. These SCOs included conservation and faith-based SCOs. Formal conservation came to Africa and North American during the colonial period. Well-meaning conservation graduates working for large-scale SCOs set wildlife conservation laws that were suited to Western societies and landscapes, but which were inappropriate for Africa and the Americas. These conservation laws set up significant wildlife reserves that effectively locked people out of their homelands, encapsulating an attempt at nature protection that has become known as 'fortress conservation' (Siurua, 2006). These well-meaning policies ignored variations in temperature and weather, prioritised the preservation of enigmatic mega-fauna often seen as pests by locals and trampled roughshod over socio-cultural practices that had kept Indigenous peoples in tune with their natural environments and enabled them to prevail for centuries. Hunting for subsistence in Indigenous homelands became reconstrued by conservation colonialists as poaching and stealing, while Indigenous peoples were settled into neighbouring regions where they faced stigma and social marginalisation (Crowe and Shryer, 1995). Indigenous environmental movements have responded in combined struggles for land, for survival, for dignity and for ancestral rights against colonial racism. Such struggles continue on Indigenous lands to this day (Gillio-Whitaker, 2019; Dominguez and Luoma, 2020; Ahia and Johnson, 2023). Indigenous peoples in the US are still active in struggles lasting over half a century against intrusions from Western capitalism (Clark, 2002). It is a hard lesson for well-meaning conservationists that attempts to redress industrial intrusions created enhanced negative side effects through eco-colonialism.

At the same time, missionaries' efforts to educate and improve living conditions tried to eradicate Indigenous knowledge while pursuing Evangelism, earning them the label 'handmaidens of colonialism' (Maxwell, 2005). Missionary societies are SCOs in so far as they – presumably – sought to improve the lives of 'others', justifying colonialism and imperialism with the 'White man's burden' to 'civilise'. Such humanitarian efforts were meant to ameliorate the living conditions and undermine revolutionary efforts following American independence and the French and Haitian revolutions (Burnard et al, 2022). Thus, humanitarian SCOs – and their successors in the 21st century discussed later – demonstrate that benevolence and good intensions are shaped by power relations and intersecting forms of inequality (Roth et al, 2024).

The emergence of racialised capitalism was thus associated with a newly developing humanitarian sensibility in Europe in the late eighteenth century. This sensibility was characterised by the confidence of having the capacity to act on behalf of human suffering and injustice, combined with a higher level of conscientiousness (Haskell, 1985a; 1985b). Humanitarian efforts included the founding of the Society for Effecting the Abolition of the Slave Trade in London in 1787, which petitioned Westminster for the abolition of the Slave Trade as well as La Société de Amis de Noirs founded in Paris in 1788 (Burnard et al, 2022). Furthermore, middle-class women were an important group of anti-slavery campaigners who engaged in boycotting the products of enslaved labour such as sugar – thus preceding contemporary fairtrade activism (Everill, 2020). The abolition of slavery resulted in financial compensation of slaveholders for the loss of their 'property' (rather than reparations for the freed slaves) and provided capital for industry, commerce, and philanthropy (Hall et al, 2014). Prominent foundations in the UK such as the Leverhulme foundation or the Rowntree foundation only quite recently (after 2020) started confronting their past and the fact that their founders benefited from slavery and other forms of forced labour.[3] Furthermore, British industrialists who were active in the abolitionist movement benefited from labour exploitation in Britain. This means that humanitarian SCOs are riddled with contradictions, advocating for change (for example, the end of slavery), while maintaining class and racial privilege.

Moreover, far from being passive, Britain's enslaved and colonial subjects were agents in the fight against slavery and for decolonisation as Gopal (2019) demonstrates. She describes the alliances and transnational moral communities of colonial insurgents and British dissidents. Gopal (2019) provides examples of violent and passive resistance, mutinies, revolts, and wars across the British Empire. Of course, such resistance could also be observed in other Empires as the Haitian Revolution (1791–1804) demonstrates (James, 2001 [1938]). The leaders of nationalist movements found allies in a range of SCOs including voluntary organisations, trade unions, and political parties (Maxwell, 2005). Indigenous leaders not only instigated uprisings and mutinies, but they also inspired dissident movements in Britain (Gopal, 2019).

SCOs thus played a role in emancipatory movements fighting for national independence and civil rights. Commonwealth soldiers who fought in the British Armed Forces and African American soldiers in the US military in the two World Wars defending democracy, were confronted with racism and ongoing discrimination in peace time (Gopal, 2019). African Americans' citizenship rights were the basis for military mobilisation, but, after the wars, people of colour faced discrimination and segregation. Similarly, women were excluded from work in male-dominated sectors of the labour market, where they had replaced men during the war. Rather than being recognised for their contributions, women and ethnic minorities were asked to make space for White native men when they returned from military service. Commonwealth soldiers were not only confronted by a lack of recognition but also by continued racial discrimination at the end of the wars. In the first half of the twentieth century, transnational networks of those active in independence movements and those working to end racial inequality emerged (Slate, 2015). One example is Marcus Garvey's Universal Negro Improvement Association (UNIA), a mass movement that was active in the US, Africa, the Caribbean, Europe, and Australia in the 1920s (Slate, 2012). Furthermore, SCMs in the US who mobilised for civil rights travelled to India to meet with Gandhi and learn about non-violent resistance (Slate, 2012). Thus, anti-racist and anti-colonial SCOs became intertwined and included a range of SCOs, including faith-based organisations. Slate (2015: 5) notes that the Bandung conference in 1955, the first intercontinental conference of people of colour, 'marks both the summit of colored solidarity and its incipient decline'. Subsequently, the leaders of the newly independent states deemed state building, economic development and the Cold War more important than 'transnational solidarities of color' (Slate, 2015: 5). The emphasis of mobilisation shifted from the 'self-determination of colored peoples against imperialism and white supremacy' to human rights of individuals against repressive regimes (Slate, 2015: 5).

Other SCOs engaged in humanitarian endeavours provided support and care for victims of war and conflicts. Two of the most prominent humanitarian SCOs are International Committee of the Red Cross (ICRC), which was founded by Henry Dunant in response to the Battle of Solferino (1859), and the Salvation Army (1865) (Redfield and Bornstein 2011). Throughout the 20th century, humanitarian organisations such as the Save the Children Fund, the International Rescue Committee (IRC), Oxfam, and CARE emerged in response to wars and conflicts to support refugees and other victims of war and to address poverty. These SCOs were involved in providing relief including food, shelter or medical support in disaster and crisis organisations. Some of these SCOs transformed over time and became multi-mandated organisations later providing both relief and development assistance, engaged in service provision as well as advocacy.

Following independence movements and de-colonialisation processes, development assistance was introduced in the late 1940s resulting in continuities and discontinuities between the colonial government and the emerging aid system (Cooke, 2003; Kothari, 2006). Humanitarian SCOs were particularly prevalent in former British colonies. Over 500 humanitarian SCOs could be found in five former British colonies alone (Burnard et al, 2022). The 1980s debt crisis resulted in a further proliferation of SCOs in humanitarianism and a restructuring of international development. This resulted in the rise of NGOs and in the 1990s some large international NGOs (INGOs) including Oxfam, Médecins sans Frontières (MSF/Doctors without Borders), CARE and Save the Children began to dominate the sector of humanitarian SCOs (Donini, 1995). This internationalisation of humanitarian SCOs has been compared to the expansion of multinational corporations (Simeant, 2005). In addition to the big international SCOs, there is also a multitude of smaller national and international organisations (Swidler and Watkins, 2017). At the end of the 1990s, a broad coalition of SCOs mobilised for debt relief under the banner of Jubilee 2000 (Saunders and Papadimitriou, 2012).

The rise of SCOs in the provision of assistance – both internationally and domestically – is an expression of neo-liberalism. This involves privatisation and a re-structuring of the welfare state. This has significant consequences for the resource mobilisation of SCOs, some of which must now bid for contracts (Watkins et al, 2012). (We discuss the ways in which these organisations garner resources in Chapter 4.) These transformations resulted in a growing mobilisation of SCOs in the Global North and South, and SCOs took on important functions in disintegrating nation states and in the delivery of development cooperation. SCOs were perceived as more cost-effective and closer to constituencies than governmental organisations and thus ideally positioned to implement 'bottom-up' development (Kamat, 2004), in contrast to failed 'top-down' approaches that had been delivered by large bureaucratic institutions including governments, and bi- and multilateral organisations. SCOs thus took on a central role implementing projects and mediating between donors and communities.

Furthermore, the complex emergencies of the 1990s challenged the Dunantist tradition of humanitarianism, which emphasises neutrality as a precondition for humanitarian aid. Humanitarian organisations have not only been instrumentalised by the parties involved in the conflict but also by donor countries (Schade, 2007), which is probably most famously reflected in the 'hearts and minds' approach during the war in Afghanistan when Colin Powell referred to NGOs as 'force multipliers' (Powell, 2001).

The 1990s were also characterised by the globalisation of faith-based SCOs (Barnett and Stein, 2012). Various factors contributed to this development, including the growth of the Christian right in the US and of political Islam, the rise of identity politics and decline of communism, the emergence of a transnational civil society and the support of diaspora communities for humanitarian and development assistance (Tomalin, 2012). The growth of Muslim aid agencies is a good example of the interaction between SCOs and can be understood as a response to Western Christian and secular aid agencies. To counter the aid of Christian and secular Western aid agencies, which were feared to be motivated by Christian missionary evangelism, several Muslim relief organisations emerged. These organisations were operating in Ethiopia, Chad, and Somalia and responded to disasters such as the famine in the Horn of Africa. Increasing oil revenues and the spread of communication technology underpinned solidarity efforts for Muslim victims of conflicts and natural disasters (Petersen, 2012). Historically variable contexts shaped different generations of transnational Muslim aid: The da'watist NGOs, which emerged at the end of the 1970s, understood aid as 'simultaneously material and spiritual'; jihadist NGOs were shaped by the war in Afghanistan and emphasised justice and militancy; solidarity NGOs emerged during the war in Bosnia in the 1990s and distanced themselves from da'wa and jihad, adopting mainstream humanitarian principles and rejecting any involvement in conflict; and finally 9/11 and the War on Terror resulted in the emergence of secularised Muslim NGOs due to stricter regulations and control (Petersen, 2012). The relationship between these generations of transnational Muslim SCOs to other faith based and to secular organisations varies.

At the beginning of the 21st century, the legacies of colonialism are still reflected in the huge inequalities between and within countries and in on-going environmental racism (Sultana, 2022). It is now long established that the people who experience the worst environmental pollution are marginalised people, often of colour (Bullard, 1990). One famous example is the struggle of the Ogoni people of Nigeria against oil giant Shell from the 1990s to present. Appropriation of land, dangerous gas flares and significant oil spills have blighted the lives of many, while Shell has purportedly been reluctant to share any of the profits. The peaceful Ogoni protests for political autonomy and environmental rights in the mid-1990s, collectively known as the Movement for the Survival of Ogoni People, were heavily repressed and the campaign leader Ken Saro-Wiwa was brutally executed. This struggle is important to mention not only because it can foreground environmental racism but also because it took years before Western SCOs came to assist. Initially, there were not enough negative repercussions from repression for human rights SCOs to feel compelled to join, and the emphasis given to political autonomy was off-putting for green groups. Eventually Amnesty International, Human Rights Watch, and Greenpeace joined the struggle, which has helped the cause become well-known across the world. SCOs continue to fight for the rights of the Ogoni peoples (Obi, 1997; Demirel-Pegg and Pegg, 2015). In 2022 a group of nine widows of peaceful protesters who had been assassinated in complicity with Shell lost their attempt to sue the oil giant. Whereas mostly peaceful front-line activists are labelled 'eco-terrorists' and persecuted, corporations that destroy the environment and cause the death of humans and other species are not (yet) held accountable (Gallagher, 2023).

Despite the ongoing endeavours of UN agencies, bilateral organisations and SCOs (we assess their achievements in Chapter 7), poverty and conflicts persist and are worsening not least due to climate change. Racial stratification, the most significant legacy of colonialism, shapes all sectors of society, even the SCOs that seek to address global inequality (Roth, 2015; de Jong, 2017; Khan et al, 2023). In 2020, the BLM movement, which emerged in 2013, achieved a global acknowledgement of racism and racial stratification in all societies and organisations. Protesters toppled statues of slave traders and others who were responsible for and benefited from exploitation and subordination, while mainstream organisations declared their solidarity with the BLM movement. The BLM movement resulted in widespread promises of main-stream organisations to 'decolonise' and to address racial (in)justice. This includes SCOs engaged in humanitarianism and development and resulted in calls for 'localisation' and the end of 'White saviourism' (Khan et al, 2023). To summarise this thread, a variety of SCOs underpinned and responded to racialised capitalism. The growth of SCOs – both in size and number – is an expression of neo-liberalism, that is the privatisation of services and responsibilities previously taken up by the state, which we discuss further in the next section.

Thread two: from socialism to neo-liberalism

In the 19th century, socialism – in addition to humanitarianism and environmentalism – emerged in response to the growing inequalities introduced by racialised capitalism. Socialism is often identified with state socialism, but it encompasses a very wide variety of approaches that range from cooperatives and workers associations to revolutionary organisations. In countries like Russia and China, revolutionary organisations were successful in establishing state socialist societies, which provided subsidised housing, education, and medical care and thus offered social rights. However, political and civil rights were significantly restricted if not absent during state socialism. Characteristic of repressive regimes, the development of a civil society was constrained by surveillance and the incarceration or expulsion of dissidents. Nevertheless, as noted in the beginning of the chapter, dissident groups met in the private sphere, for example around kitchen tables (Miethe, 1999) and contributed to the end of state socialism. Before, during, and after state socialism, in many countries around the world socialist parties also became part of democratically elected governments and shaped social democratic and other welfare states. In this section of the chapter, we focus less on socialist SCOs, which seek to transform the class-structure, than on benevolent, charitable organisations, which perpetuate class-differences but also provide welfare and respond to the needs created by unequal capitalist societies.

In the industrialising nations of the Global North a variety of SCOs addressed social inequalities and needs associated with industrialisation and urbanisation processes. They resulted in the formation of trade unions and cooperatives as well as settlement houses such as Toynbee Hall in London (Himmelfarb, 1990; Briggs and MacCartney, 2011; Hartley, 2019) and Hull House in Chicago (Deegan, 1988). While some of these organisations were engaged in solidarity and mutual assistance, others were driven by benevolent and charitable impulses. Moreover, Weinbren (2007) argues that charities and mutual aid groups cannot be strictly separated, as both involve elements of reciprocity. Following Skocpol (1992), we argue that these SCOs not only addressed social problems but also prefigured the welfare state. Thus, they represent a step towards guaranteeing social rights – namely access to education, healthcare, housing, pensions, and other public support. Welfare states are grounded in a variety of SCOs. Such organisations include charitable and benevolent societies founded by middle-class reformers and humanitarians providing support to immigrant and working-class communities in urban centres. It is important to keep in mind that this benevolence encompassed elements of regulation, for example ensuring employment and training for employment (Adams, 2007). Some mutual societies and self-help organisations emerged in association with labour movements. The mutual aid and private insurance groups that emerged in the 19th century (van Leuwwen, 2007) are not only precursors of state pensions and private insurance companies, but also comparable to contemporary micro-credit programmes. Such brotherhoods represented early insurance systems to which each member contributed and received support in times of need.

Thus, although the debate around 'the mixed economy of welfare' is associated with neo-liberalism and the restructuring or dismantling of welfare states at the end of the 20th century, it can, in fact, be observed in many countries since the 19th century (Harris and Bridgen, 2007). Skocpol (1992) describes the role of women's organisations for the emergence of the US welfare state with respect to the protective legislation and support for mothers and their children. In European countries, welfare state formation was closely related to the formation of trade unions and workers associations (Korpi, 1978; Esping-Andersen, 1990). In the mid-20th century, Keynesianism or state intervention was introduced to address economic downturns and associated unemployment to prevent poverty and inequality, but also to strengthen capitalist democracies and avoid the spread of socialism. As noted previously, there is a long-standing debate about the relationship between the welfare state and the third sector. In times of shrinking welfare states, SCOs tend to take on services previously provided by state agencies. Neo-liberalism thus not only includes a shift from the state to the market but also to the third sector and thus SCOs. As Bridgen and Harris (2007) point out, a variety of SCOs have consistently played a role – albeit a changing one – in the mixed welfare economy. Moreover, supplementary, complementary, and adversarial models of government-non-profit sectors can be distinguished (Young, 2000).

As noted at the beginning of the chapter, the fall of the Berlin Wall in 1989, and the break-up of the USSR in 1991 ended the Cold War and marked the end of state-socialism in Eastern Europe. It was widely perceived as the 'end of history' (Fukuyama, 1989) and the victory of capitalism. These developments reinforced neo-liberalism and increased the role of SCOs in the provision of domestic welfare and overseas aid. Furthermore, the increase of conflicts after the end of the cold war resulted in a growing number of humanitarian interventions and the growth of NGO budgets (discussed earlier). These developments brought military and civilian actors in contact with each other: a trend that intensified after 9/11 and the start of the Global War on Terror (GWOT). Security measures related to the GWOT significantly impacted the mobilisation of SCOs. The beginning of the 21st century was shaped both by the increasing significance of anti-globalisation or global justice movements and the political and military response to the terrorist attacks on the World Trade Center in New York and other targets in the US as well as other countries. Alter-globalists met at World Social Forums and protested outside the meetings of political and economic world leaders. The battle of Seattle in 1999 had brought together a broad coalition of labour, environmentalists and other groups pursuing social and environmental justice. However, a global justice week organised by a broad coalition of SCOs, which was planned to begin on 11 September 2001 in Washington, DC, was prevented by the previously mentioned terrorist attacks (Gillham and Edwards, 2011).

While 9/11 and the GWOT constrained the mobilisation of SCOs, the end of the Cold War also resulted in a revival of civil societies in Eastern Europe, and we will now return to addressing the impact of the transition from socialism to capitalism on women's organisations in Central and Eastern Europe that we briefly discussed in the beginning of this chapter. After 1989, a multitude of SCOs emerged in former socialist countries, including women's organisations, which initially did not necessarily prioritise gender issues (Roth, 2007; 2008). However, over time – and in response to funding opportunities – some of these organisations started to focus on women's rights (Einhorn, 2006). They thus provide a good example for the impact of funding on the changing agendas and strategies of SCOs, which we will discuss in subsequent chapters. These women's organisations included successor organisations of the former state socialist women's councils, while others grew out of the dissident movements that were concerned with peace, human rights and environmental issues during socialism (Einhorn, 1993; Einhorn and Sever, 2003). In addition to SCOs that were a result of the transformation of earlier organisations, explicitly feminist groups emerged, including the *Unabhängiger Frauenverband* (UFV) (Independent Women's Association) in the former East Germany (Hampele Ulrich, 2000). The formation of these women's SCOs responded to women's exclusion from politics and labour markets, and the loss of care services in the context of shrinking social services. Furthermore, the formation of women's SCOs reflect a growing awareness of gender inequality, and are an expression of the more general emergence of civil society in Central and Eastern Europe (CEE) (Watson, 1997).

It is important to note that immediately after 1989, Western SCOs, foundations, governments, international organisations (UN, International Monetary Fund – IMF), and the EU set out to strengthen civil society and assist the transformation to capitalism (Wedel, 2001). Several aid organisations (including USAID (United States Agency for International Development), the US Department of State, Ford Foundation, Soros' Open Society Institute, UNIFEM,[4] and so on) supported organisations that addressed women's issues such as domestic violence and supported anti-trafficking programmes. However, the collaboration between Western SCOs, feminists, and foundations, and women's organisations in CEE was far from smooth, despite the fact that Western SCOs wanted to support the development of civil society and women's activism in the CEE countries. Meanwhile women's organisations in the transformation countries consciously sought allies in the West – as well as in other CEE countries. The East–West collaboration was shaped by the unequal relationships between aid donors and aid recipients and different understandings of feminism and women's needs (Ghodsee, 2004). However, this is nothing new as previous conflicts between women from the Global North and South at UN conferences demonstrate. Similarly, differing experiences of living under (former) state socialism and in democratic capitalist (welfare) states shaped encounters between Eastern and Western women. What we want to emphasise here is that the end of socialism and the funding provided by Western donors shaped the relationships between women's SCOs in Europe. The conflicts between Eastern and Western women and women's organisations highlight the diversity of 'women's' interests, which are associated with inequalities – with respect to class, race, ethnicity, and other markers of difference. Conflicts within and between women's organisations are shaped by the positionalities – in class-stratified, racially stratified, heteronormative societies White heterosexual middle class cis-women are differently positioned than women who belong to ethnic minorities, are homosexual, working class or trans-women (of course, any combination of these aspects of privilege and discrimination are possible) (Emejulu and Bassel, 2023). Similarly, women in East European post-socialist societies were differently positioned than women in Western capitalist societies. Moreover, it is important to keep in mind that Western capitalist societies also represent different gender regimes (Walby, 2009) with consequences for women's political participation (Roth and Saunders, 2020).

Neo-liberalism and the associated welfare state retrenchment since the 1980s have resulted in growing inequality in recent decades. Workfare policies of New Labour in the UK and other social democratic or centre left parties around the world have contributed to stagnating and falling wages and an increase of precarious working conditions. Even in Sweden, the paradigmatic social democratic egalitarian welfare state has been eroded by neo-liberalist policies and experienced worsening working conditions, a rise in youth unemployment, and urban segregation (Schierup and Ålund, 2011; Schierup et al, 2018). Neo-liberalism has been pursued to an even greater extent by conservative governments and the effects of public sector cuts have been instrumentalised by anti-immigrant organisations. The global financial crisis and the subsequent widespread austerity measures at the beginning of the millennium resulted in a resurgence of populist movements from the left and from the right. Both types of populist movements address problems associated with neo-liberalism, criticise domestic and international political and financial elites and make appeals to 'the people' (Mudde and Kaltwasser, 2017), but how they conceptualise 'the people' varies considerably. Populist movements from the right tend to be racist, heterosexist, and homophobic whereas populist movements from the left seek to be inclusionary and intersectional, trying to mobilise across race, class, gender, sexuality, and nationality. But it is also important to mention forms of populism on the left that are aligned with global justice movements and attempts to create broad coalitions of progressive movements (women, LGBTQIA+, civil rights, and so on) representing the 99 per cent. Syriza, Podemos, the Indignados and Occupy all emphasised solidarity across differences and bring together cross-class and other heterogeneous coalitions (Roth et al, 2014; Saunders et al, 2016; Flesher-Fominaya, 2020) and socialist counter-movements have sought to continue to mobilise against neo-liberalism (Dean and Maiguashca, 2018). However, to some extent working-class voters who were traditionally aligned with and supported social democratic parties have turned to right-wing populist movements in various European countries (Front National, UKIP [United Kingdom Independence Party], AFD [Alternative für Deutschland (translated; Alternative for Germany)]). In recent years, elections throughout Europe and in the US brought wins for populist movements, which we will discuss in the next section.

Thread three: from fascism to right-wing movements

The interwar period (1919–39), did not only see the emergence of humanitarian organisations and welfare states but also the rise of fascist movements in Germany, Italy, Spain, and elsewhere. Fascist movements emerged in nations that had been defeated in World War I, as well as those that had been victorious (Passmore, 2017). Furthermore, these fascist movements had highly heterogenous constituencies, encompassing supporters from all social classes and – at least initially – diverse ideologies. Fascism emerged from a 'whole range of veteran, religious, and charitable groups, bourgeois clubs, women's groups, et cetera' (Passmore, 2017: 585). However, many of these politically heterogeneous groups, that had formed during and after the war, were right wing and all were opposed to communism. Although not everyone involved was committed to violence, fascism included 'bourgeois self-defence organisations, often paramilitary' (Passmore, 2017: 584). As in other countries, fascist organisations such as the Nazi Party in Germany were not just middle class. However, Fisher (1996) found that the German Nazi Party was less successful recruiting workers in regions with strong Catholic and strong social democratic cultures. The authoritarian regimes, which emerged from fascist organisations restricted civil rights, violently repressed dissidents, and destroyed trade unions and parties on the left. Dissident and resistance movements could only undertake clandestine actions, which risked incarceration and death for participants, for example of the members of the Weisse Rose.

The end of World War II brought the defeat of fascist regimes in Germany, Italy and Japan, while fascism continued in Spain, Portugal and Greece. The UN in 1944 and the European Economic Community (EEC) in 1957 were formed in the hope that such transnational alliances could promote peaceful relations and prevent wars among member states. The Allied Forces defeated and occupied Germany and engaged in a denazification process, which – temporarily – removed teachers and other civil servants from their positions if they were alleged to have ties to the Nazi Party. However, Payne (2006) notes that 'the denazification policy actually strengthened the neo-Nazis in the post-war years' (p 216). Thus, post-fascist right-wing movements existed in Europe and the US long before the Great Recession of 2007/2008 (Virchow, 2017). For example, in West Germany 'new right' groups emerged as early as in the 1950s and nationalist movements became more prominent after the unification of East and West Germany in 1990 (Bitzan, 2017; Virchow, 2017). To some extent, these far-right movements represented a backlash against the progressive movements of the 1960s and 1970s, whereas the West German student movement of the 1960s was a response to the failed denazification of the Federal Republic of Germany. This is a further example of the interaction between SCOs.

Populist movements from the right engage in 'othering', emphasise traditional gender roles and gender binaries and exclude ethnic minorities, immigrants and minority religious groups. How enemies are perceived varies across Europe and the US (Blee, 2017) – far-right groups in the US perceive Jews and non-Whites as enemies, but in Europe Islam and immigration from Asia and Africa are framed as threats. Just as anti-Semitism and racism can also be observed in Europe, immigrants are facing discrimination in the US as well. What far right and populist movements from the right in Europe and the US share is the fact that they are anti-feminist, anti-immigrant, homophobic movements that seek to 'take back' the country in the name of supposedly 'native' (White) populations (Bhambra, 2017a; Bobo, 2017; Narayan, 2017). Much media attention has been devoted to those who feel left behind by structural transformation and so-called 'identity politics' that promote the rights of ethnic minorities, women, and LGBTQIA+ people. It is important to note that the supporters of anti-immigrant and anti-gender politics are seeking to defend their privilege and include White, middle-class, well-educated men and women (Roth, 2018).

In the US, the Tea Party was established in response to Barack Obama's presidency in early 2009. Its active participants have tended to be White, male, middle-aged, and older, and regular evangelical Protestant churchgoers (Skocpol and Williamson, 2012). As small business owners largely enjoying above average incomes, they cannot be seen as economically marginalised. The success of the Tea Party has been attributed to the combination of grassroots mobilisation, advocacy groups promoting an ultra-free market, and conservative (social) media (Skocpol and Williamson, 2012). Some recent ethnographic studies examined the supporters of the Tea Party in the US (Skocpol and Williamson, 2012, Hochschild, 2016) and the English Defence League (Pilkington, 2016). Right-wing organisations like these represent an important reminder that not all SCOs are progressive, indeed some are advocating to preserve privilege and inequality.

Far right and anti-gender movements are not identical, but they partially follow similar patterns. They reject the notion that gender is socially constructed and fluid. They assert that there are two biological distinct sexes – men and women – with different characteristics and roles. That means that they reject gender equality and homosexuality, and do not recognise transsexuals. The Catholic Church plays a crucial role for the emergence of anti-gender movements (Kuhar and Paternotte, 2017; Pavan, 2020; Graff and Korolczuk 2021). The rise of populist forces in Europe and elsewhere represent a 'culturalist response to structural crises' and reaction against the 'neoliberal consensus' (Kováts, 2018). Rather than addressing the socio-economic inequalities exacerbated by neo-liberalism, right-wing populists attack human rights, as well as gender and LGBTQIA+ equality legislation and discourse (Kováts, 2018; Verloo and Paternotte, 2018; Graff and Korolczuk, 2021).

Both in the US and Europe, the rise of nationalist, anti-immigrant and racist movements is accompanied by the election of far-right parties such as the Alternative für Deutschland (Alternative for Germany) in Germany, National Front in France, the Freedom Party of Austria, the Polish Law and Justice party, the Progress Party in Norway, Fidesz, and Jobbik in Hungary, and the Sweden Democrats to name a few are associated with a significant rise of hate crimes. Cunningham (2018) argues that it is important to distinguish between the rise in hate crimes, which are enabled by the historically variable context, and the growth of hate organisations, which are responding to a threat and seeking to preserve the status quo and therefore should be understood as 'reactive mobilisation'. The emergence of hate organisations thus represents another example of SCO interactions – with the contemporary context, with each other, and the SCMs that engage with them. The Trump administration provided an opportunity that fosters the rise in hate incidents, this development has been well documented by the Southern Poverty Law Centre (SPLC) (Cunningham, 2018). Hate crimes have also increased in the UK after the EU Referendum and in many European countries a growing number of racist and anti-Semitic attacks have been noted. It is important to note that despite the notion that Brexit and the support for Donald Trump represented the rise of those 'left behind' (Dodd et al, 2017), both were supported by cross-class coalitions (McVeigh and Estep, 2019). Indeed, middle-aged and older middle-class college-educated men and women were well-represented among the supporters of the campaigns to Leave the EU and to 'Make America Great Again'. Indeed, they were even more likely to support Brexit and Trump than working-class voters (Walley, 2017; McCall and Orloff, 2017; Virdee and McGeever, 2018). Thus, just like the fascist movements of the 1930s, the populist movements that emerged in the second decade of the 21st century are cross-class mobilisations and must be understood as interacting with progressive SCOs.

Conclusions

In this chapter, we have both highlighted the importance of SCOs in bringing about social change, and how historically variable contexts enable and constrain SCOs and SCMs. We provided a broad overview over the role of SCOs in social, political, cultural, and economic developments in a historical and global perspective. The concept of historically variable contexts is central to our argument here. These contexts are important for understanding how the structures and strategies of SCOs are shaped by and shape their relations to local, national, inter-, and transnational contexts. Moreover, a historical perspective on the development of SCOs, as well as the theories and concepts explaining them, is useful for understanding path dependent developments and contemporary practices and processes. In the following chapters, we will further analyse how governmental structures at the local, national, regional, and global levels are targets for SCOs and sometimes also provide resources in the form of financial support or legitimacy. In the next chapter, we will describe the strategies of SCOs and further explore how they shape and are shaped by their relationships to the state, which matter in multiple ways. While we emphasise the need to look beyond the state to broader economic, cultural, and social and technical contexts, we note that the state provides a legislative context in which these organisations operate, some activities can be constrained (for example protest) while others are supported (service provision). Thus, state–SCO relations comprise policing as well as providing financial support. SCOs' relationships to the state and transnational structures are intertwined with the strategies that SCOs employ to which we turn next. This involves moving away from a perspective on incumbent/challenger relationships and broadening the perspective from contentious politics to also include insider activism and prefigurative politics.

3

Ways of Making Change

In the late 1990s and early 2000s, the global justice movement (GJM) came to prominence around the world. It first grabbed the attention of journalists, academics and the public through large and oftentimes disruptive summit hopping demonstrations that coincided with meetings of the World Bank, the International Monetary Fund, the G20, G8, and G7. But a closer examination of the movement reveals, behind the scenes, multiple repertoires, strategies, and tactics tailored to specific grievances localities and settings. It is for this reason that Tarrow (2005) referred to the participants involved in these apparently global mobilisations as *rooted cosmopolitans*. While some of the SCMs associated with the GJM came together for big international demonstrations, they and many of their counterpart SCMs were rooted to locally situated concerns and shaped by more localised sets of geographically and historically variable contexts.

Some scholars consider the GJM as a 'movement of movements' (della Porta and Mosca, 2005; Cox and Nilsen, 2007) because it brought together a range of causes including environmentalism, humanitarianism, workers' rights, and other struggles for equality. Together, the SCOs involved in the GJM used a range of strategies to seek justice for people and the environment across the globe. A useful way of thinking about the GJM is as a call for, in Paul Kingsnorth's words, 'one no, and many yeses'. This means that while the GJM universally rejects neo-liberal forms of capitalism that generate injustices (the 'one no'), there were multiple ways to take action to begin to redress these injustices (the 'many yeses'). These ranged from marches, occupations and riots through to hacking and reconnecting electricity supplies, reclaiming land, guerrilla gardening, and helping others in need.

The GJM provides a useful lens to examine the repertoires, strategies, and tactics of SCOs, and to illustrate how social change efforts are multi-faceted and shaped by geographically and historically variable contexts. It also shows the ways in which SCOs work together strategically (and sometimes less strategically) in chains of interacting strategic repertoires. This does not only apply to the GJM as we will show in this chapter.

Our argument in this chapter is that a moving and interacting pool of SCOs employs a variety of tactics that are shaped by their strategies, which in turn are shaped by historically variable contexts (including SCMs' perceptions of those) as we outlined in Chapter 2, and in accordance with their values and goals. After briefly introducing this argument, and conceptualising tactics, strategies, and repertoires, we define and provide a contextualised overview of the overlapping and evolving tactics, strategies and repertoires of SCOs through the lens of a selection of causes: struggles for democracy and independence, environmentalism, humanitarianism and gender equality. This allows us to elaborate on how the political and historical contexts, values and goals of SCOs, in interaction with one another, shape their choice and use of tactics and the forming of strategic repertoires. Woven into our analysis is a discussion about the affordances of ICT for delivering tactics, and some thoughts on whether they have transformed the repertoires of SCOs. Even though we do not have space for a comprehensive survey of *all* tactics employed by SCOs, our focus on causes allows us to illustrate the synergies between, affordances of, and potential trade-offs, of different tactics.

We illustrate the central argument of this chapter in Figure 3.1. The overlapping circles at the centre convey the ways in which SCOs use a range of tactics, either on their own or through engagement with coalitions, networks and alliances with other SCOs that employ different tactics (a theme we pick up in more detail in Chapter 6). The triangle illustrates how the range of tactics used is shaped by historically variable contexts, and the goals and values of SCOs and SCMs.

As we have indicated in Chapter 2, the shape of the historically variable context – including different authoritarian and democratic regime types – matters for SCOs and SCMs repertoires. Thus, the relationships between SCOs and the (welfare) state change overtime and shape SCOs' activities. Furthermore, the activities of SCOs are rooted in the *values* of their leaders and members and are related to their *goals*, which are both closely interrelated. As we explain in more depth in Chapter 7 (on the outcomes of SCOs), their goals vary from helping a small group of beneficiaries, to incremental policy change, through to programmatic change. Demands for different types of change result in different emphases given to *strategies* geared towards reform (for incremental change) or radicalism (for systemic change).

Goals are tightly linked with values, which are also central to shaping SCOs' tactics, strategies, and repertoires. This is exemplified by SCOs that hold the value of non-violence and therefore eschew militancy.[1] Let us now do some conceptual work in relation to tactics, strategies, and repertoires before we discuss specific strategies associated with the causes of democracy/ independence, environmentalism, humanitarianism, and gender rights.

Figure 3.1: Key factors influencing the tactics of social change organisations

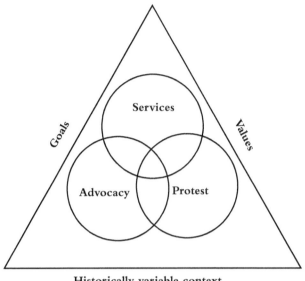

Historically variable context

Tactics, strategies, and repertoires

SCOs pursue a broad range of different *tactics*, which we broadly categorise in three sometimes overlapping categories: protest (including revolutions and uprisings, non-violent direct action, demonstrations and vigils), advocacy (including bargaining, influencing the public and lobbying government and other targets), and service provision (directly helping themselves and/or others with goods and services). Tactics are not the same as strategies but are decided in relation to them. Whereas tactics are activities – specific tools – implemented to achieve a strategy, a *strategy* is a broad plan about what needs to be achieved in interaction and/or conflict with others (Meyer and Staggenborg, 2012). In this sense, strategies relate to the *goals* of SCOs and their *values*. We find Jasper's (2013) military analogy useful here: whereas a strategy is the overall battle plan, the tactics are the means used by 'lower officers ... to implement the commander's strategy during the battle' (Jasper, 2013: 1262). SCOs are strategic in the sense that they work with and against other actors to achieve their goals.

Repertoires, a term initially developed to help understand how changes in contentious action came to emerge in the UK in the 17th century (Tilly, 2008), represent broader patterns and combinations of tactics that – in their stronger form – are more or less scripted but with small innovative changes. Repertoire shifts usually happen gradually as social and political contexts change and as SCOs respond to one another. Tilly (2008) shows how repertoires of contentious politics in the UK shifted from food riots to the archetypal social movement repertoire of marches and lobbying targeted at national government that we still recognise today. This repertoire emerged from factors such as the reduction in the power of local landlords, the centralisation of power to London, and the adaptation of funeral processions. Although the tactics of SCOs vary from organisation-to-organisation, and to a lesser degree from sector-to-sector, we wish to draw attention to the fact that there have been shifts in repertoires as the boundaries between pressure groups, voluntary organisations, social movements, and NGOs have become increasingly fluid. ICT have also facilitated shifts in repertoires that were unforeseen before the advent of Web 2.0, changing patterns of networking among SCOs and SCMs. The fluidity of repertoires is partly illustrated through slow changes in strategies – and therefore tactics – of different types of SCO over time but is also illustrated in part by the work of unpaid volunteers and paid staff members who oftentimes belong to more than one organisation (Chapter 5).

Digital repertoires involve the use of ICT to support SCOs and perform social change tactics (Van Laer and Van Aelst, 2010). It is important to recognise that ICT and social media allow extensive global interaction and quick dissemination of SCOs messages. But there are also downsides. Digital inequality (Halford and Savage, 2010) precludes many from participating, and many observers are alarmed by the ways in which the internet opens opportunities for state surveillance and repression (Tufekci, 2017). In addition, it is more difficult to build trust, and decision-making might be hampered by a 'tactical freeze' (Tufekci, 2017).

The effect of ICT on the strategies and tactics of SCOs reflects the overall argument of our book and of this chapter in particular. The external impetus of changing opportunities provided by ICT within a varying technological context has resulted in significant shifts in the way that some SCOs mobilise and perform tactics. Some have endorsed their use and others have reacted against it or founded and used subterranean social media networks. In turn, the creative use of ITCs has come to shape the functionality of ITC platforms.

When social media were introduced some 20 years ago it was believed that ICT might completely transform organising for change into a fluid online set of activities that can function independently from SCOs (Bennett, 2003). Instead, we argue that there is a range of evolving digital repertoires across SCOs that are more and less fluid. Together, these have the potential to attract the support of SCMs who are to a greater or lesser extent familiar and comfortable with technology. These repertoires function alongside each other in an increasingly hybrid division of online and offline labour. The digital repertoires of SCOs vary from being entirely *internet-based*, for example, online petition sites like Change.org or 38 Degrees (Karpf, 2016) and self-help social media feeds, to being *internet supported*, that is making minimal use of ICT simply to contact members (Van Laer and Van Aelst, 2010). This means that while some digital activism is only carried out online, most digital communication of activists underpins more or less frequent face-to-face interaction. Van Laer and Van Aelst (2010) also distinguish low and high threshold actions. Internet-supported and low-threshold repertoires include making online donations, changing consumer behaviour, and recruiting SCM participants or volunteers. Actions that are internet supported and have a high threshold include participation in a transnational demonstration. ICT make it much easier to organise and learn about such events and activities. Similarly, the participation in a local vigil or providing mutual aid in a neighbourhood represent internet supported low threshold activities. On the other hand, there are actions that are internet-based and have a low-threshold such as online petitions, reading and sharing advocacy reports, and virtual sit-ins. Hacktivism and intense participation in online support groups represent forms of high threshold internet-based activity.

Rather than fully replacing traditional SCO activities, ICT and social media have increasingly transformed these activities. Rallies and demonstrations are announced on social media in addition to posters, leaflets, more and more replacing telephone trees or mass-emails. Meetings can be held online or in person, as well as hybrid. These developments started before the COVID-19 lockdowns, but since then have become even more widespread. We thus follow Bennett and Segerberg (2012) and Pavan (2014) in noting the hybridity of connective (online) and collective (on- and off-line) action. On- and off-line forms of organising for change intersect in important and creative ways. How does this relate to offline tactics?

Spheres of action: ways of classifying tactics

Van Laer and Van Aelst's (2010) notions of low- and high-threshold online activism draw upon the work of McAdam (1986) who distinguished between high- and low-cost and high- and low-risk off-line activism in the pre-internet era. McAdam (1986) coined these terms in relation to SCOs that focus on protest, but, as we now illustrate, they are just as applicable to the broader SCO universe. Low-risk actions include peaceful approved demonstrations, drafting press releases and donating to service delivery organisations. Examples of high-risk actions include illegal occupations and activities that are criminalised such as accessing abortion, disseminating and consuming illegal drugs, or helping migrants. However, what constitutes high-risk depends as much on the context as on the activity itself. For example, in repressive regimes even exchanging information online can be high-risk (or, as Van Laer and Van Aelst, 2010 put it, high threshold) and in societies in which homosexuality is stigmatised, if not criminalised, being 'out' can be risky (Taylor and Raeburn, 1995). Moreover, even academics carrying out research and speaking out about racism and right-wing politics are at risk (Ferber, 2018). Among low-cost actions we could include throwing some money into a beggar's collection bowl, whereas high-cost actions include procuring expensive drugs to support citizens' health, or time-consuming participation in grassroots discussions (for more on how these concepts have been applied to protest focused SCOs, see Tarrow, 1998; Taylor and Van Dyke, 2007).

Another way to classify spheres of action, as 'insider' or 'outsider', is based on the *targets* of the action (insider or outsider advocacy) and the *location* of the action (insider or outsider activism). Lobbying, a form of insider activism, requires an SCO to be on open-doors terms with political decision-makers, which includes having opportunities to draft legislation and to be closely and comprehensively consulted. This means taking the 'long march through the institutions' as Rudi Dutschke, a leader of the West-German student movement of the 1960s, put it (Schelsky, 1974: 346). Feminists within the Catholic Church and the military changed these organisations from within through interest-group participation and, as Katzenstein (1998) put it, *unobtrusive mobilisation*. Furthermore, women who were underrepresented in US politics, used *insider tactics*, such as 'lobbying, testifying, writing legislation, providing public education, mobilising constituencies, and supporting women's candidates' to get *outsider* (women's) *issues* (such as reproductive choice, violence against women, economic inequality and so on) on the agenda (Spalter-Roth and Schreiber, 1995: 105). Based on a study of 19 US women's organisations, some of them active since the first wave of the women's movement at the end of the 19th century, Spalter-Roth and Schreiber (1995) examined the tactical choices of these organisations in the 1980s. They found that the differences between radical and mainstream feminist organisations started to blur, and the organisations professionalised and mastered the 'art of insider politics', learning to function as interest groups (p 113). *Insider activism* takes place *within* institutions or the workplace where the institution itself is transformed and used as a vehicle for change.

Insider activism has found increasing scholarly attention, particularly in the context of the women's movement, where it has been studied as 'state feminism' (Stetson and Mazur, 1995; Kantola, 2010). Not only have the successes of insider feminism been celebrated, but also scholars have revealed the risks of compromising the values of SCMs who can find themselves caught in a difficult and messy place in between the targets and aspiration of fellow activists and the rules they need to follow within their institutions (Browne and Bakshi, 2013). The institutionalisation of gender equality as well as the adoption of environmental sustainability goals, which resulted in appointing officers and establishing departments or working groups in mainstream organisation, represent further examples of insider activism.

Outsider activism refers to mobilisation outside of institutions including peaceful protests, direct action, or community organised soup kitchens. SCOs, for example grassroots organisations, can have outsider status, but through connections to insider activists (for example, members of Green parties or government commissions) have access to material and non-material resources. As we will discuss later (Chapter 5), SCMs might simultaneously or successively be involved in insider and outsider activism and serve as brokers between different SCOs. Closely related to the question of insider and outsider status is the professionalisation of SCOs. As we discuss in more depth in Chapter 4, professionalisation can constrain an organisation to insider channels and distance it from its grassroots supporters. Central to our argument here is the fact that insider and outsider activities often work in synergy to obtain social change.

Some activists refer to the application of pressure from above and below as 'political sandwiching' (Roth, 2007: 475). Insider and outsider activism and pressure from above and below are not the same. Pressure from above refers to initiatives from transnational organisations (for example the UN or the EU) or legislative change, for example the adoption of anti-discrimination legislation. Such legislative change might have been brought about through protest (outsider activities) or lobbying (insider activities), but usually a combination of both. Since adopting progressive legislation is not the same as implementing it, pressure from below is important to hold legislators accountable.

Now that we have distinguished low- and high-cost and low- and high-risk forms of social change making from each other, and introduced the interplay between insider and outsider activities (note that we have more to say about the relationships between SCOs in Chapter 6), we discuss the tactics used by SCOs. We make, once more, the argument that different types of SCOs need to be holistically analysed as they influence one another and work together to achieve social change in planned and unplanned ways. We begin our account with higher-risk and higher-cost tactics and move step-by-step to lower risk strategies. Thus, we begin with protest, and then move on to look at advocacy, and finally service provision and submerged networks/prefiguration. We do not put any of the tactics of SCOs 'in a box' but instead illustrate the ways in which different tactics are deployed simultaneously in struggles for social change.

Exploring tactics through the lens of causes

We begin with violent uprisings and revolutions illustrated through struggles for democracy and independence. We start here because these activities – when successful – secure the democratic conditions in which other SCOs can flourish. From there, we move to consider non-violent protest, illustrated through the Arab Spring, and the cause of environmentalism. For environmental struggles to thrive, civil and political rights must first be secured. However, direct action results when activists sense a democratic dead end as tactics focused on institutional change fail to deliver the changes required (Saunders, 2009a). Environmental SCOs also engage in more routine demonstrations and rallies as a way of raising public awareness, and as a form of lobbying for change. We use environmentalism and humanitarianism to discuss the ways in which SCOs deploy more routine demonstrations and lobbying. Humanitarian organisations are better known for their advocacy work and service provision, so we use them to explore the intersections of protest and advocacy work. Finally, we illustrate service provision by focusing on the cause of gender equality. As with the other causes we explore, feminist struggles engage in a range of tactics. They became semi-institutionalised in the 1980s as they helped to deliver a range of women-centred services including reproductive health services, rape/battering crises centres and childcare facilities. These examples sit alongside many other services provided by SCOs, including bookstores, health food stores, cafes, magazines, and social enterprises, which serve as hubs connecting SCMs and the wider public. These more every-day focused SCOs help guarantee continuity in social change struggles through times of reduced activity and visibility. In other words, they serve as submerged networks (Melucci, 1989) and abeyance structures (Taylor, 1989), which keep people interested in the causes, even if only from behind the scenes. As such, they provide important infrastructures for SCOs and the people who participate in them. They can also be considered as prefigurative politics (Yates, 2015) as they provide services that are otherwise unavailable.

Protest

When we think about protest in the early 2020s, the first things that come to mind are probably large-scale civil liberties marches against COVID-19 restrictions, demonstrations to stop or re-start the counting of ballots from the US presidential election, acts of civil disobedience by Extinction Rebellion, or a gathering to pay tribute to BLM. But protest is actually more varied than this. What is protest? Protest consists of a multitude of forms of action by individuals or groups that seek to change aspects of the political, social, or cultural status quo (della Porta and Diani, 2006). According to Quaranta (2017: 2), 'the repertoire of protest and contentious politics ... range from mild forms of action, such as petitions or boycotts, to more routinized forms, such as demonstrations, to even illegal or violent forms'. Although we might usually not think of petitions and boycotts as protest, they are frequently identified as forms of protest in classic studies about political participation (Marsh, 1974; Barnes et al, 1979) as well as more contemporary ones (Benson and Rochon, 2004; Quaranta, 2014). Political participation is usually classified as violent where there is violence towards persons, but it sometimes also incorporates violence against property (Rootes, 2003).

Violent protest manifestations and non-violent uprisings

Violent manifestations consist of uprisings and riots that damage property and sometimes people. Uprisings can be classified as revolutions when they bring about regime change – in particular, democratisation – by successfully replacing (or significantly modifying) political power holders with an alternative preferred by insurgents. Skocpol (1979) posits that revolutions emerge when the following conditions are present: the old regime is based on traditional forms of economic organisation that exploit the working classes; there is a crisis that the current system cannot accommodate; a rebellion (or, as we put it, 'uprising') emerges; and a new – totally different – transformed regime emerges. Riots are shorter-term episodes, but are otherwise similar to uprisings. Uprisings and riots are usually the result of extreme discontent throughout large swathes of a population (McAdam et al, 2001).

Violent protest manifestations have played a central role in bringing about social change over the last four centuries. For example, they have been credited with ending feudalism; fighting for the end of slavery and colonial rule; and securing the rights of women, workers, ethnic and sexual minorities. The complex interplay of a variety of tactics employed by SCOs means that violent protest manifestations do not exist in a vacuum. Some previously peaceful SCOs turn violent in response to social and political conditions, some use multiple tactics and others work in networks with actors across the violent to non-violent spectrum. Indeed, Malm (2021) argues that many historic episodes of organising for change, usually misremembered as entirely peaceful struggles, were successful precisely because of the interplay between violence, threats of violence, property damage, civil disobedience, and more respectable forms of organising for change. Especially prior to the availability of ICT and social media, SCOs played an important role mobilising participation in violent protest manifestations.

We begin by discussing the interdependency of the political context and the tactics of SCOs fighting for independence from colonial rule. As we illustrated in Chapter 2, this represents a historical starting point for modernisation processes and has paved the way to (more or less) democratic regimes. Based on Foran (2005), we will illustrate the evolution of different tactics in periods of major social change through a discussion of the Algerian independence war, the first great anti-colonial revolution in the 20th century. We then turn to the peaceful Arab Spring uprisings. These cases allow us to survey a wide range of SCO tactics within the context of revolutions for post-colonial independence and the transformation of repertoires of action in North Africa from violent action to peaceful occupations, which inspired protests around the world.

The story of the bloody battles for Algerian independence (1954–62) shows how a hard fought revolutionary struggle emerged from institutional activism (in political parties). It reveals the dynamic interplay between insider and outsider activism and factional splits between SCOs willing to be violent and those eschewing violence – but whose actions *together* helped, eventually, to bring about social change. These SCOs were further complemented by the engagement of service providing SCOs. The peaceful Arab Spring protests, in contrast, are frequently used to illustrate the complementary nature of on- and off-line forms of activism, but this case perhaps best illustrates a turning point in the establishment of the repertoire of assembling in squares that is now commonplace across the world. Both stories illuminate the importance of dynamic historically variable contexts (Chapter 2) in shaping organising for change.

In Algeria, a French colony since 1830, SCMs left the French Communist Party to form the Algerian Popular Party (APP), which was banned in 1939 and re-emerged as Mouvement pour la Triomphe des Libertes Democratiques (MLTLD) (Foran, 2005). Some members of MLTLD formed the paramilitary organisation Organisation Speciale (OS) which considered revolutionary action. After OS was shattered by the French rulers the MTLD split, and the leadership chose to pursue non-violent action. Former OS members formed a new clandestine organisation, the Comité Revolutionaires pour l'Unite et l'Action (CRUA). In 1954, CRUA began the Algerian anti-colonial social revolution (1954 to 1962) and announced the Front de Libération Nationale (FLN). Within the first two years, the FLN successfully mobilised the major anti-colonial organisations and broad swathes of Algerian citizens across gender and class, and rural and urban populations (Foran, 2005: 97–9). Between 141,000 and 1.5 million Algerian revolutionaries, which included rural and urban groups, men and women, and almost the entire urban Muslim population, lost their lives in this anti-colonial social revolution (Foran, 2005). Although involving severe losses, these protests for independence succeeded. The FLN received moral support from the international community, including the UN, and material aid from North African countries including former French colonies such as Tunisia and Morocco. The use of torture was condemned by French trade unionists, youth, and intellectuals, who participated in large demonstrations against the French government, which sent troops to Algeria to in response to the anti-colonial uprising. After an attempted insurrection within the French Army in 1958, de Gaulle became president of France and in 1959 proposed the self-determination of the North African colony in response to ongoing mass demonstrations and street violence in Algeria. In 1962, a referendum was held and 90 per cent of the French population voted for Algerian independence, which was declared in July 1962 (Foran, 2005: 103).

Less than 60 years after Algerian independence, a new wave of unrest occurred in North Africa and West Asia, which included peaceful protests and occupations of squares. This so-called 'Arab Spring' has its roots in street protests following social media coverage of the self-immolation of the Tunisian street vendor Mohamed Bouazizi who set himself to fire after being humiliated and beaten by the police (Khondker, 2011). Protests and civil unrest followed, while demonstrations and strikes were organised by trade unions and lawyers. The government reacted with repression, but the army turned against the leadership and the leader of the one-party-state left the country a month after Bouazizi's death (Meyer, 2021: 44).

Tunisia's 'Jasmine Revolution' encouraged and inspired uprisings in other North African and West Asian states including Algeria, Bahrain, Egypt, Jordan, Libya, Syria and Yemen, but none of them removed the existing regime as quickly and successfully as the uprising in Tunisia. In fact, Syria experienced a long-lasting civil war that resulted in significant refugee movements and a refugee crisis as we discussed earlier (see Introduction). Street protests in Egypt brought together various groups of dissidents who were united in their opposition to President Hosni Mubarak. The attempt of the Egyptian government to shut down internet providers and thus undermine the online mobilisation had the paradoxical effect of increasing the number of street protesters (Meyer, 2021: 48). Furthermore, the Egyptian administration failed to enforce a curfew and prevent the occupation of Tahir Square where hundreds of thousands of protesters came together. The protests led to the resignation of Mubarak who a year later was replaced by the leader of the Muslim Brotherhood, Mohamed Morsi. Morsi's attempt to establish Islamic rule resulted in further protests by liberals, Christians and secularists. Subsequently, a state of emergency was declared and eventually the former Defence Minister Abdel Fattah el-Sisi became prime minister and democratisation processes in Egypt stalled (Meyer, 2021: 49).

Overall, the attempts to democratise Egypt were only partially successful. However, the occupation of Cairo's Tahir Square in spring 2011 inspired world-wide occupations like the Occupy movement, which started in

New York in September 2011, and other anti-austerity movements such as the 15-M in Spain. We discuss other, similar, mobilisation outcomes in Chapter 7. Digital technologies played a central role in these mobilisations and the uprisings during the Arab Spring and have been somewhat misleadingly termed 'Twitter revolutions'. Therefore, it is important to emphasise the hybridity of online- and offline mobilisation. Social media brought protesters together and they could share images and recordings from various occupations around the world. Tufekci (2017) provides a nuanced assessment of the affordances of social media during the Arab Spring and in other contexts. These affordances include many paradoxes – social media can undermine state-controlled media, but at the same time they can also be employed for surveillance, be censored, or be used for propaganda. Furthermore, bringing together large numbers of people in 'leaderless' movements can stall decision-making and make it more difficult to build trust (Tufekci, 2017). In addition to social media, networks (Volpi and Clark, 2019) and 'nonmovements' of collective actors without recognisable leadership and organisation (Bayat, 2010:14) mattered during the Arab Spring.

Non-violent non-systemic protest manifestations

In this section, we continue to look at the engagement of SCOs in non-violent protest manifestations through the lens of the struggles to halt environmental degradation and mitigate climate change. Similar to violent protest manifestations, non-violent protest manifestations are also organised and mobilised by a range of SCOs and also engage people who are new to organising for change. The environmental struggle is a good lens through which to view SCOs' engagement in a broad range of non-violent protest manifestations, including non-violent direct action, civil disobedience, occupations, and more routinised forms of protest like demonstrations, boycotts, and petitions. The case of non-violent environmental action is also a textbook example of how different SCOs working with these tactics influence each other and shape one another's strategies (Saunders, 2013). Before we dive into the environmental cause, we first do some brief definitional work.

Non-violent direct action aims to practise the principle of peaceful resistance, which has roots in the Gandhian principle of *Satyagraha*, which – in short – recognises that the aggrieved should be able to express their demands, and that they peacefully accept any damage to them inflicted by their opponent. Being the receiver rather than the giver of violence is oftentimes a conscious strategy intended to provoke a moral response in the opponent and therefore to halt the oppression (Parekh, 1997).

An *occupation* is the forceful taking or holding of a public or private space to achieve or resist social, political or cultural change (Palacios-Valladares, 2016).

An occupation can last anywhere between a few minutes to months, years or even decades. It might be a temporary roadblock (for example, Extinction Rebellion), a long-term squat for living in or a long-term social centre (for example 56a), a week-long symbolic occupation (for example, the Camps for Climate Action – see Saunders and Price, 2009; Saunders, 2012) or a more enduring camp such as Occupy or Greenham Common (Roseneil, 1995; 2000; Feigenbaum, 2010; Feigenbaum et al, 2013; Eschle, 2017; Eschle and Bartlett, 2023; Kerrow et al, 2023; Mackay, 2023). Occupations are a form of civil disobedience, along with non-violent direct action.

Demonstrations are street protests, that can be defined as 'collective gatherings in a public space whose aim it is to exert political, social and/or cultural influence on authorities, public opinion and participants through the disciplined and peaceful expression of an opinion or demand' (Casquete, 2006: 247). They take place in a variety of forms: marches/parades, rallies, vigils and picketing. Due to space constraints, we confine our account here to marches, which vary from ritual parades to more spontaneous marches. Ritual parades are scheduled events – often annual – that commemorate a historical event or mark an upcoming event (Klandermans, 2012). Typical among ritual events are the annual May Day labour marches across Europe that usually take place on International Workers Day to raise attention to workers' rights (Peterson and Reiter, 2016).

We distinguish three different types of environmental SCOs – the conservationists, 'newer' environmentalists, and newer still radical activists (Dalton, 1994). In the West, recent manifestations of non-violent direct action environmental protest have drawn heavily on the repertoires of the radicals of the 1990s. New innovations are striking from school (Global Climate Strike) and purposefully seeking arrest (Extinction Rebellion, until April 2023). Although our account of environmental protest is Anglo-centric, we wish to draw attention to the fact that Western environmentalists have incorporated Indigenous people's environmental protest repertoires (Gilio-Whitaker, 2019; Ahia and Johnson, 2023) into their own praxis: non-violent direct action and blockades are common forms of resistance outside of Western contexts.

Although there are precedents, the first conservation organisations to emerge in the UK were established in the 19th century and include the Open Spaces Society (established 1865), the Selborne Society (1885) and the Royal Society for the Protection of Birds (RSPB, 1889) (Green, 1981; Lowe, 1983; Clarke, 2004). Conservation organisations are often characterised as advocacy or hands-on conservation-oriented in their tactics, which we will discuss in the next section, but they have more radical roots than many remember and continue, to this day, to engage in protest. Let us give two examples. In July 1871, the Open Spaces Society mobilised thousands of people to attend a protest in Epping Forest to protest against plans to fence it off to prevent public access. The RSPB began its life as a women's only organisation that protested against the sale and wearing of hats adorned with plumes from birds, and sought to encourage its members to avoid eating all birds except – for some reason – ostriches. Over time, it broadened its remit to the management of nature reserves for birds, including purchasing significant tracts of land. It has also organised significant citizen-science bird surveys and engaged in educational activities, including the Young Explorers scheme for young bird enthusiasts.

The Open Spaces Society and the RSPB are classified as conservationist organisations, but they continue to engage in many protests alongside their conservation work. The Open Spaces Society arranges regular protest walks, including to request protection for Clapham Common in London. The RSPB protested in 2002 against an airport proposal at Cliffe in North Kent, which would have destroyed internationally important habitat for birds. In 2006, it was part of a significant coalition to Stop Climate Chaos, surprising many commentators by organising coaches to deliver hundreds of its supporters to the 50,000-or-so strong march and rally (Saunders, 2008a). Annual climate change marches have continued to be a feature in the streets of London in the run up to the United Nations Conferences on Climate Change. The summits themselves are also met with significant climate demonstrations. In 2015, the Paris summit witnessed tens of thousands of protesters, initially protesting peacefully. This turned violent when members of the French Gilets Jaunes (Yellow Vests) movement staged counter protests against proposed climate mitigation solutions. The Gilets Jaunes contrasted the 'end of the world' with 'the end of the month' (their pay packet), thus challenging the sustainability agenda and framing it as an elite concern that disregards people's material needs (Martin and Islar, 2021). That does not mean that the Gilets Jaunes (a highly diverse movement) are necessarily against green politics, but that they emphasise that environmental justice needs to include social and economic justice (Wilkin, 2021).

In the 1970s, a new type of environmental SCO emerged, which was concerned with humans' increasingly apparent negative effects on natural environments and global environmental systems (Atkinson, 1991; Doyle and McEarchen, 1998). These SCOs, which include Greenpeace and Friends of the Earth, were stimulated by a new tranche of radical environmental literature that warned of the dangers of pesticides (Carson, 1962), the limits to economic growth (Meadows et al, 1972) and the need for a new ecological paradigm (Catton and Dunlap, 1978; 1980).

Greenpeace protests, which, to this day, include disruptive direct action, have been based on the strategy of 'bearing witness' to environmental problems and sharing this with the public via daring mediagenic stunts (Dale, 1996; Weyler, 2004; Born, 2019). Greenpeace emerged in 1971, when a small group of anti-nuclear activists hired a boat that was barely seaworthy to bear witness to – and to attempt to intercept – nuclear weapons tests that were active off the coast of Amchitka, Alaska. It failed in its original mission because the boat broke down, but a new wave of environmental lobbying making creative use of press stunts was born. Although the organisational structure and other functions of Greenpeace have changed markedly since 1971 (Saunders, 2014), Greenpeace continues to bear witness. In summer 2020, an issue of its *Connect* magazine for supporters brought the public's attention to overfishing from giant super trawlers, oil tankards at sea, penguins in peril, plastic pollution, forest fires in Poland, and destruction of tropical forests from the industrial meat and other industries.

Greenpeace and Friends of the Earth, however, have both been heavily critiqued by a third group of more radical environmental protesters, who consider that their approach is too incrementalist in the face of escalating environmental threats. The new wave of environmental activism emerged in the early 1990s in the UK when the anti-roads movement took off. It was a response to the then Conservative Prime Minister Margaret Thatcher's announcement of the roll out of the largest road building programme in Britain since the Romans. It destroyed Sites of Special Scientific Interest as much as beloved parks, streets, and homes. For reputational and legal reasons, the by then established and professional 'new' wave organisations – Friends of the Earth and Greenpeace – were unable to get involved in a series of radical actions including illegal parties on development sites, tree camps, underground tunnels and sabotaging construction equipment (Wall, 1999).

The UK tradition of direct-action environmentalism has continued through multiple SCOs including the Camps for Climate Action, which occupied sites close to environmentally damaging infrastructure (for example, Heathrow Airport and Kingsnorth Power Station) for one week, organised multiple discussion and educative forums, planned and conducted direct action, and glorified lobbying, and tried to prefigure an environmentally sustainable lifestyle (Saunders, 2012). Greenpeace did not engage directly with the climate camps but used its own tactics to stop the Kingsnorth Power Station. In 2008, Greenpeace-UK won a landmark trial against the power company E-ON, which took six Greenpeace-UK activists to court under charges of criminal damage to the tune of £30,000. The SCMs had been planning to write 'Gordon Bin It' (directed at then prime minister Gordon Brown who authorised planning permission) on the flue of an existing power station where construction of a new coal fuelled trial carbon capture and storage facility was planned. The participants were arrested part way through the job. But an eight-day long court case, supported by US climate scientist James Hansen, concluded that they were not guilty of criminal damage. The judge found that the SCMs had a lawful excuse in that they were trying to protect the Earth, which is of greater economic value than the damaged property.

More recently Fridays for Future (Doherty and Saunders, 2021), Uprising of the Last Generation (Kaufer and Albrecht, 2022), and Extinction Rebellion (Saunders et al, 2020; Hayes and MacGregor, 2023) have upped the ante for the climate change cause. This global wave of environmental activism is carried by a new generation of what Pickard (2019) calls 'do-it-ourselves' protesters. Fridays for Future began when Greta Thunberg took a stand for the future of young people by taking Fridays off school to protest outside the Swedish Parliament for tougher action on climate change. Thunberg has become a celebrity SCM for her powerful speeches and has motivated several global days of action in which school children – around the world – have stayed off school on Fridays. For example, Nakabuye et al (2020) report that 20,000 Ugandan youth supported the demands of the movement. In Germany, the group Aufstand der letzten Generation (Uprising of the Last Generation) formed in August 2021 and engaged in a wide range of direct actions, including hunger strikes, occupations, and blockades, and gluing oneself to art works (Kaufer and Albrecht, 2022). In the UK, Extinction Rebellion is a network of local SCOs and other support groups that engages in multiple attention-raising stunts. It is most famous for its national rebellions, which have blockaded parts of the City of London to try to stop business as normal and force decision-makers to act on climate change. Its strategy 2018-2022 of encouraging wilful arrest – which is being radically rethought at the time of writing – is designed to overwhelm the police and judiciary to make decision-makers wake up to the need for change. While Fridays for Future and Extinction Rebellion emerged in 2018 and responded creatively during the COVID-19 pandemic, Uprising of the Last Generation emerged during the pandemic. All three initiatives made creative use of ICT by organising online forums to engage people with the cause. At the same time, during the COVID-19 pandemic, restrictions to civic rights have been widely justified to prevent the spread of serious infectious disease. For example, the UK Government's Police, Crime, Sentencing and Courts Bill 2021 (PCSC), sought to place restrictions on the right to protest (Uthayakumar-Cumarasamy and Calderwood, 2021), resulting in 'Kill the Bill' protests (Walker, 2023).

It is important to keep in mind that environmental SCOs use a wide repertoire of strategies including non-violent protest manifestations, advocacy work (for example, Forum for the Future, which seeks to shape businesses for a greener future), and service provision (for example, organic food cooperatives and green magazines such as *Resurgence & Ecologist*). Moreover, SCOs working primarily in other fields have developed climate change and sustainability action plans and targets.

Environmental SCOs do not work in isolation on environmental causes. In recent years, well-established environmental organisations have 'faced south' (Rootes, 2006) just as many development organisations have 'turned green' (Saunders, 2008a). The 2006 climate change march we mentioned earlier, to which RSPB mobilised hundreds of its supporters, was significant for another reason. It was the work of a coalition (see Chapter 6) of SCOs, which, as one of us has previously written, represented the 'first time that aid, trade and development organisations (ATDOs) have become involved in a broad coalition coalescing on a specific environmental issue' (Saunders, 2008a: 1511). In the next section, we focus on advocacy and lobbying through the lens of humanitarian SCOs. We discuss the factors that have facilitated the shifting repertoires of some of them into protest.

Advocacy and lobbying

Let us first briefly define advocacy and lobbying. In short, *advocacy* is an attempt to influence political decision-makers for or on behalf of a social group. It can involve research, the compilation of reports and using the media to share stories that can assist in the creation of social change. The term *lobby* is derived from a facile interpretation of where lobbying takes place – that is in the lobby of parliament or the legislature – but in practice it takes place in multiple locations including MPs' offices (surgeries), other government offices, in cafes or restaurants, and, increasingly, online. Clemens (1993) argued that women invented lobbying – or influencing politicians – because they lacked political rights. Excluded from mainstream political participation, they appropriated the organisational structure of the 'club' (Clemens, 1993). While fighting for political rights, women and other excluded groups thus engaged in alternative forms of political activism. In addition to lobbying, they also engaged in buycotting – purposefully buying ethical or environmentally friendly products. In countries with a generalist civil service, like Britain, lobbies can be very useful for helping decision-makers who are pressed for time to understand the terms of reference of a social or political issue (Grant, 2018). It is important to mention that not all lobby groups seek progressive social change. Quite to the contrary, many are fronts for corporate interests, some of which are significant donors to political parties (Rowell, 2017).

SCOs that focus on humanitarian relief and development organisations have generally been regarded as being engaged primarily in service provision and advocacy. Scholars have tended to see them through this lens because they are hierarchically organised, are – or at least have historically been – tactically moderate and tend to engage in at least one of the following: fundraising, raising public and political awareness, and humanitarian relief. Humanitarian SCOs' emphasis on advocacy is arguably a result of the constraints of charity law (at least in the UK and the US), their willingness to accept government funding, their tendency to be distracted by emergency appeals, and because they work with exceedingly complex multi-level issues (Saunders, 2009c).

We will now illustrate the overlapping and complementary strategies of such SCOs primarily through a discussion of the emergence and development of the humanitarian sector in the UK. As we noted earlier, early forms of humanitarianism concerned abolitionism (see Chapter 2), the ending of slavery. British women who were involved in the abolitionist movement boycotted sugar and other goods that were produced by slaves thus prefiguring fairtrade activism (Everill, 2020). Furthermore, from the 19th century until the 1950s, humanitarian SCOs focused mostly on offering relief in Europe, oftentimes to help people suffering after war. One example of a British SCO are the Quakers who established the Friends Foreign Missionary Association in 1868, and whose first mission was providing relief for towns and villages destroyed as a result of the Franco-Prussian war (1870) (Wilson, 1952).

Save the Children was created in 1919 in the UK in response to the suffering of children caused by World War I and the Russian Revolution (Gnaerig and MacCormack, 1999, Daughan and Fiori, 2015). It is one of the oldest and largest humanitarian organisations. One of the founders, Dorothy Buxton, was involved in left and pacifist organisations. She withdrew from visible leadership in order to depoliticise the public image of the organisation inviting her sister Eglantyne Jebb to become the face of the organisation (Baughan and Fiori, 2015). In 1920, the Save the Children Union was founded in Geneva under the patronage of the ICRC, after the first affiliations were founded in Canada and Australia; over time the union encompassed member organisations in 40 states in the British Empire and Europe. In 1988, the federation renamed itself Save the Children Alliance (Gnaerig and MacCormack, 1999). In the early 21st century, the Save the Children Alliance pursues political solidarity in its programmatic work and is fighting for children's rights. This globally active multi-mandated organisation responds to humanitarian emergencies, launches global campaigns (for example, against child marriage), promotes health and nutrition, delivers education programmes, is active in child protection, advocates child rights governance and seeks to end child poverty (https://www.savethechildren.net/what-we-do/).

During the Spanish Civil War (1936–39), and in particular after World War II, humanitarian SCOs (1950s–60s) became more overtly political. After World War II, alongside the provision of relief, humanitarian SCOs such as Save the Children and Oxfam engaged in advocacy work (Black, 1991). This included public criticism of the Allied Powers' blockades of Germany through distribution of highly controversial leaflets (Saunders, 2009c). Furthermore, the formation and transformation of humanitarian SCOs was informed by colonialism as well as decolonialisation (Ryfmann, 2011; Slim, 2011). In the UK, traditional organisations such as *Rotary* clubs and the *Women's Institute* took on international issues in film screenings, lectures and 'International Days' thus involving middle-aged, middle-class members in discussion of decolonisation and its consequences (Bocking-Welch, 2018). Politicisation lengthened and deepened in the 1960s as the emphasis shifted towards 'teaching men to fish' rather than providing them with fish. This era saw SCOs engaging in significant advocacy work, while also helping people in need to establish local self-support networks and their own self-sufficiency strategies to avoid famine and re-establish devastated communities. The 1960s *Freedom from Hunger Campaign*, for example, was a coalition of 76 SCOs that raised public awareness and funds, ran educational campaigns in schools and, by 1964, had supported nearly 250 projects in 61 countries worth £6 million. By the mid-1960s, in the UK the Disasters Emergency Committee was established, which relieved some of the pressure on SCOs to respond to emergencies and allowed them to think more politically and strategically.

One of the most prominent French humanitarian organisations, Médecins sans Frontières (MSF), was founded in the context of the Biafran war, which the founders of this SCO identified as genocide (Terry, 2002). The founding members of MSF felt constrained by humanitarian law insisting on impartiality and neutrality. In addition to providing relief, they felt the need to expose what was going on during the Biafran war (Rieff, 2002). The newly founded organisation adopted the principle of *témoingage* – the duty to bear witness (Davey, 2015). MSF's concern with publicising human rights violations became influential far beyond France and led to a new type of humanitarian organisation. MSF's *Sans-Frontierisme* is grounded in the history of the French Left, which is informed by the acknowledgement of complicity and resistance during Nazi occupation and the support and disillusionment with anti-colonial independence movements (Davey, 2015). Financially independent from governmental and intergovernmental organisations, MSF is critical of the aid system and able to set its own agenda. This includes advocacy work, critique of the aid system, drawing attention to forgotten crises and being vocal with respect to the refugee crisis. More than 20 years after starting the Access Campaign, which called for the lowering of the price for HIV/AIDS treatment (Fox, 2014; Davey, 2015), MSF has documented the unequal distribution of and calls for equal access to COVID-19 vaccines (https://msfaccess.org/covid-19-action).

More and more, SCOs were overtly framing poverty in the Global South as political: colonialism and global inequality were increasingly considered to be the root cause of poverty. The SCO War on Want in the UK established its strategy of combining the tactics of vigorous research, lively presentation, and intensive lobbying, perhaps best illustrated in its well-known campaign against powder-based breast milk replacements that ended up being supported by an international boycott against Nestlé (Luetchford and Burns, 2003). However, overtly political goals and activities were frowned up by the UK Charity Commission. In 1995, the Charity Commission's emphasis shifted from charities being requested to stick to 'bandaging the wounds of society' rather than preventing those wounds being inflicted in the first place, to allowing them to 'advocate or oppose changes in law and policy if this helped them to achieve their charitable objectives' (Saunders, 2009c: 49). It is important to keep national differences between SCOs in mind; British NGOs tend to rely more on state funding than French NGOs (Stroup, 2012). In contrast, French NGOs represent the 'Dunantist' tradition and insist on independence from the state and criticism of government policies (Davey, 2015).

In the UK, the relaxing of Charity Commission regulations paved the way for a new phase of humanitarian SCOs' development, from the late 1990s onwards. This phase has seen the emergence of significant campaigns – not restricted to advocacy, but also drawing on social movement repertoires involving protests and street demonstrations. Examples include Jubilee 2000 (which called for the unpayable debts of poor countries to be wiped), the Trade Justice Movement (a coalition of 00 organisations that opposed conditionality on indebted countries); Make Poverty History, The Big Ask and the Stop Climate Chaos Coalition. Each has mobilised tens of thousands of protesters to the streets in addition to high-level advocacy – such as carefully interrogating and critiquing the high-level documents of the International Monetary Fund.

Our account illustrates that humanitarian SCOs engage in lobbying and advocacy, alongside providing relief and engaging in service provision, activities for which they are best known. They are living, interacting, and ever-developing bodies, responding to human needs and redressing the political causes that put people in need first. As well as their increasing participation in protest, local, national and international SCOs provide services in the form of humanitarian assistance including emergency relief, which involves medical support, food, and shelter in human-made and natural disasters across the globe. Some of the biggest and most prominent organisations like Oxfam and Save the Children have a head office in global cities, regional offices, and field offices in the countries where they are carrying out projects, illustrative of their deployment of tactics at multiple levels (Krause, 2014; Roth, 2015) including in transnational advocacy networks (Keck and Sikkink, 1998).

There is, then, a close link between lobbying and service provision (which we further discuss later) as SCOs can help to write guidelines for implementation of their suggestions and sometimes engage in monitoring them. The use of lobbying by disadvantaged groups – historically and presently – illustrates a merging of institutionalised and non-institutionalised repertoires. As noted previously, women lobbied long and hard to be represented by institutionalised forms of politics, they made use of (a range of) non-institutionalised forms to do so – including, but not restricted to advocacy and lobbying (more on this, later). Participation in institutionalised and non-institutionalised forms of politics continues to be intertwined (Roth and Saunders, 2019). We explore the intertwining of institutionalised and non-institutionalised tactics in the next section through the lens of feminist organisations.

Service provision and knowledge production

As discussed in Chapter 2, SCOs play an important role in neo-liberal societies in which social welfare services are contracted out and in which competition, commodification, and individualisation play an ever-increasing role (Brandsen and Pestoff, 2006; Clayton et al, 2016). In this situation, the services provided by SCOs are crucial for the survival of disadvantaged and minority sectors in society. Such services are oftentimes provided in informal spaces such as self-help groups, DIY networks, and grassroots community organisations (Bassel and Emejulu, 2017; Craddock, 2021; Jupp, 2022). Many SCOs provide social service provision to sectors of society in need (NCVO, 2014; Salamon and Sokolowski, 2016) such as befriending older people, running a youth club, or supporting refugees (NCVO, 2014). Self-help, self-care, and self-organising are not only important for personal support but become 'DIY autonomous spaces in which survival is radical action' (Bassel and Emejulu, 2017: 82; see also Craddock, 2021; Jupp, 2022). We consider these forms of mutual support as prefigurative politics.

We discuss service provision largely through the lens of feminist and women's organisations because they illustrate well the complexities of the services provided by SCOs. On the one hand, women have for a long time been excluded from influential organisations and from influential positions within such organisations (Acker, 1990). On the other hand, women have formed a wide variety of feminist organisations, which have contributed to social change (Martin, 1990; Ferree and Martin, 1995). Moreover, in a more general sense, the care work provided by SCOs tends to be gendered and undervalued (Baines, 2011; McDonald and Charlesworth, 2011; Eschle, 2023). It is also important for us to shed light on the strategies of women's organisations because of the long and hard struggles feminist movement scholars have faced in the shape of resistance from both those they study and the male-oriented academe (Freeman, 1995). Before we delve into a discussion of feminist organisations, let us briefly reiterate that we are approaching feminism and women's movements from an intersectional perspective (Crenshaw, 1991; Roth, 2021). We are aware that women's experiences and positionality vary widely across class, race, ethnicity, sexuality, nationality, and many other markers of difference. We want to remind the reader that neither are all feminists female, nor are all women feminists. Finally, we want to stress that the achievements of gender equality movement have important consequences for women, men and those who refuse binary gender-constructions. When we thus refer to women's movements and women's organisations in this section of the chapter, we want the reader to remember the diversity of women's interests. Furthermore, our account builds on research on movements for gender equality, which are frequently referred to as women's movements.

SCOs that seek to promote gender equality and women's interests engage in a wide range of activities, including protest and advocacy. While we acknowledge the enormous contributions and multi-faceted tactics of gender equality and feminist SCOs, here we are focusing on service provision and knowledge production. Feminist organisations have been defined as 'the places in which and the means through which the work of the women's movement is done' (Ferree and Martin, 1995: 13). They take on a variety of shapes, forms and strategies not restricted only to the grassroots/participatory service delivery we primarily focus on in this section.

A very important type of feminist organisation are women's shelters, which emerged in the 1970s in many countries. These shelters provided support for women and children who were at risk from, or had already suffered from, domestic violence. By 1976, there were approximately 90 domestic violence refuge centres for women in Britain (Pugh, 2000: 324). In the 1980s, women's SCOs became increasingly enmeshed in service provision in the 1980s, as they undertook 'municipal feminism' (Bruegel and Kean, 1995) – working to protect women's interests in their local councils via women's committees and helping with other services to protect women's interests. As in other countries, feminist service provision SCOs developed to take on a staggering range of roles and organisational forms, including rape crisis centres, health clinics, battered women's refuges, bookstores, cafes and restaurants, theatre groups, credit unions and more (Ferree and Martin, 1995). The municipalisation of feminism in the UK was met with mixed feelings, with some SCMs and commentators going so far as to suggest that it was 'a means of containing women while side-stepping the underlying conditions that made the service necessary' (Griffen, 1995: 8). Radical feminists became disenchanted that the movement was departing from its women-centred, collective, and non-hierarchical origins and it was seen as the beginning of a decline of women's activism (Lovenduski and Randall, 1993). However, volunteers in a service providing – perhaps seemingly apolitical – rape crisis centre were motivated by a desire to help women and perceived their involvement as political participation (Weiss, 2022). Moreover, at the beginning of the millennium radical feminism, which focuses on patriarchy and male violence and promotes 'women-only' spaces, re-emerged and brought together different generations (Mackay, 2015).

As we have shown in the previous chapter, the formation of SCOs is shaped by the social, political, and historical context. But the values and goals of

SCOs also matter. Values and goals drastically shape the strategies and tactics deployed by service-focused feminist SCOs. In rape crisis centres (Matthews, 1995), feminist health clinics (Morgen, 1995), and battered women's centres (Arnold, 1995), for example, the nature of services provided varies among SCOs we might crudely categorise as radical and reformist. Moderate feminist organisations tend to align themselves with conventional service provision. They focus on being strategically effective and face few dilemmas in accepting state funding (except for criticism from their more radical counterparts). More radical service providing feminist SCOs, however, seek fundamental change in the way society is run and so emphasise not only effective services for women in crisis but also experiment with new ways of running those services. In line with feminist ideology, the more radical organisations try to set up alternative feminist communities, they focus on self-help (to help women become autonomous), challenge conventional social relations, and take an active stance against racism and homophobia (Arnold, 1995). Radical feminist health clinics, for example, have focused on providing women-centred, affordable, and accessible services that stress lay-involvement in all phases of care alongside measures to make abortion accessible to grant women with their own reproductive rights (Morgen, 1995). Service-providing SCOs like the Chicago Abortion Fund, which was established in 1985 by a coalition of predominantly White middle-class women, led organisations to support poor and working-class communities transformed into a Black-led organisation that combined service provision through outreach with advocacy and mobilisation for reproductive justice (Daniel and de Leon, 2020).

Women's SCO service-provision is thus – for some such SCOs – closely aligned with advocacy. In the US women's movement, state funding was oftentimes paired with an expectation to deliver not only services, but also advocacy and educational programmes (Reinelt, 1995). The close relationship between advocacy and service provision is perhaps best illustrated by thinking about women in need of refuge. Such women require considerable help from many quarters: liveable welfare benefits, help with childcare, affordable housing, and the provision of protection from perpetrators by (and including) the police and the courts. For SCOs, this results in a combination of service provision and advocating for women in need of a better social support network. But the extent to which feminist SCOs reach out to different institutions to deliver their tactics varies. Some radical rape crisis centres, for example, have historically, at least, purposefully avoided contact with the police for fear – after witnessing police responses to left-wing activism more generally – of being subject to surveillance, and because of a belief in police ambivalence, or, worse still, hostility, towards women in need (Matthews, 1995; see also Mackay, 2023). While outsider feminists might be ideologically purer and thus find it easier to maintain a strong bond with their grassroots, they may not be able to secure financial resources to survive. Insider feminists might need to make some compromises, but they will have resources to enable them to try to stick as closely as possible to their principles while not excluding ordinary everyday women (Spalter-Roth and Schreiber, 1995).

We illustrate the relationship between goals and tactics further through a German feminist SCO, the women's cooperative WeiberWirtschaft (this section draws on Roth, 2016), which provides support for entrepreneurial women. It is feminist in its ideology, guiding values, goals, outcomes and its founding as part of the women's movement (Martin, 1990: 116), even if it differs significantly in tactics from other women's SCOs. In contrast to most feminist organisations, which focus primarily on political and cultural change, the cooperative WeiberWirtschaft is unusual in that it is primarily an economic organisation and enterprise supporting women's employment. The cooperative seeks to support women's employment by providing affordable office space, it supports founders of women's enterprises with access to loans and expertise, provides on-site day-care and engages in sustainable practices (Roth, 2016). It also represents a real utopia in the sense that it is guided by the values of equality, democracy, and sustainability (Wright, 2013).

This cooperative is embedded in the transformations of German, European, and global women's movements (Wichterich, 2010; Ferree, 2012). In the 1970s, autonomy – which included a distancing from political parties and trade unions – played a major role for the West German women's movement and shaped the outsider tactics in which it engaged. As time moved on, this changed. With the creation of the Green Party and of women's representatives and women's equality bodies in the 1980s the integration of West German feminists in mainstream political institutions began. This process became even more intense after German unification (1990). The subsequently increased presence of women in politics and business and the adoption of policies seeking to facilitate the reconciliation of work and family life can be seen as an outcome of the women's movement (see Chapter 7). However, the affinity between (liberal) feminism and neo-liberalism has been noted (Fraser, 2009). In a tricky way, the demands of women's movements for self-determination, self-reliance, individual liberty, and autonomy are compatible with the logic of globalised markets. What does this mean? Neo-liberalism involves the transfer of tasks that were previously covered by the state, to private sector or civil society as well as an emphasis on personal responsibility and efficiency. This meets with feminist demands for self-determination and opens possibilities for women's NGOs and gender consultants. Kantola and Squires (2012) characterise these changes as a shift from *state feminism* to *market feminism*. While it is welcome that the expertise and services of feminists are paid adequately, the reliance on project and performance-bound funding encompasses the risk of co-optation and de-politicisation.

In addition to formal SCOs, it is important to consider the services provided by a variety of more ephemeral groupings. As we have demonstrated in the previous chapter, the political context matters tremendously for a variety of organisational forms. In the eighteenth century, coffee houses and salons played an important role for the emergent public sphere in feudal societies (Habermas, 1989). Throughout the 20th century, authoritarian regimes forced dissidents underground and prevented the formation of formal organisations. However, even in democratic societies, safe spaces and submerged networks play an important role for marginalised groups and movements 'in the doldrums'. The National Women's Party in the US played a significant role as an 'abeyance structure' between the first and second wave of the US women's movement (Taylor, 1989). Throughout Western democracies, hundreds if not thousands of feminist and anti-capitalist social centres exist, hosting archives on social change, providing updates on campaigns and spaces to learn skills for social change (Hodkinson and Chatterton, 2006). One example is the Feminist Library, in London Peckham, which has been archiving feminist history since 1975 and supports research, activist and community projects and is run by volunteers (www. feministlibrary.co.uk). Feminist bookstores represent important spaces for the creation, dissemination and archiving of new forms of knowledge. Prior to the establishment of gender studies courses at universities and feminist journals, bookstores and small feminist publishers provided information that was otherwise inaccessible. One famous example is the book *Our Bodies Our Selves*, which was written by a group of women who later formed the Boston Women's Health Book Collective (Stephenson and Zeldes, 2008). Frustrated with the ignorance and lack of empathy of doctors, the women who met in 1969 at a women's liberation conference started to compile a list of 'good' doctors and upon realising how little they knew about their bodies started to learn about women's health. In 1971, the first edition of *Our Bodies, Our Selves* was published. By 2008, it had been published in 23 languages (Stephenson and Zeldes, 2008); by 2022 it had been available in 34 languages. The book was regularly updated, most recently in 2011, and now has a website https://www.ourbodiesourselves.org. Feminist and other progressive bookstores provide spaces for SCMs to share knowledge and experiences.

Conclusions

As we have demonstrated in this chapter, SCOs engage in a wide variety of overlapping and often mutually useful tactics and strategies shaped by historically variable contexts, the actions of other SCOs and the values of SCOs and SCMs. The repertoires they use diffuse across sectors and countries, often with only small innovations on what has gone before. Some

SCOs emerge as a reaction to perceived weaknesses of their forebears as did direct action roads protest networks; and those providing services to people struggling for their lives during and after the Algerian revolution. In particular, we have illustrated the ways in which varieties of SCO engage in a range of tactical responses even when working on the same cause. The diversity of tactics and diffusion of repertoires across countries and causes illustrates how the conceptual boundaries thought to separate SMOs from NGOs and voluntary organisations are actually rather arbitrary. This underlines the importance of our concept of SCOs, which highlights the similarities, differences, and complementarities of a range of organisations involved in bringing about (or resisting) social change. As we show in more depth in Chapter 6, the tactics of SCOs facilitate or hinder collaboration and conflict among them.

While it may sometimes be useful to analytical distinguish varieties of SCO based on their different strategies, we argue that it is problematic to focus on one type of action because struggles for social change are creative interplays of protest, advocacy, and service provision. It is therefore unfortunate that existing scholarship tends to give separate treatment to protest-focused (social movements), advocacy-focused (NGOs) and service-based (voluntary) organisations, or criticise the NGOisation and depoliticisation of SCOs. In contrast, we believe that it is important to note that SCOs that pursue joint causes engage in different tactics with different outcomes, which we discuss in Chapter 7.

Perhaps one of the most important values shaping SCOs' strategies and tactics is their stance on entering into partnerships with state agencies, or even on whether they should accept funding for them. This has led to disputes among radicals and reformists across a range of different causes, and also to a richness of tactics. Gaining access to local and national governments and intergovernmental organisations can distance NGOs from the constituencies they are representing (Lang, 2013; Carroll and Sapinski, 2015). Sustainable organising for change – no matter in what form it comes – requires accountability to values and to constituencies and contribute to empowerment (Kilby, 2006). We pick up these debates in the next chapter, which discusses the consequences that choices of strategies and tactics have for the mobilisation of resources; a well as the consequences that resource choices have on strategies and tactics.

4

No Such Thing as a Free Gift: The Sources and Consequences of Resource Choices

Founded in 1971, Médecins sans Frontières (MSF, Doctors without Borders) is one of the largest and most prominent humanitarian organisations. According to its website,[1] in 2021, the organisation received 97.1 per cent of the funds it raised (€1.94 billion) from more than 7 million individual donors and private institutions (private companies and foundations). The organisation explains that relying on 'individuals donating small amounts ... helps to ensure our operational independence and flexibility to respond at a moment's notice to the most urgent crises, including those that are under-reported or neglected'.[2] MSF furthermore explains that less than 2 per cent of the total funds raised come from government funding and, since 2016, in opposition to the damaging migration deterrence policies, MSF refuses to take funds from the EU, its member states, and Norway. The SCO also eschews the acceptance of funding from companies and industries that are in conflict with the provision of medical humanitarian work, for example pharmaceutical and biotechnology companies; extraction industries (such as oil, natural gas, gold or diamonds); tobacco companies; and arms manufacturers).[3] The organisation thus has strict policies on its funding sources. It is clear in its determination to turn down financial support from sources that contradict the values of MSF. This allows MSF not only to decide where and how to allocate its resources but also to speak out against the policies and actions of governments and companies. In 1999, MSF was awarded the Nobel Prize in recognition of its pioneering humanitarian work around the world.

In this chapter, we discuss the different resources needed to carry out the work of SCOs. These material and non-material resources include people, knowledge (experience and expertise), money to pay salaries, travel costs and accommodation, goods, access to media and meeting space, and much more.

We also examine how these resources are mobilised and argue that decision making processes about access to resources are a central part of organising for change. As our introductory vignette discussing MSF's fundraising strategy demonstrates, some SCOs consciously avoid and refuse support that would constrain their ability to speak out, criticise, or to engage in disruptive action. However, even these organisations depend on the support of many small donors or of volunteers who provide time, commitment, and expertise. We argue that all resourcing choices involve a cost-benefit balance, for example, applying for grants and accepting donations both enables and constrains SCMs. Resourcing decisions have consequences that result in sets of actions, interactions, and reactions, between donors and SCOs, among different various SCOs pursuing similar goals with different means, among SCMs and SCOs, and among SCOs and beneficiaries. No resource choice is perfect, but accepting grants and other forms of support from government and formal institutions does not automatically result in selling out. Rather, it requires compromises that shape strategies as well as outcomes. Sometimes it leads to important forms of insider activism. Resources often come with a variety of strings attached and open a range of different opportunities for further work.

To make these arguments we refer to various theoretical and conceptual approaches to resources from different subfields of SCO studies. We draw on resource mobilisation from social movement theory (McCarthy and Zald, 1977), institutional isomorphism (DiMaggio and Powell, 1983) from the literature on voluntary organisations, and notions of accountability from the literature on NGOs (for example Kilby, 2006; Bawole and Langnel, 2016). We also draw on the notion of 'protest businesses' (Jordan and Maloney, 1997), which highlights the resource similarities between large-scale SCOs that mostly engage in protest and those that mostly engage in advocacy.

The chapter is structured as follows. We begin with the distinction between material and non-material resources; next we consider how resource demands are related to the strategies and tactics of SCOs. This is followed by a discussion of the sources from which SCOs obtain resources and how this relates to their goals and values. Finally, we address the consequences of resource choices. We discuss SCMs in the following chapter.

Material and non-material resources: concepts and definitions

Resource mobilisation theory emphasises the centrality of resourcing to protest-focused SCOs (McCarthy and Zald, 1977). We apply this perspective to SCOs in general, starting with the basic premise that without moral, cultural, social-organisational, human and material resources (Edwards and McCarthy, 2004; Edwards et al, 2018), SCOs would not be able to function (Oberschall, 1973: 280). Material resources include paid staff, space (for working in and/or operating services from), equipment, travel and accommodation costs, and access to data or servers to host websites or databases in the case of ICT. Non-material resources include moral, cultural, and social-organisational goods (Edwards and McCarthy, 2004; McCarthy et al, 2018). According to Williams (1995: 127), 'cultural resources can be thought of as the symbolic tools that movements wield in their efforts at social change, be they formal ideologies or symbolic-expressive actions'. Cultural resources vary between SCOs and are not easily interchangeable from one SCO to another because they are bound up with organisations' ideologies and values. Additional non-material resources include media coverage, stakeholder access, legitimacy, and celebrity or elite endorsement as well as open-source software. Many of the resources required by SCOs are connected with their staff and volunteers: staff need to be paid salaries, staff and volunteers need equipment to perform their jobs, and many staff and voluntary roles need a space in which their activities can take place.

It is important to keep in mind that different SCOs draw on different types of resources and that there is an interplay between material and non-material resources. Edwards and McCarthy (2004) identify that 'resource availability enhances the likelihood of collective action' and identify this to be 'generally taken for granted among contemporary analysts of social movements' (p 116). While it is true that an SCO with significant financial resources might be able to foster some types of non-material resources much more easily than a nascent or resource poor organisation (and vice versa, non-material resources can play an important role for obtaining financial resources), material resources are simply less essential for some types of SCOs. Indeed, many thousands of SCOs thrive on small budgets. Some SCOs with few financial resources can mobilise hundreds or thousands of volunteers to support their goals or as in the case of MSF, hundreds of thousands of small donations. In the next section, we give an overview over different types of resources generated and gathered by SCOs.

Different tactics, different resource needs

The diversity and different combinations of SCO tactics and the range of contexts in which SCOs operate, necessitate the mobilisation of different types and amounts of material and non-material resources. Table 4.1 provides examples of different types of resources required by organisations with different organisational structures and functions. The table is not intended to be comprehensive but rather to give an idea of how resource needs vary across varieties of SCO. We have simplified the types of SCOs on two dimensions (primary function) and size (small and grassroots versus large

Table 4.1: An illustration of the variety of resources required and garnered by social change organisations

	Service provision	Advocacy	Protest
Large and professionalised	**Material:** Salaries for professional staff, including CEO; Computers with WiFi or internet access; Equipment, data to access internet; Extensive travel/ accommodation costs; Field site rental/ maintenance; Property for headquarters and regional offices. **Non-material:** Volunteers; Moral authority; Celebrity endorsers; Social media; Branding. **For example: Shelter UK**	**Material:** Salaries for professional staff, including CEO; Computers with WiFi or internet access, data to access internet; Travel/accommodation costs for research and attendance of meetings; Property for headquarters. **Non-material:** Volunteers; Moral authority; Celebrity endorsers; Social media; Branding. **For example: Amnesty International**	**Material:** Salaries for professional staff, including CEO; Computers with WiFi or internet access, data to access internet; Occasional travel/ accommodation costs to plan and attend protest events; Property for headquarters. **Non-material:** Volunteers; Moral authority; Journalist endorsers; Collective action frames; Social media; Branding. **For example: Greenpeace International**
Small, grassroots collectives	**Material:** Limited equipment (personal to SCMs); Donations (for example, of food); Computers with WiFi or internet access equipment, data to access internet. **Non-material:** Volunteers; Social media. **For example: Truro Foodbank**	**Material:** Limited equipment (personal to SCMs); Computers with WiFi or internet access equipment, data to access internet. **Non-material:** Volunteers; Moral authority; Social media. **For example: Sisters Uncut UK**	**Material:** Limited equipment (personal to SCMs), perhaps squatted property; Computers with WiFi or internet access equipment, data to access internet. **Non-material:** Volunteers; Moral authority; Prefigurative actions; Collective action frames; Social media. **For example: Earth First! UK**

and professional). Note that these do not represent ideal types, but rather are illustrative of a continuum – many SCOs are between the extremes we present (on both axes), and, as we established in Chapters 1 and 3, many have multiple functions, that is not just service provision, advocacy *or* protest but often a combination of two or three of these broad tactics. Note that the type of resources needed are actually quite similar across different strategies. What differs, however, is the *amount* of resources that are required for different activities, and how the resources are mobilised, and distributed within the organisation.

There are two crucial differences between the resource needs of large and professional SCOs, and small grassroots SCOs that function as collectives. Large and professional SCOs usually require a large membership that pays membership fees or gives donations to pay highly skilled professionals whereas grassroots collectives require a smaller amount of people for basic functioning even if thousands are mobilised to, say, a demonstration. However, small specialised grassroots organisations also might involve professionals working pro bono, drawing, for example, on legal or medical expertise. Large organisations, partly as a function of their staffing requirements, also have significant expenditure for offices, equipment, and travel. This means that large-scale SCOs have a high need of mobilising financial resources.

This contrasts with small grassroots groups that might be able to hold meetings in public houses or private homes. The nature of the space available in private homes is dependent on resources of SCMs: some SCMs crowd into bedsits to organise, others are able to meet in a bespoke space (for example, the office over the garage, or a large private home). Organisations that offer some kind of services oftentimes need office space for full- or part-time working staff and service-users. This applies also to organisations that pursue research and advocacy, for example into environmental, equality, human rights or social justice issues. In addition to office space, they might also need a location to archive documents and other artefacts, including cloud-based storage online. Organisations that use ICT not only need access to devices and an internet connection but also the knowledge to benefit from the affordances of ICT and to be versed in data protection practices and legislation (Fielker, 2021).

Organisations that provide social services or are engaged in humanitarian aid and development cooperation also need spaces to provide those services. SCOs that are active overseas need travel money to reach the destinations, and depending on the service that they provide, need medical equipment, tools and devices to clean water or build shelter. Some professionalised SCOs become 'complex transnational bureaucracies', which adopt strategic planning and management and the adoption of internal staff guidelines, as well as recruitment of staff with a professional background. For such organisations, the professionalisation of human resources departments and paid staff is becoming more standard (Ryfman, 2011; Slim, 2011; Stroup, 2012).

By way of illustration, at the time of writing Amnesty International had 2 million members and 2,600 members of staff (amnesty.org), which contrasts significantly with countless micro-charities that are too small to even register for charitable status. The balance of staff to members/volunteers varies significantly across SCOs. Whereas Amnesty International has a huge base of mostly passive members, it also has a significant number of staff. This contrasts with the 'poor people's movements' that Piven and Cloward (1979) studied: the roles in those movements were voluntary rather than paid but also very active. Piven and Cloward (1979) stressed the power of poor people's movements. In their view, although such movements are resource poor in conventional terms, 'industrial workers' and 'defiant Blacks' achieved concessions precisely because they were not led by inert hierarchical bureaucracies whose militancy is constrained. Instead, thousands of strikers and individuals engaged in mass civil disobedience that was a powerful but relatively resource-lite force for change. We can apply a similar argument to some types of service providing SCOs, like foodbanks, which rely heavily on donations of food and volunteers. But the reliance on volunteers is not without consequences. Such work can be empowering for volunteers, but it also might be unfair to the SCMs who are at the heart of the work, due to an unhealthy reliance on their unpaid labour (Sbicca et al, 2019). The radical environmental SCO Earth First! is similar in some ways to the poor people's movements that Piven and Cloward (1979) researched. Earth First! is purposively set up as a network. It has no formal organisational structure (and therefore no accountability as an organisation), no premises, no equipment and no staff. But it has, at times, mobilised hundreds of individuals to participate in civil disobedience under the motto of 'no compromise in defence of Mother Earth' (Wall, 1999). Anyone who is deeply connected to the Earth and ascribes to a deep ecology perspective can set up a local Earth First! group or participate in one.

Earth First! does not have an operational budget and relies on volunteers for ideological reasons, first and foremost to remain independent and unconstrained by funding requirements. If resources are required, they are provided by local groups and activists themselves. Thus, Earth First! relies on its constituency rather than external supporters. If you need a monkey wrench to do the task at hand, then it is your responsibility to go and buy or borrow one. This is similar to other small, grassroots, collectives but contrasts markedly with the operational budgets and equipment required by their large-scale professional counterparts.

In contrast, Greenpeace International (which is the co-ordinating body of 27 independent national and regional organisations across the world, rather than the sum of them), for example, had a total turnover of €90,243,000 in 2019. From this, nearly €38,000 was provided in the form of grants to national and regional Greenpeace organisations, nearly €11,000 was spent on campaigns, around €2,500 on media and communications, almost €7,000 on global engagement and funding and €14,380 on organisational support (Greenpeace International, 2020). Among other things, Greenpeace International requires significant resources for funding its scientific laboratories (hosted by the University of Exeter in the UK), for its high-tech equipment used in direct action campaigns, its fleet of ships and smaller boats for its at-seas missions and for maintaining this equipment. It also has specialised staff working on campaigns, in public relations, on logistics, with its finances and more.

Small and large SCOs also differ with respect to the need (that large-scale organisations have) for professionalised media and communications strategies. In grassroots collectives, these functions are often taken care of in-house at little extra cost using the do-it-yourself skills of volunteers and their home internet connections. In contrast, the need for large-scale professional SCOs to maintain their organisations means that marketing, website development and maintenance are essential resources for them (while at the same time requiring resources) – particularly as the sector has become more competitive due to the 2008 financial crisis, the impact of the COVID-19 pandemic, the Ukraine war, and – in the case of the UK – Brexit. Writing about large SCOs, and Amnesty (Belgium) in particular, Vestergaard (2008) claims that 'while ... social change, which is the ultimate goal of such an organisation, may be aided by donations that allow the organisation to go about its business, the arousal and maintenance of public social awareness is its fundamental prerequisite' (p 472). Large-scale SCOs have become increasingly professional with respect to marketing, fundraising, and branding. They work increasingly to market logics, seeking to gain customer loyalty through brand recognition. Amnesty International illustrates well the brand orientation of large-scale SCOs. Its brand is founded on its name and logo but also its mission, vision and values (Urde et al, 2013).

Service-providing SCOs, in particular humanitarian organisations, are equally likely to use the resource of celebrity endorsement as their advocacy and protest-oriented counterparts (Richey and Brockington, 2020). Celebrity endorsement has drawn significant attention to advocacy and protest causes. Prominent examples include the media event Band Aid and the music group Radiohead supporting environmental causes (Clément, 2017). Furthermore, Brian May, the guitarist for the rock group Queen, spearheaded the UK campaign against badger culling, and the celebrity cook Jamie Oliver participated in a Food Revolution campaign in 2015 that saw stars like Ed Sheeran, Jazzy B, and Paul McCartney working on a song with others to support the cause. The BBC's Children in Need, an annual televised fundraising appeal, has been one of the most prominent examples of celebrity endorsement in the UK. The show has worked with hundreds of unpaid celebrities to raise over £1 billion for over 3,000 charities since 1980. Emerging in 1927 as a radio appeal, it launched a televised appeal in 1980 that has continued almost annually since (although in 2020–21 it was disrupted by COVID-19). Celebrities like Madonna, Angelina Jolie, and Ben Affleck have been involved in various humanitarian causes (Richey and Brockington, 2020; Budabin and Richey, 2021).

One further significant difference between types of SCOs refers to their need for moral authority, which varies according to their primary functions. Service-provision focused SCOs often provide basic needs to their beneficiaries. In the case of Shelter, this is housing; for the Truro Foodbank in Cornwall in the Southwest of the UK, it is food supplies. Although these services are morally motivated, and, as we discuss later, should ensure accountability, the fact that they are providing basic needs means that moral authority is not as important as it is for organisations like Amnesty International, Greenpeace International and Earth First! SCOs use framing as a resource to attract the support of individual donors and active volunteers. Their framing identifies the prognosis for the issue they are addressing (prognostic framing), their diagnosis (diagnostic framing) and motivational framing – to try to persuade people to engage. Some SCOs additionally use injustice frames (Benford and Snow, 2000). Injustice frames are one way of taking the moral high ground, but some organisations will instead use moral outrage (Jasper and Poulsen, 1995). The moral stance and broader goals of SCOs are also important given their significant impacts on their fundraising strategies. Greenpeace International, for example, refuses, for ethical reasons, to accept financial donations from corporations or the government because it believes that this would compromise its values and its moral authority. As our vignette at the beginning of the chapter demonstrated, MSF takes a similar approach, refusing funding from particular sources that would compromise its ability to speak out against injustice. This also applies to some gender equality SCOs as we discussed in the previous chapter (Chapter 3). While reformist organisations are happy to accept state funding, radical ones will seek to challenge conventional social relations and therefore would eschew it.

For many SCOs, volunteering roles are fairly active but also relatively non-specialist. Simply believing in the moral stance of the SCO, alongside having commitment to participate is enough to get involved. Foodbanks, for example, require non-skilled staff to weigh, sort and date food, to give out food parcels and more (see, for example, truro.foodbank.org. uk). For other types of SCO, internships are competitive and require skills and experience. A three-day a week three-month unpaid internship with Starfish UK (a small international development charity working with children orphaned or made vulnerable through HIV/AIDS) often seeks to appoint graduates, who are experienced in the use of communication technologies, and text- and data-processing software, and have good communication and research skills. This means that the organisation relies on the qualifications of the unpaid intern as well as on the fact that the interns can (or rather: must) support themselves without getting an income from the SCO. Whereas Earth First! emphasises the importance of commitment to the cause and Starfish UK stresses the importance of skills, both rely on the financial independence of SCMs and interns. Some SCOs carry out training courses that might be mandatory for their volunteers. This applies in particular to organisations which deal with vulnerable communities, for example disaster relief organisations. Such SCOs must have access to qualified trainers that are either volunteers of the organisation, offer the training pro bono, or are paid by the organisation.

The sources of SCOs' financial resources

As we have established, the activities of large-scale professional protest and service-providing SCOs require large sums of money in order to carry out their activities. However, there are also financially resource-lite SCOs (Piven and Cloward, 1979). Resource mobilisation theory (McCarthy and Zald, 1977) argues that external resources are crucial for the emergence and success of SCOs, although internally and externally generated resources are deemed equally important (Edwards and McCarthy, 2004). Churches, corporations, and governments have been important contributors to many SCOs (McCarthy and Zald, 1973). Furthermore, funding might come from individual donations or from wealthy philanthropists, for example the Bill and Melinda Gates Foundation (Dean, 2020). We explore different sources of funding before discussing the potential consequences of accepting funds from such sources.

Individual donations are collected through a variety of means. Traditional channels for raising funds (until the 1970s) depended on the people power of staff or volunteers who engaged in the selling of raffle tickets, in door-to-door collections, and from penny collection boxes in public places (Anheier and Toepler, 1997). Notoriously, in 2016, 92-year-old Olive Cooke who raised funds for the British Legion by selling poppies, killed herself after receiving a large number of fundraising requests (Dean, 2020; https://www.theguardian.com/society/2016/jan/20/poppy-seller-who-killed-herself-got-up-to-3000-charity-mailings-a-year). From the 1990s, direct mailing and chequebook memberships took over from collection tins and pots. Direct mailing has largely – but certainly not entirely – been superseded by social media campaigns and crowd funding, and cheque book memberships have become monthly Direct-Debit donations (Jordan and Maloney, 1998) and more recently PayPal contributions. Some SCOs also nowadays invite individuals to leave a legacy donation in their wills.

Philanthropy is nothing new and needs to be critically assessed (see the recent survey by Mitchell and Pallister-Wilkens, 2023). Money from philanthropists supports SCOs working in poverty relief, education, healthcare, international aid, and many more causes. In the US alone, it 'supports a kaleidoscopic non-profit sector of well more than one million organisations that accounts for approximately 10 percent of the labour force and that touches the lives of most citizens' (Reich et al, 2016: 1). Much of the money comes from exceedingly rich philanthropic agencies that draw on the wealth of individual billionaires (which seek to evade taxation). Prominent examples include the Rockefeller and Bill and Melinda Gates' Foundations. The Rockefeller Foundation was established in the early 1900s as a way to distribute some of the vast profits that Rockefeller had made from Standard Oil. The Bill and Melinda Gates Foundation (using profits from Microsoft) was established in 2000, which, among other things, provides funding for ventures related to global health. Dauvergne and Lebaron (2014) note a shift to more strategic philanthropy in the 1990s and note that 'Taking a business approach to philanthropy allows capitalists to invest in societal development without foregoing profits' (p 42). Moreover, Dean (2020) notes that the Bill and Melinda Gates Foundation is to a large extent financed through companies that engage in activities that are in opposition the foundation's goal (p 17). Although philanthro-capitalism is not a new development, it has significantly increased in the last few decades (McGoey, 2012) and has been criticised for underpinning rather than challenging structural inequalities.

The state is also a significant source of funding or SCOs, even though competition for such funding has increased as the money available has shrunk due to the effects of austerity. As we have discussed in Chapter 2 (on the big picture), one of the consequences of neo-liberalism is a shift of service provision from the state to the market and the third sector. In 2010, the Third Sector Research Centre (Mohan, 2011) reported that 36 per cent of UK-based third sector organisations received income from the public sector (Clifford et al, 2010) and that 14 per cent of them had the public sector as their most important source of finance. Moreover, those receiving public money were disproportionately located within or serving deprived communities. The dependence of the neediest sectors of the population on public finance is concerning in the face of budgetary cuts (from 2008, and which will likely be even more drastic in economic restructuring after COVID-19). Receiving grants from the state, foundations and donors has consequences for SCOs in relation to professionalisation and accountability as we discuss in the following sections.

The consequences of obtaining resources

SCOs have good reasons for accepting funding from external sources: they can help them get kick-started, they can provide resources for building organisational capacity, and they can help struggling organisations to get back on their feet. But the sources from which SCOs' garner financial resources can have significant implications, particularly in relation to two key factors: accountability and professionalisation. We describe what these terms mean before discussing their tightly interwoven consequences in relation to varieties of SCO.

Accountability

It is important to distinguish upward, downward and value accountability (Kilby 2006). SCOs have *upward accountability* to their donors: if they are bound by a contract, whether formal or informal, they will feel obliged to fulfil it. They also have *downward accountability* to the communities who are the intended beneficiaries (Kilby, 2006; Bawole and Langnel, 2016). In addition, SCOs should have a third type of accountability namely *value accountability*, which concerns the values of their members, volunteers, and adherents (Kilby, 2006).

In contrast to the rich literature that discusses the accountability (albeit mostly restricted to upward accountability) of SCOs that engage in service delivery, the concept 'accountability' is less used in the analysis of SCOs that engage in advocacy and protest (but see Lang, 2013; Stroup and Wong, 2017). This might be because many, but certainly not all, of them purposively avoid accepting funding from external sources that might jeopardise their values or image. However, even for SCOs that might be less concerned with upward accountability, because they do not seek financial support from donors, what deserves attention are downward accountability and value accountability. We suggest that conflicts about the inclusion of underrepresented groups, such as working-class women, women of colour and LGBTQIA+ communities working to secure women's rights and other causes, should be seen as debates around 'value accountability' and 'downward accountability'. Such debates concern whether the leadership of an organisation is representing its constituency or if groups are over or underrepresented as even progressive organisations are not necessarily inclusive (Strolovitch, 2007), and whether the needs of all groups are equally represented. Furthermore, paradoxically, organisations that employ direct democracy and lack formal procedures might suffer from the 'tyranny of structurelessness' (Freeman, 1972) in which some group members dominate group processes without being held accountable. Scholars of protest-focused SCOs might also overlook matters of accountability due to the fact that participation in small grassroots organisations and in sporadic protest events relies primarily on the self-funding of SCMs who participate in their spare time and may pay for travel expenses themselves (if travelling is required). This, of course, might be what leads to a middle-class bias in many types of protest. For example, in the UK SCMs engaged in Extinction Rebellion were, in October 2019, predominantly from the middle class and had flexibility in their work and surplus income to be able to travel to mass rebellions in London (Saunders et al, 2020). Many of the Extinction Rebellion rebels surveyed in October 2019 were from the more affluent southwest region of the UK and BAME people were heavily underrepresented.

Accountability matters for those rich and professional SMOs known as 'protest businesses' (Jordan and Maloney, 1997), that are not very distinct from formally organised, well-established, and bureaucratically organised NGOs. Furthermore, with respect to all of the activities of SCOs it is important to consider downward accountability and the mechanisms that are involved in order to ensure that the organisations actually benefit those they purport to help – in other words, their beneficiaries. Moreover, should it not only be applied to those obtaining donations, but also the donors – to whom are they accountable? We argue that all forms of accountability matter and that they are relevant for all types of SCOs. Our novel contribution here is to apply accountability to SCOs writ large, and to relate it not only to the mobilisation of resources but also to the representation and involvement of members and constituencies.

Although the literature on protest-focused SCOs tends to sidestep issues of accountability, it does discuss the related issues of professionalisation and bureaucratisation. Critical perspectives on the professionalisation of SCOs, particularly those in the service sector, highlight the consequences of upward accountability – that is accountability to donors, rather than constituencies – which results in a growing distance between NGOs and grassroots activists (Dauvergne and LeBaron, 2014; Choudry, 2015). Compromising downward accountability oftentimes goes hand-in-hand with a reduction in value accountability (Kilby, 2006; Lang, 2013). According to Smith (2015), the 'process of professionalisation, institutionalisation and bureaucratisation – known as "NGO-ization" is associated with the institutionalisation and de-radicalisation of movement demands' (p 612). Positive and critical perspectives on professionalisation processes often share poor conceptualisation of the notion of professionalisation, leaving the terms 'professionalisation and professionalism' as 'ambiguous and multidimensional' (Ganesh and McAllum, 2012: 153).

Professionalisation

So what do professionalisation and professionalism comprise and what consequences do they have? Although related, the two concepts refer to different aspects. Professionalisation concerns organisational form and processes (bureaucratisation, rationalisation, marketisation) whereas professionalism concerns practice and (occupational) identity (Ganesh and McAllum, 2012: 153). Professionalisation transforms protest and advocacy focused SCOs into 'formalised, knowledge intensive and professionally staffed organisations' (Andreassen et al, 2014: 336). These transformations are related to gaining access, legitimacy, and resources from governments, intergovernmental organisations, and private donors – although not all large SCOs rely on such sources. The related process of NGOisation involves gaining and maintaining access to government agencies and transnational organisations such as the UN and its agencies as well as the EU (Saunders and Roth, 2019). Such access includes representing constituencies at the local, national, and international levels as well as access to (limited) funding.

The accountability consequences of professionalisation

Access to governmental and intergovernmental resources like these might seriously jeopardise SCOs' chances of obtaining any programmatic goals (see Chapter 6). Funding through these sources will likely come with some conditionality on how the funds should be spent, oftentimes with small or specific remits rather than aspirations for fundamental social change. Through achieving *upward accountability* to donors, *downward accountability* and *value accountability* might be compromised. Tarrow (1994) puts it like this: SCOs' core values can come to match the values of the organisations they used to oppose – and they have to tame their strategies so as not to jeopardise the existence of their organisation and the jobs of their staff. Smith (2015), for example, compares the contemporary incorporation of SCOs into the political process with colonial strategies of indirect rule, that is the inclusion of local elites into the colonial administration in order to prevent mass resistance. The loss of value accountability in the pursuit of upward accountability is further illustrated with the case of feminist SCOs. Feminism is an identity to which women can feel accountable: this is, in short, the notion that they are working together to stop gender inequality (Mansbridge, 1995). When that goal becomes compromised due to funding requirements of an external agency, value accountability is lost. Thus, some feminist organisations take a form of active resistance by refusing to take state funding (Matthews, 1995). Moore (2008) takes further objection to the state funding of SCOs, arguing that it buys into a 'contract culture', which undermines the need for state-based welfare that was predicated on the need to replace charities with comprehensive basic welfare services in the first place. The acceptance of state and foundation funding for minority women's activism in the US has pulled organisations into contracts that have taken them away from areas of work that they intuitively felt would be better suited to addressing their concerns (for example, INCITE!, 2017).

For the anti-violence network INCITE!, SCOs' collusion with the state and foundations has resulted in a non-profit industrial complex that upholds rather than challenges systems of violence and oppression.

However, some SCOs that are beholden to the state also work to critique it by trying to achieve downward accountability and perhaps jeopardise upward accountability as a result. In relation to grassroots organisations, Lang (2013) demonstrates that the local state can strengthen grassroots groups by providing them with funding while strengthening democratic decision-making and public advocacy. This means that upward accountability (to the state, which is providing resources) can sometimes be combined with downward accountability (towards beneficiary constituencies) without compromising the values of grassroots groups (value accountability).

Regardless of the sources of funding, it has long been established that professional and large-scale organisations have a tendency to weaken their connection with the grassroots (downward accountability) as well as their values (value accountability) as they grow and mature (see, for example, Lang, 2013; Stroup and Wong, 2017). Schumacher (1973) wrote of the benefits of small organisations: they are able to be more 'active and intimate', to better allow 'creative freedom'. They therefore can prevent organisations from becoming 'moribund and a desert of frustration' by involving everyone (Schumacher, 1973: 227). We might contrast Schumacher's idealised small organisational form with Michels' (1911) 'iron law of oligarchy', which posits that too much orderliness in a large organisation can, instead, result in alienation of the cadre as power becomes concentrated in the hands of a few (see Saunders, 2009b). In a large organisation, volunteers might consequently end up not participating in the core functions of an SCO, but only in the more 'mundane work of sending in the funds, selling raffle tickets, or buying goods from catalogues' (Jordan and Maloney, 1997: 118). For Jordan and Maloney, who refer to such organisations as 'protest businesses' (Jordan and Maloney, 1997: 118) 'there is as much danger in glamorising this as in describing it as being meaningfully involved in the political process'. But funds are needed, and without large organisations, public awareness of many progressive causes would be stifled.

Significant size increases combined with professionalisation processes result in organisations having – and consequently increasingly relying on – significant budgets. They thus might appear to be putting organisational maintenance before their charitable causes or beneficiaries. Greenpeace, for instance, has been criticised for being more interested in real estate than campaigning. It is also known as an organisation that picks its battles carefully, partly in relation to marketability and winnability, which can sometimes make communities struggling with environmental pollution or unwelcome infrastructural development decisions feel abandoned. If your local environmental problem matches on to one of Greenpeace's five to six campaign areas, then count yourself lucky (Saunders, 2013). Similarly, in the early 1990s, Friends of the Earth (England, Wales and Northern Ireland) faced the choice of a legal challenge against its occupation of the site of the M3 motorway extension (through Twyford Down, near Winchester in the South of England), which had the potential to wipe the assets of the company, or to continue to engage in an occupation. Its need for organisational survival meant that – to the disparagement of groups of non-violent direct activists – it chose to withdraw from confrontations with bulldozers (Saunders, 2013).

However, the 'iron law' is not so much a law as a tendency (Walker and Martin, 2018). It is possible for large SCOs to 'bend' the iron law of oligarchy, by having processes to ensure the continued involvement of grassroots SCMs; just as it is possible for smaller organisations to fall into the trap of an informalised oligarchy. As noted earlier, Freeman (1972) wrote about latent power in small horizontally organised SCOs, which is what happens when those who are in friendship groups or are more experienced inadvertently exercise power. These people in-the-know can come to dominate processes and procedures unless steps are taken to avoid this 'tyranny of structurelessness' (Freeman, 1972). Nevertheless, usually power can be more easily redistributed in small horizontal SCOs, compared to larger ones, through caucuses as well as through skills-sharing and training. Saunders' (2009b) study of 208 global justice SCOs found that although larger organisations might be more likely to become oligarchic and to distance themselves from their grassroots, this is not universal. Some SCOs, like Indymedia – a global network of independent media centres – did surprisingly well at including grassroots SCMs. Thus, the inclusivity of an organisation might depend more on the ethos and practices of its leaders than the size of the organisation.

By imposing a sense of inevitability, the iron law of oligarchy has some similarities with the concept of institutional isomorphism. Whereas the former term is used to refer to trade unions (in its initial conception) and SMOs (thereafter), the latter – institutional isomorphism – is a not too dissimilar term used to understand the NGO sector. We discuss it more fully in Chapter 6, but it is, in short, the idea that organisations become increasingly similar to one another as they adjust their functions to comply with the bureaucratic procedures and contractual obligations associated with receiving government grants (DiMaggio and Powell, 1983). As with the iron law of oligarchy, some organisations can resist institutional isomorphism, by either holding true to their values or through path dependencies that entrench them in existing routines (Ramanth, 2009). Institutional isomorphism is different from the iron law in that it can be more easily applied to smaller-scale SCOs.

Just as downward accountability from SCOs to the grassroots is jeopardised by obtaining grants and professionalisation processes, so too can international professional SCOs lose downward accountability to national chapters or national support agencies. These changes are associated with a loss of autonomy of country operation and – taking the example of humanitarian SCOs – a shift to newly regional management structures 'with a new breed of NGO manager that emerged who oversees programme planning and reporting systems and rolls out new initiatives across the organisation instead of simply administering projects' (Slim, 2011: 37). For example, a former head of human resources found 'no fundamental difference whether the business is a corporation or a humanitarian organization like CARE' with respect to managing organisational staff (Stroup, 2012: 91; see also Maier and Mayer, 2016).

Within the humanitarian aid industry, the growth in budgets, agencies, and personnel led to a critical evaluation of the impact of aid and the need for professionalisation, accountability, and coordination of aid efforts (Walker and Russ, 2011). This debate originated in the late 1980s but intensified after the Rwanda Crisis of 1994, which had revealed massive shortcomings in aid delivery (and therefore in downward accountability to beneficiaries) (Walker, 2004; 2005; see also Roth, 2012). The critical reflection of the aims, conditions, and obstacles of carrying out humanitarian aid led to the development and dissemination of standards for the delivery of humanitarian assistance (Buchanan-Smith, 2003; Walker, 2004; 2005). The development and adoption of standards and codes of conduct play an important role for fundraising and the recruitment of qualified staff and volunteers. However, the newly introduced standards were written from the perspective of Western humanitarian SCOs. This was not unproblematic, given the need to respect local cultures, inclusion of local capacities and beneficiaries, and thus downward accountability (Hilhorst, 2002; 2005). Especially when professionalisation involves standardisation, it is important to consider whether presumably universal principles reflect local principles and practices, and therefore might potentially disadvantage SCOs in the Global South. There is a thus a risk that standards might constrain creativity and improvising skills, and that they might marginalise and weaken Global South organisations. Standards may even be open to political abuse (Hilhorst and Schmiemann, 2002; Dufour et al, 2004; Vaux, 2006). Thus, there is a tension between the usefulness of standards given the high turnover in humanitarian assistance and the risk of marginalising local knowledge (Redfield, 2008).

Moreover, while humanitarian SCOs engaged in promoting codes and standards highlight their contributions to a promotion of 'best practice', there is so far little evidence of the impact of these initiatives on performance (Crack, 2014). In fact, the proliferation of standards resulted in additional reporting tasks typical of audit cultures and might further drain the resources and energy of humanitarian organisations. A further risk associated with the introduction of standards is that it could prevent an open discussion of problems out of fear that admitting to weaknesses could jeopardise the

SCOs. Especially after the sex abuse scandal in which Oxfam and Save the Children were involved in 2018 (staff paid for sex with the survivors of the Haitian earthquake), SCOs are under a lot of scrutiny and it is clear that the adoption of standards does not prevent misuse. Critics warn that as long as the introduction of standards is based on peer regulation and lacks independent assessments, the most significant impact might be the creation of new job opportunities for accountability managers (Crack, 2014), rather than improving accountability itself.

Despite these concerns, it is important to note that professionalisation can also have positive consequences. For example, professionalisation has allowed SCOs to perform media advocacy, to engage in litigation, and to generate public support incredibly effectively. Thus, professionalisation affords both advantages and disadvantages, which shape the strategies and tactics of SCOs. Multiple studies that have evaluated the impact of SCOs on legislation and support for anti-discrimination, development, humanitarianism, and human rights have tended to associate success with professionalisation (Keck and Sikkink, 1998; Martens, 2005; Barnett, 2011; Watkins et al, 2012). However, as we discuss in Chapter 7, this could be a rather limited conception of success: a small goal achieved through policy channels might actually have less impact than an on-the-ground set of service provisions – such as feeding the hungry and providing refuge for battered women. Organisations that are not professional have less chance of long-term organisational survival (Zald and Ash, 1966). Formalisation and professional leadership can contribute to the continuity of SCOs and thus to their sustainability (Staggenborg, 1988). But some small-scale SCOs also thrive, partly through their steadfast commitment to their principles, which shape their resource choices.

Other consequences of resource mobilisation

We now discuss a selection of additional issues that arise from resourcing choices, including the increasing dominance of larger organisations in a competitive field, the broader societal consequences of philanthropy, and the broader implications of branding and marketing strategies.

In an economy working under strain, competition for resources among SCOs increases in intensity (see Chapter 6). But SCOs that already have resources can invest those resources to generate more resources still, perhaps to the detriment of smaller SCOs. They have the resources to sub-contract funding agencies, or to sustain their own fundraising division. Better-funded organisations are also more likely to be able to fund expensive social media or paper-based/letter box campaigns. However, as Fisher (2006) has shown, this approach to fundraising can undermine grassroots activism. Furthermore, sub-contracting might stifle SCOs' development of innovations in social change (Clifford and Backus, 2010), which have driven many of the significant social changes we examined in Chapter 2. Statistical analysis of a broad range of SCOs listed in the UK-based Charity Commission Register (n=41,732) reveals that the largest SCOs are better able to further grow, although this does not always preclude small-scale organisations from professionalising (Clifford and Backus, 2010).

While the contributions of philanthropists allow advancements and contributions to causes in need, it is worrying that a handful of billionaires increasingly shape societal developments more than governments or the will of the public. Bill Gates, for example, has been conceived of as the global head of worldwide education, health, and technical development by virtue of being rich rather than because he has been voted in through democratic processes and procedures (Reich, 2016). Billionaire philanthropy has a legitimacy deficit: its wealth effectively allows it to buy consent to rule, and to shape global health governance, and its influence goes largely uncontested by virtue of Bill Gates' charisma (Harman, 2016). Similarly, the Rockefeller Foundation has been critiqued for using dirty money. Standard Oil, which raised the money, has been implicated in environmental damage, monopolistic business practices and resistance to its workers joining trade unions. Moreover, can a group of trustees be trusted to distribute vast sums of money in a way that is, overall, beneficial for society? Wealthy philanthropists might, therefore, overall be seen as threatening to the principles of democracy (Reich, 2018).

Charisma also matters in the media and for celebrities, both of which are important resources for many SCOs. However, there is an issue – even and perhaps especially among SCOs that do not require significant financial resources – about who within an organisation ends up speaking for the organisation. In the course of our own work, a media spokesperson for the Camp for Climate Action (UK) told us in an interview how she felt uncomfortable being the voice of a horizontal movement comprising many voices (Saunders, 2012).

As noted previously, celebrities can be an important resource for SCOs, but they might also contribute to the spectatorship of suffering and compassion fatigue. They can also alter the claims of movements, sometimes taming them. Analysing Children in Need, Lloyd (2018) discusses how celebrities raising money for the cause is celebrated on this UK-based BBC show. The show is about celebrating the raising of money, without much contextualisation of how the money is spent and what it achieves. In her words: 'Money and fundraising appear to have become the measure of charities' success and the focus for the celebration of charitable action, instead of being judged on how much they impact on the lives of beneficiaries' (Lloyd, 2018: 130). The emphasis on celebrating fundraising exists in part because Children in Need funds children's charities based on grant applications it receives, making it difficult to link money raised with its beneficiaries.

Thus, downward accountability is underplayed by the celebration of fundraising. This is one reason why the show lacks universal appeal. For some viewers who participated in Lloyd's (2018) focus groups, the show is a series of adverts for celebrities and charities that glorifies suffering, which makes for unbearable viewing.

In their analysis of two US-based controversies in the 1990s, Meyer and Gamson (1995) critiqued the ways in which celebrities redefined SCOs' demands for social change, making them less conflictual and universalising alternative discourses. Celebrities must carefully negotiate their own identities as SCMs in a way that does not jeopardise their own personal brand. However, they also might get involved or start SCOs to build their own brand, as discussed by Budabin and Richey (2021) in 'Batman Saves the Congo'. Members of the public are aware of this and might therefore see them as 'profit-making constructions' (Meyer and Gamson, 1995: 201). They conclude that 'if celebrities, manufactured by entertainment industries, must carry the water for the politics of protest, perhaps this reflects more substantial distortions in society' (Meyer and Gamson, 1995: 202). At the same time, they noted how these causes may have faded to oblivion considerably more quickly in the absence of celebrity endorsement.

ICT and social media as game changers

The role that ICT and social media play for SCOs (and any other type of organisation) can hardly be overestimated. First, let us unpack what we mean by ICT – information and communication technologies. They include hardware (computers, mobile phones, smart phones) and software (programmes and applications). Social media sites such as Twitter/X, TikTok or Facebook are hosted on servers (hardware), can be accessed by a variety of more or less mobile devices (desktop computer, smart phone) via data (mobile data, WiFi) employing a variety of applications and programmes (software). Once a user has obtained a device, has data access, and (paid or unpaid) programme or application, use of ICT might seem 'free'. However, even unpaid applications have a cost because the use of social networking sites 'propertizes personhood' (Skeggs and Yuill, 2016) by tracking user data, for example on Facebook, even beyond the social networking site. Consequently, 'social media protest is now completely enframed by capital' (Skeggs and Yuill, 2016: 392). While SCOs have been active on an international and transnational level long before the widespread use of ICT and social media, these technological developments have had a tremendous impact on resource mobilisation. First and foremost, they represent resources themselves. Keeping digital inequalities (Halford and Savage, 2010) in mind, the cost of sending out emails to list members or disseminating messages via Twitter/X, Facebook and other platforms is much cheaper than printing and posting letters or leaflets for those who have access to devices, data and know how. Of course, they will only reach those who are signed up to email lists, Twitter/X and Facebook, and who engage with the information they have been sent. Websites and chatrooms provide resources to download information or to exchange support and experiences with other members. However, whether intended audiences see certain social media posts depends on the algorithms of the social media sites (Skeggs and Yuill, 2016; Tufekci, 2017). For example, (so far) anecdotal evidence suggests that since multi-billionaire Elon Musk bought Twitter in 2022 and renamed X in 2023, users experience changes in their timelines. While 'connective action' (Bennett and Segerberg, 2012) and 'networked' activism (Tufekci, 2017), which rely on the use of social media to recruit, mobilise, and coordinate participants, might render some conventional SCO activities as obsolete, we note that SCOs still play an important role and adopt the use of ICT and social media to provide information about their activities, recruit supporters and members, engage in crowdsourcing and so on.

ICT and social media have made it easier for SCOs to reach broad audiences, but it does not necessarily increase their influence because they must compete with thousands of other messages seeking attention through the same channels. Earl and Garrett (2016) warn us of the dangers of overloading people with information, of the ways in which social media produce echo chambers that foster selective attention, of bias and of associating serious concerns with entertainment. ICT – whether internet based or not – can also contribute to what Vestergaard (2008) calls compassion fatigue. As a society, we have become desensitised to horrific images of impoverished and starving children and habitat destruction, which are oftentimes culturally inappropriate. Such images have significant ethical implications as questions are raised about how they might (mis)represent others. Chouliaraki (2006) identifies three paradoxes in relation to 'the spectatorship of suffering' (which is also the title of her book). First, she worries that spectatorship fictionalises stories of suffering and can result in spectator indifference. Second, the shrinking of physical distances by mediatisation anchors spectacles into viewers' life worlds, which suggests that the blame for 'compassion fatigue' might lay at the feet of the media itself. Third, images of suffering invite us to take pity, which is an emotion that evokes powerlessness, even if we are persuaded to donate some money to a cause as a consequence. The depiction of vulnerable beneficiaries, in particular children, has been criticised as 'poverty porn' (for example, Bhati and Eikenberry, 2016).

ICT and social media raise important questions with respect to accountability and professionalisation. First, whereas organisations are accountable to donors, members and beneficiaries, it is much harder to decipher to whom those posting on various platforms are accountable. The payment of membership fees indicates some kind of identification with and support for an organisation. Does crowdfunding indicate similar commitment? SCOs tend to have assemblies in which members decide about the strategy of the organisations and/or a board of directors, which oversees the activities of an organisation. To whom are those posting on networking sites accountable and how representative are they? A large membership indicates a lot of attention, but that does not necessarily imply approval or representativeness. Moreover, the existence of bots raises important questions about the quality and consequences of social media discourse.

Furthermore, ICT and social media necessitate further consideration of professionalisation processes. On the one hand, this includes the skilled use of ICT and social media to raise the profile of organisations and contribute to fundraising and the delivery of services. On the other hand, the skilful use of ICT and social media can supplement or even displace professional services. For example, blogging and micro-blogging sites provide the basis for citizens' journalism. When activities of SCOs are not covered in the mainstream media, alternative internet-based forms of communication play an important role. The websites can also disseminate legal or medical information and advice. Over the past decades, e-health has grown significantly, for example in the context of the prevention and treatment of HIV and AIDS. Such e-health initiatives include government efforts as well as third sector organisations (Masilela et al, 2013; Van Zyl et al, 2014; Osunyomi and Grobbelaar, 2015) and raise concerns regarding the privacy and security of sharing and storing personal data.

Conclusions

In this chapter we have argued that in addition to context and values, resources matter for the choices of tactics. We have used the concepts of resource mobilisation, accountability, and institutional isomorphism to explore a range of resourcing dilemmas in SCOs. We have shown not only how obtaining resources impacts on the strategies of SCOs but also how their values and tactics determine which resources SCOs are open to receive. In Figure 4.1, we show the overall argument of the chapter. Resources are provided by a range of sources from individuals through to transnational organisations, which are used in moral, cultural, socio-organisational, human, and material ways. These resources shape SCOs' ability to garner further resources. They are used to support the primary tactics of SCOs – whether that be protest, advocacy, service provision, or a combination. These tactics (particularly protest and advocacy) have value accountability to their grassroots supporters and (particularly for service provision) downward accountability to their beneficiaries. Moreover, they have upward accountability to their donors. In this chapter, we have also illustrated how resource demands of SCOs are shaped as much by professionalisation processes as they are by the primary function of SCOs. The resource needs of bureaucratic protest businesses,

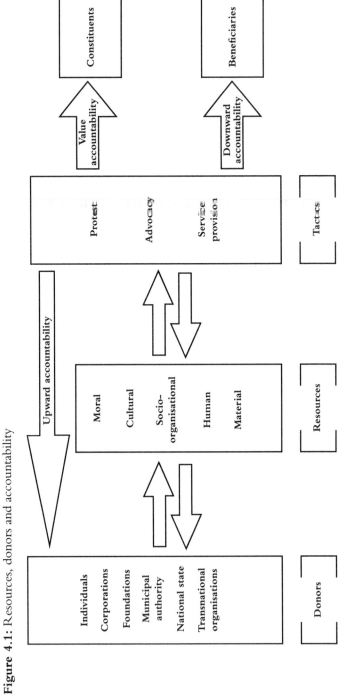

Figure 4.1: Resources, donors and accountability

professionalised advocacy organisations and large-scale service organisations are similar in many ways (skilled and differentiated staff, office space, media support, brand name and so on), even if different forms of equipment might be required depending on their issue specialism. Resourcing choices are thus implicated in complex cycles of actions, interactions and reactions – with donors, with other SCOs, with SCMs, with beneficiaries and with constituencies. We have shown that the concept of accountability is particularly useful to understand how beneficiaries and grassroots supporters lose out in the face of government funding and/or through the processes of professionalisation. We also illustrated how the resources are tightly related to the people who work within SCOs. It is people who have jobs or volunteer roles, people who use equipment, and people who engage in debates about legitimation and accountability. We discuss people – SCMs – in the next chapter.

5

People Making Change

In the autumn of 2011, thousands of protesters in multiple cities across the world – from Australia to Mongolia – put up tents to occupy prominent sites in cities to protest against the international financial system. Under the slogan of 'We are the 99%' they were particularly responding to the financial crisis and austerity measures. Our own research on the Occupy movement shows that these protests attracted many people who were new to organising for change. However, the camps also attracted experienced SCMs who had participated in multiple causes. Life history interviews with SCMs like Mike, a man in his forties, who participated in Occupy London, illustrate how the involvement in SCOs is embedded in everyday lives.

We interviewed Mike, who came from a working-class background, in November 2011. He remembered that during his childhood and youth, his mother supported the Labour Party and was involved in the Greenham Common protests of the 1980s against the stationing of cruise missiles during the Cold War. He was socialised into attending marches and direct actions and started to become aware of different movements through going to protests at an early age. He remembers meetings of SCMs while he was growing up and that his mother hosted members of the Polish Solidarność (Solidarity) movement. They were staying with Mike and his mother on an exchange basis at the beginning of the 1980s, when Solidarność was starting to take shape to bring about changes in communist Poland. Mike went to university, and at the time of the interview was self-employed and had several children. He told us that fatherhood was his main motivation for being politically active. He was concerned that his children would not have the same opportunities that he has had and was concerned about their economic situation and the state of the environment. Before getting involved in Occupy, he had participated in various campaigns organised by several environmental SCOs. He had been involved in Camps for Climate Action and had also run a local environmental campaign. When he realised that his local environmental campaign got bigger, he approached larger and more established organisations such as Friends of the Earth and Greenpeace because he felt that he did not have enough experience to deal with the significant campaign that he envisioned. However, he stressed that he preferred being independent from organisations. He perceived Occupy London as bringing together SCMs pursuing different causes that are all involved in peaceful protest, he mentioned 'women's groups, environmentalist groups, anti-capitalist groups, anarchist groups'. He felt that what united the heterogenous constituencies in the camp was their effort to communicate peacefully. This contrasts with sexism and sexual violence that have been observed in some camps (Eschle, 2018; Eschle and Bartlett, 2023). He rejected the anti-capitalist label of Occupy and believed in reform, rather than overturning the system. Furthermore, he could draw on his professional skills to contribute to Occupy.

This vignette illustrates several of the arguments of this chapter. We argue that in order to understand the involvement and participation of SCMs in SCOs it is useful to employ a life course perspective. Our interviewee, Mike, has been an activist in a range of causes and deployed professional skills to further them. We also argue that people involved in SCOs, who we call SCMs, are SCOs' most important resource. Without individuals like Mike, the Occupy London camps – and many other SCOs – would not come into existence. SCMs are the founders, leaders, members, volunteers, and supporters that drive the work of SCOs. In Chapter 1, we began to introduce the range of roles in which SCMs engage. In this chapter, we address how SCMs are recruited through push and pull factors, the benefits, and costs (including burnout) of involvement and the effects on individuals of professionalisation processes. We also show how being an SCM intersects with the wish to have or not to have children and experiences of parenthood.

As we have already noted, we recognise that SCMs do different things simultaneously or consecutively, paid and unpaid. We also note that the professionalisation and precariousness of many SCM roles can impact on the sustainability of being an SCM and experiencing burnout (Cox, 2010; Gorski, 2015; Roth, 2016). Shifting priorities or disillusionment might lead to dropping out, but they can also cause SCMs to try out new strategies, and result in intermittent patterns of involvement that include boundary-crossing (Roth et al, 2023).

The overall argument for the chapter is illustrated in Figure 5.1. The diagram illustrates some of the different patterns of participation that SCMs can take over their life course. They may be *persisters*, *boundary-crossing persisters*, *abeyances* or *boundary-crossing abeyancers*. Boundary crossers switch from one organisation to at least one other. They might cross causes (for example, humanitarianism, environmentalism, feminism) and/or varieties of SCO (services, advocacy and protest). In the diagram, we illustrate boundary crossing across varieties of SCO. A persister remains with one organisation

Figure 5.1: Social change makers' trajectories of participation across the life course

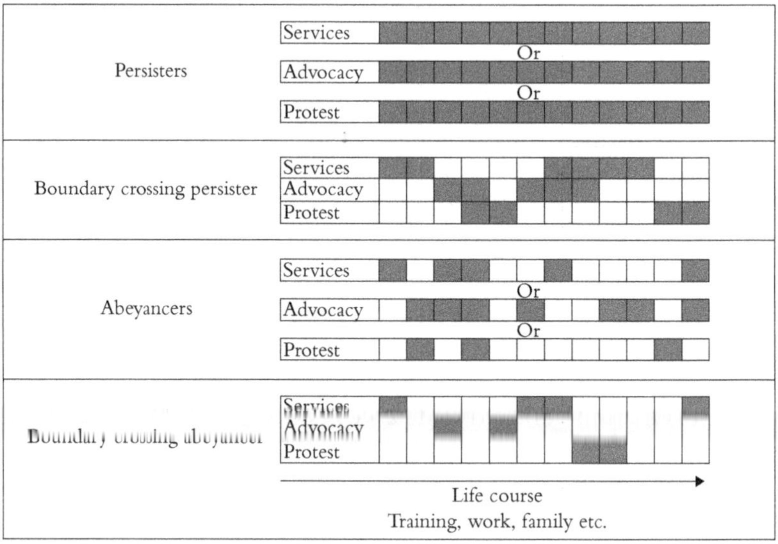

for a long time. A boundary crossing persister remains a persistent SCM but switches across organisations. Abeyancers dip in and out of one organisation; and boundary crossing abeyancers dip in and out of different types of organisations. Note that the life course interacts with patterns of participation, which also interacts with historically variable contexts that shape political generations. We now discuss recruitment to SCOs, the costs and benefits of involvement in SCOs, and the effects of professionalisation processes on SCMs.

Recruitment into social change organisations

First, let us start with those who have yet to become SCMs: the general public or *bystanders*. If they can be convinced about the goals of a SCO, this would transform them into *adherents* (McCarty and Zald, 1977). Convincing the general public or specific communities of the aims of an SCO contributes to disseminating the goals of the SCOs and mobilising financial and other resources as we discussed in the previous chapter. Adherents share the values and goals of a SCO without actually taking part actively or financially supporting it. This means that SCOs need to convert adherents into *constituents*, who do not only support the goals of an SCO, but also support it through individual acts, for example a donation or attending an event, or more regular support, for example volunteering. Some volunteers might take on leadership positions or become staff members of SCOs.

There is no magic recipe to ensure the recruitment of volunteers. We discuss recruitment in two ways – through pull and push factors. Pull factors refer to things that SCOs do to attract volunteers, whereas push factors refer to aspects of everyday life and the life course factors that might make individuals predisposed to becoming SCMs.

Pull factors for SCM recruitment

Recruitment of volunteers is more difficult for organisations that work in a high-risk or high-cost situation (see Chapter 3 and Marx 1999), and for small grassroots organisations that do not have an established reputation (Lynch and Smith, 2010). Moreover, newcomers who are joining small grassroots organisations can be perceived as disruptive (Blee, 2012). There are perhaps two main reasons that more established organisations have the ability to more easily recruit volunteers. First, they likely have better resources for an effective recruitment campaign. Second, mention of a well-known voluntary organisation looks much more impressive on one's curriculum vitae than a lesser-known local organisation that might be viewed as parochial or with scepticism by a prospective employer. However, this matters less for organisations in which elderly volunteers are active (Harflett, 2014). Organisations vary with respect to the requirement of high levels of mobility and physical activity from their volunteers. SCOs that rely on younger volunteers are likely to have higher turnover of volunteers because young people are more likely to be building careers and will be more likely to move on quite rapidly (Hager and Brudney, 2008).

Hager and Brudney (2011) refer to the difficulties of recruiting volunteers as a matter of 'nature' or 'nurture'. Recruitment problems related to 'nature' are due to the nature of an organisation: its issues, its size, its remit and its staff–volunteer ratio. They are not things that a manager or leader is able to easily fix. Recruitment problems related to 'nurture' are, by contrast, fixable by strategic action. A 'nurture' feature might include the adoption of volunteer management plans that 'include screening and matching volunteers to appropriate assignments, developing written policies for volunteers and their duties, providing training to volunteers, and recognizing them for their contributions to the organization' (Hager and Brudney, 2011: 142). Other aspects of nurture include having a paid volunteer programme supporter and a supportive organisational culture for volunteers. While it is easy to see how these can support volunteers, Hager and Brudney (2011) do not consider the interaction between nature and nurture arguments. A small-scale organisation (a weakness on the 'nature' side), for example, will not be able to afford to appoint a member of staff to a volunteer management position (a weakness on the 'nurture' side).

Other nurture volunteer recruitment strategies are advertising in a variety of places, and making use of volunteers to recruit other volunteers. However, while professionalised volunteer recruitment might have advantages, it also has some weaknesses. Fisher (2006) makes the case that the outsourcing of canvassing is actually undermining progressive politics because it 'reinforces the role of citizens as spectators' (p 112). She emphasises that 'meaningful membership' requires deep-rooted connections to local communities. Similarly, Eliasoph (2011) critically evaluates the work of city-sponsored after school youth programmes and notes that 'plug-in' volunteers might not only be unhelpful, but can be 'downright destructive' (p 127). Moreover, it is important to not only assess the strengths and weaknesses of recruitment processes of established and professionalised SCOs, but also the dynamics of nascent groups. Blee (2012) surveyed 60 emerging groups in Pittsburgh who were pursuing a wide range of causes. Only one of these organisations had a (part-time) paid staff member; these groups drew on 'existing ties of occupations, place and class' (p 7). Not all of them survived and some changed in direction. Blee (2012) examines the path-dependent development that accounts for their survival and demise.

The conservative Tea Party in the US represents a very successful example of grassroots mobilisation. Skocpol and Williamson (2012), identified nearly 1,000 groups in 2011, two years after the first local Tea Parties emerged in response to the election of Barack Obama. Many of these groups were led by retired, and semi-retired members as well as small business owners (Skocpol and Williamson, 2012: 93). Inspired by the mobilisation success of the Tea Party and responding to the election of Donald Trump in 2016, local Indivisible groups formed quickly making use of ICT. Within one year, about 6000 Indivisible Groups formed across the US (B. Roth, 2018). This means that successful mobilisation does not depend on professionalisation, which might contribute to or undermine the participation in SCOs. We return to professionalisation at the end of this chapter. Now we discuss the 'push' factors for recruitment – the different life spheres and life stages in which recruitment occurs.

Push factors into SCM recruitment

One of the most commonly used 'push' theories in relation to SCOs that focus on protest is the notion of biographical availability, which refers to having the time to participate in SCOs by virtue of having fewer family or job commitments (McAdam, 1986). As we mentioned earlier, McAdam (1986) initially developed the concept to explain high-risk activism in Freedom Summer – a form of risky civil rights activism in southern states in the US. But biographical availability matters differentially for different tactics (Roth and Saunders, 2022; Roth et al, 2023). A life course perspective is preferable because it helps us understand participation in varieties of SCO in the broader context of SCMs' lives. Signing an online petition, donating online to an advocacy organisation, or re-tweeting a micro-blog post on a social media platform (low cost) take seconds, whereas the participation in direct action or providing services to people in need of support requires preparation, training, and substantial commitment of time (high cost). While high-cost activism involves substantial time spent participating in SCOs – and, perhaps consequently burnout – high-risk activism concerns participants' freedom, health, and lives. In fact, biographical availability has little effect in predicting the extent to which people participate in low-risk street demonstrations (Saunders et al, 2012). Moreover, family and work responsibilities also did not prevent individuals participating in solidarity movements in Central America (Nepstad and Smith, 1999), as we will demonstrate in this chapter. But first we turn to examine the broader historical contexts in which SCMs' life courses are situated and look at political generations in which they find themselves.

Historically variable contexts give rise to political generations which Mannheim (1952) defined as age groups that upon entering social life undergo formative experiences that produce distinct and lasting perspectives. The concept of political generations is a useful lens to examine the SCMs that formed the humanitarian organisation MSF. They were shaped by the experience and memories of the Holocaust and longer histories of resistance and complicity of the Left in France and other countries. Davey (2015) traces the emergence of MSF through the involvement of Jewish activists in internationalist and universalist causes and notes the relationship between *Tiers Mondisme* (Third Worldism) and the New Left, the US civil rights movement, and movements opposing the Vietnam War. SCMs involved in these struggles have been shaped by their experiences. The Algerian Independence War (discussed in Chapter 2) represented 'one of the most important sites of intellectual mobilisation in contemporary France' (Davey 2015: 59) and *Tiers Mondistes'* (SCMs participating in *Tiers Mondisme*) militancy. Individuals' support for this revolution crystallised the thinking of the French Left around 'colonialism, power, revolution, and violence' (Davey 2015: 65). Their support for anti-colonial movements encompassed the Cuban and Vietnamese struggles. However, the *Tiers Mondistes* started to perceive Cuba, the USSR, China, and Cambodia as repressive and solidarity turned into disenchantment. The French activists became increasingly concerned with the situation of foreign political prisoners and shifted to *Sans-Frontiérisme*. Like *Tiers-Mondisme*, *Sans-Frontiérisme* deals with occupation, resistance, and genocide, but differs in framing and tactics. Davey (2015) argues that the memories of the Holocaust were central to informing the early humanitarian ideas of *Sans-Frontierisme*. Whereas *Tiers-Mondisme* justified 'left-wing violence as necessary resistance to oppression' (p 177); in contrast, *Sans-Frontiérisme* 'made human rights the cornerstone of future campaigns' (p 178), based on the recognition that the Left was also capable of significant examples of repression and even genocide. Davey describes how this resulted in individuals turning 'against ideology' (p 212) in the 1970s and the (media-driven) campaign around assistance for Vietnamese boat people, which is highly relevant in the context of the contemporary refugee crises.

World War II and the Holocaust did not only matter for the French Left, but for other political generations around the globe. The student movement and the terrorist Rote Armee Fraktion (Red Army Faction, RAF) in West Germany were motivated by a confrontation with the Nazi past, the half-hearted de-Nazification in post-War West Germany, and opposition to authoritarianism. Fietze (1997) describes the student movement of the 1960s as the first global political generation (see also Horn, 2017). Similarly, dissidents in the East German Peace movement opposed the socialist regime because they did not want to be complicit with authoritarianism. Women in the GDR (German Democratic Republic) peace movement felt that they owed it to their children to fight for their convictions even if this involved risking prison sentences (Miethe, 1999). They perceived their parents as complicit with the Nazi regime, and they did not want to be accused by their own children of not standing up to the communist regime.

The confrontation with fascism mattered not only for political generations in Europe but also for other parts of the world. African American soldiers who had served in Europe to defeat Nazi Germany were confronted with racism when they returned to the US (Slate, 2012). Similarly, Commonwealth soldiers who had fought in the British Armed Forces experienced racism in the UK (Gopal, 2019). The unequal treatment between White and non-White soldiers after the war fuelled civil rights movements. The involvement in the war production also mattered for women who upon the return of men from the war experienced exclusion from better-paid male dominated sectors of the labour market, which they were able to enter during labour shortages (Milkman, 1990).

Milkman (2017) identifies Millennials as a new political generation, which she contrasts with the 'Boomers'. In contrast to earlier political generations, millennials are highly educated and 'digital natives' (Milkman, 2017). Based on her analysis of four progressive movements (Occupy Wall Street, BLM, Dreamers and movements against sexual assault on campus) in the US, Milkman (2017) notes that Millennials emphasise intersectionality and combine the emphasis of redistribution of the old left with the emphasis of recognition of the new left and thus represent a 'new, new left' (see also Feixa et al, 2009). However, not all Millennials promote progressive causes on the left. Based on a comparison of cohorts surveyed between 1982 and 2012 Grasso et al (2019) observe that younger generations moved politically to the right and support authoritarian values. Whittier (1995) developed Mannheim's concept further and distinguishes between cohorts and *micro-cohorts*. She notes that participants shape the collective identity of SCOs. Long-term members provide continuity while new recruitment and turnover contribute to change. Micro-cohorts, which differ in political socialisation and their perspectives on key issues, join SCOs at different stages and thus contribute and (re-) negotiate the development of SCOs.

Socialisation processes throughout the life course – in the family, at the workplace and in SCOs – as well as structural factors account for recruitment into SCOs. Caregivers consciously and unconsciously, positively and negatively contribute to the political socialisation of children. 'Red-diaper babies', for example, grew up in communist households and participated in the second wave of the women's movement (Weigand, 2001). Similarly, growing up in and raising a family in which political commitment plays a central role can contribute to the motivation to pursue a career in SCOs as our vignette of Mike at the beginning of the chapter illustrates (see also Frantz, 2005). This applies for example, to SCMs in the peace movement (Sisk and Duncan, 2006; Sommers-Flanagan and Sommers-Flanagan, 2006; Eschle, 2023), LGBTQIA+ parents (Averett, 2016), and those engaged in community and environmental activism (Fuentes, 2013) as well as in health-related issues (Ryan and Cole, 2009).

The concern for the lives of family members, and the ethnic community (and social class) can motivate women to get involved in social justice issues (Naples, 1998). In Los Angeles, the grass-roots organisation Mothers of East Los Angeles (MELA) mobilised Mexican immigrants, supported by Catholic priests and city and state level Mexican-American politicians, against a planned prison and an incinerator in their neighbourhood (Pardo, 1995). As 'mothers' they understood themselves initially as defenders of the neighbourhood, but over time they worked together with environmental groups across the state. Identifying as a mother thus can play a crucial role for the involvement in environmental justice organisations (see also Bell and Brown, 2010). The 'politics of care' (Jupp, 2022) also plays an important role for anti-austerity activism in which mothers and other community members fight against the closure of day care centres and other welfare state and austerity cuts. Of course, community involvement is not restricted to parents and other adults, but also includes environmental and social justice activism of youth (Shah, 2011). Parents can be role models and the experience of participating in a demonstration, attending an anti-authoritarian day care centre or a Waldorf school, or growing up in shared housing can influence children's future political participation. This does not mean that children of leftist, anti-racist, feminist parents necessarily share the beliefs of their caregivers.

Workplaces also represent important contexts for recruitment into SCOs. One of the oldest types of SCOs that seek to improve the working conditions of employees are trade unions, which employ various tactics. These include disruptive protest events such as strikes; advocacy work in the context of legislation and policy making; collective bargaining; and the provision of legal advice and support for their members. Full-time trade unionists, women's, and minority officers are active on behalf of their constituencies, act as mentors, recruit union members, and involve union and non-union members in events (Roth, 2000; 2003; Kirton and Healy, 2012). Their participation in strike action or the experience of having received support from the union can act as political socialisation and lead to joining or increased union involvement. In addition to trade unions, other SCOs represent interests of women, ethnic minorities, sexual minorities, the disabled, and others experiencing health issues, while trade unions have also created subcommittees and caucuses that serve diverse constituencies.

Trade unions and other workplace organisations are not the only networks that play a central role for the recruitment into SCMs. Being connected to SCOs through formal and informal networks contributes to disseminating ideas and to recruiting SCMs to various activities. (In the following chapters we examine the contact between SCOs and the mobilisation outcomes of SCOs.) Different 'structures of association', which play a role for mobilisation, can be distinguished: trans-movement, indigenous, and pre-figurative structures (Polletta, 1999). Trans-movement structures bring together SCMs from across varieties of SCO and are characterised by extensive ties, 'well-equipped to identify opportunities, not well-equipped to supply leaders or mobilizing frames, or to recruit participants' (Polletta, 1999: 9). Indigenous structures consist of community organisations, such as churches and other religious communities, which provide a space for communities to develop a response to social and political issues. They are characterised by dense ties and are 'well-equipped to supply leaders, local participants, and mobilizing frames; but not to identify extra-local participants' (Polletta, 1999: 9). Both trans-movement and indigenous structures take for granted a physical presence rooted in existing social movement activism or community organisations. In addition, online-based free spaces are increasingly important and, as we discuss later, digital prefigurative action can turn into offline involvement. Polletta's (1999) examination of trans-movement sectors applies to the multi-sectoral SCO alliances and networks we are exploring throughout our book, particularly in Chapter 6.

Organisational ties – which generate structural availability – have attracted significant scholarly attention, particularly in the resource mobilisation and social networks literature. Organisational ties refer to the membership in organisations – these could be SCOs, but they could also be religious organisations, sports clubs, workplaces, in short, any organisational setting. However, the role that multi-sectoral SCO networks play for recruitment depends heavily on the context, including the culture and type of organisation or protest event to which someone is recruited (Diani, 2011). While overlapping networks can bolster the diffusion of mobilisation efforts, at the same time SCOs might compete for the resources that SCMs have to offer (Cress et al, 1997). Religious organisational ties play an important role in oppositional and religious SCOs and constitute important indigenous structures facilitative of SCO tactical repertoires in a broad range of contexts. Examples include the US civil rights movement (Morris 1984), South African Apartheid opposition (Walshe, 1991), dissident movements in Eastern Europe (Kubik, 1994; Torpey, 1995), liberation theology in Latin America (Smith, 1991), and the solidarity movement in Central America (Passy and Giugni, 2000; Nepstad, 2004). Studies of Occupy camps in different countries (Juris, 2012; Pickerill and Krinsky, 2012; Roth et al, 2014, Milkman 2017; Eschle 2018; Eschle and Bartlett, 2023) found that it attracted veteran activists who had participated in multiple organisations and protest events as well as novice participants. Yet, attempts to consider the relationship between multi-sectoral SCO networks and indigenous structures, while taking into account less active forms of participation based on prefigurative politics, are rare.

ICT and online recruitment as push and pull factors

In recent years, online activism has become increasingly important and instead of being detached from SCOs, digital activism is embedded in the everyday life of SCMs and SCOs (Van Laer and Van Aelst, 2010; Tufekci, 2017). Social networking sites are frequently used to mobilise online as well as offline (Harlow and Harp, 2012; Costanza-Chock, 2014). Digital activism can be prefigurative and recruit participants in offline protest events (Mercea, 2012) or it can contribute to movement retention (Bunnage 2014). We defined prefigurative action in Chapter 1 when we introduced service provision, arguing that the provision of charitable or mutual aid can prefigure statutory support, for example healthcare, education, pensions, and other welfare benefits. So what is meant by digital prefigurative action? Mercea (2012) argues that through digital prefigurative action newcomers are recruited into activism. This means that bystanders might first support a cause online – through expressing their agreement with a post on social media, re-posting, or contributing original posts – thus being transformed into adherents, before getting involved in offline events.

Given that increasing access to the web in the past two decades has offered new opportunities for movement recruitment and participation, scholars have examined the role of the web for social movement mobilisation and the extent to which it might be transformative. The current COVID-19 pandemic has forced third sector organisations to shift face-to-face meetings and activities to online activities and make greater use of ICT (Fielker,

2020; Gronberg et al, 2021; McMullin, 2021; Seibert et al, 2021; Chevée, 2022). New information and communication technologies lower the costs of joining collective action (Eaton, 2010; Tufekci, 2017), although it is not clear whether purely virtual ties sustain SCO participation (Diani, 2000). Bunnage (2014) examined how activists stay involved in online activism when they reduce – temporarily or permanently – offline involvement.

Branding and the use of new media play a central role for solidarity activism, which requires little time and effort. However, while the click of a mouse to sign a petition or make a donation requires little time and effort, such online involvement can be less satisfying than actual participation in SCOs. Thus, ICT – especially in the context of social media – enable mutually constitutive interaction between offline and online dimensions of SCO participation (Costanza-Chock, 2003; Garrett, 2006; Van Laer and Van Aelst, 2010; Olcese, 2014; Tufekci, 2017). Computer-mediated communication (CMC) is not only relevant for 'super-activists' who have connections to SCOs (Van Laer, 2010) but also for those previously unaffiliated. However, Nielsen (2013) highlights exclusionary aspects of digital and networked technologies and the need for reflexivity. Digital inequality (Halford and Savage, 2010) encompasses not only lack of access to devices and data, but also the knowledge of how to employ these devices or navigate online spaces. For example, SCMs might have access to mobile phones rather than smart phones, or they might use data on pay-as-you-go plans rather than longer plans. Furthermore, they might have limited or extensive awareness of digital surveillance and the digital footprint they are leaving. Schradie (2018) found significant class differences in digital activism and notes 'The internet reproduces class inequality, rather than operating as a mechanism of egalitarian participation' (p 71). Her data revealed that 'the gap in online participation was embedded in access, skills, empowerment, and tools' (p 64) and that working-class participants made less use of social media than middle-class participants. This has important consequences not only for SCMs but also for SCOs, for example trade unions, that seek to mobilise working-class constituencies.

Mercea (2012) recognises that participation in protest events is rooted in a communicative act through which private concerns regarding a public issue are assembled and articulated and identifies three levels of participation: mobilisation, identity-building, organisational transformation. These levels are distinct from online organising for change, which is only taking place online. This, of course, also applies to SCOs that engage in service-provision and advocacy. In fact, the COVID-19 pandemic has accelerated the shift to online and hybrid forms of working in a broad range of SCOs. The use of ICT is both important for internal communication with staff, trustees, and volunteers, as well as externally with donors and clients. It still requires further investigation how the use of ICT affects trust relationships in SCOs' internal and external relations (Fielker, 2021). Mercea (2012) highlights the intersections of online and hybrid forms of organising for change and compares mobilisation into high-risk and low-risk tactics. CMC is important for the mobilisation of the previously unaffiliated, but Mercea notes scepticism about the contribution of the internet and argues that trust is developed in face-to-face interaction. He therefore argues that CMC did not seem to contribute in a fundamental way to the formation of a movement identity among the participants of the two events he studied. Although low risk participants might have appropriated movement identity by the event organisers, high risk-activism appealed primarily to constituencies from the environmental movement. Mercea (2012) concludes that movement identity may be articulated but not constructed through CMC. Thus, he observes primarily reinforcement effects and argues that this will not change before SCOs are willing to open up decision-making to prospective participants on Web 2.0 platforms. SCOs might have different reasons for not doing this including the absence of trust, misgivings about security of the platform, and scepticism about the commitment of the blog audience to organisational goals for restricting online discussions to existing members. At the same time, social media platforms such as Twitter/X and Facebook open up the debate to members and non-members. Engaging in digital organising for change is a characteristic of the Millennial political generation (Milkman, 2017). In the next section, we address the benefits and costs of participating in SCOs and how participation can be sustained over time.

Variations of involvement in social change organisations

The involvement in SCOs, for example voluntary organisations, varies over the life course (van Willigen, 2000; Tang, 2006; Borgonovi, 2008). While the involvement in voluntary associations drops during the transitions from adolescence to young adulthood, a role-related (work, family) peak in the middle years can be observed (Wilson, 2000), which differs by gender (Parry et al, 2021). Although retirement does not seem to draw people into volunteering, those who are already engaged in voluntary organisations tend to increase the time they devote to volunteering (Wilson, 2000). Thus, there is considerable evidence demonstrating that volunteering varies across the life course. Another key finding is that volunteering is strongly related to well-being. We will discuss the outcomes of social change making on the individual level in the next chapter; in this chapter we focus on the pathways of SCMs.

Engagement with SCOs (whether volunteering or protesting) can result in a number of pathways for individuals. According to Corrigall-Brown

(2012), they may decide to leave volunteering or protesting behind entirely, they may intermittently dip in and out of such activity, or, they might become a small group of people who 'persist' in SCO participation. Those who dip in and out, as well as those who take on a lifetime task of SCO engagement, are likely to be motivated to continue through 'individual abeyance structures' – that is, 'overlapping networks of individuals, ideologies, goals, and tactics' (Corrigall-Brown, 2012: 12). The argument here, however, seems relatively weak given that the factors that account for initial participation, sporadic participation, and persistent participation are pretty much identical. Cress et al (1997) challenge this assumption and find, with data from a probability sample of 1,587 voluntary memberships across a 15-year time period, that what pushes SCMs away from participation is often competition for their attention from other organisations (Cress et al, 1997). However, organisational competition is likely to be but one factor. It is often not SCMs' ideological commitment that falters, but rather that their life circumstances change, rendering participation more difficult at times (Stoker and Jennings, 1995).

More attention has been paid to the recruitment into social change making than retention (Corrigall-Brown, 2012; Bunnage, 2014) and disengagement (Fillieule, 2015). Moreover, most existing studies that examine the persistence in and disengagement from SCOs have in common a focus on the involvement in one particular movement, one particular SCO or one particular SCO tactic (usually a form of protest). For example, Passy and Giugni (2000) studied members of the Swiss solidarity movement. They found that those who experienced a congruence of life spheres (activism, work, and family) stayed involved in the movement whereas those who experienced a disconnection of the life spheres – for example, living with a partner who did not share the same political goals, or making career changes – tended to withdraw from the movement. However, their study did not include whether former participants had moved on to other SCOs associated with other causes, for example environmentalism. Downton and Wehr (1998) who studied participants in the peace movement found that a congruence of life-spheres contributed to sustaining activism. They present the example of a peace commune which shared making a living and raising children. Corrigall-Brown (2012) considered different SCOs and identified four different trajectories of participation: persistence, transfer, individual abeyance, and disengagement. *Persisters* stayed active in the same movement, those who *transferred* moved their participation to another cause; *individual abeyance* characterises those who interrupted their participation and resumed it later on whereas *disengagement* does not involve a return to activism. Corrigall-Brown (2012) employs a broad definition of 'contentious politics', which includes 'participation in both civic and community SMOs and activities, including demonstrating, rallying, marching, and protesting' (p 11). However, she does not include occupational activism (Cortese, 2015) which we discuss later when we turn to professionalisation and paid staff members of SCOs.

As we argued at the beginning of this chapter, in order to gain a fuller understanding of the sustainability and trajectories of participation in SCOs it is important to think about participants as 'boundary crossers' (Lewis, 2008; Kyle et al, 2011; Roth, 2015; 2016; Roth et al, 2023) who move between different sectors and between paid and unpaid activism over their life course. Such boundary-crossing has significant consequences for coalition building and contacts between SCOs, which we will discuss in the next chapter (Chapter 6). Based on our analysis of several waves (1991–2008) of the British Household Panel Survey (BHPS) (Roth et al, 2023) we suggest expanding the patterns of participation identified by Corrigall-Brown (2012) and add the following trajectories: *boundary-crossing persisters* and *boundary-crossing abeyancers*. Boundary-crossing persisters have been active throughout the entire time-period but they moved between different causes and SCOs. Boundary-crossing abeyancers have been active on and off, switching between different causes and SCOs. We found that among a representative sample of the British population almost 75 per cent had been involved in volunteering at some point over a time-period of 17 years, almost a third were *abeyancers*, 16 per cent were *boundary crossing abeyancers*, 10 per cent were *persisters* (in one cause), and 2 per cent were *boundary crossing persisters* (consistently volunteers but in different sectors). This demonstrates that people's patterns of membership in voluntary organisations changed significantly across the nearly two decades we studied. Many more people are *abeyancers* and *boundary crossing abeyancers* than are *persisters* who stay with the same cause.

Moreover, other research of ours on involvement in trade unions (Roth, 2003) and humanitarian SCOs (Roth, 2015) demonstrates that SCMs alternate between paid and unpaid engagement in SCOs, which is not captured by the BHPS, which only asks about associational membership.

Our research thus builds on and further develops the notion of 'biographical consequences' (McAdam, 1989) of organising for change, addressing the impact activism has on personal and professional life spheres (see Chapter 7, addressing outcomes). McAdam (1989) found that former participants of the *Freedom Summer* campaign were more likely to work in helping professions; however, he does not identify these occupations as a form of activism. We are acknowledging a broader spectrum of strategies in which SCOs and SCMs engage and perceive some forms of employment as *occupational activism*. Participation in SCOs can also lead to a variety of careers, especially when the boundaries between political activism and volunteering is not drawn too strictly (Eliasoph, 2013). Thus, volunteering in Amnesty

International as a student can be helpful for a career as a lawyer, participation and interest in autonomous movements can contribute to an academic career and voluntary participation in political parties and trade unions (Roth, 2003) and humanitarian organisations (Roth, 2015) can lead to full-time positions. In order to understand the sustainability of participation in SCOs it is important to comprehend what being a social change maker means.

Identities of social change makers

As we stated in the Introduction to our book, we prefer to use the term *social change makers* rather than activists. One reason is because who counts as an activist varies widely in the literature as well as among those engaged in SCOs. Bobel (2007) notes that women involved in menstrual activism distinguished between 'doing activism' and 'being activists', which might overlap – or not. Even women with similar patterns of involvement differed in whether they identified as 'activists'. Some stated they felt that they did not meet the 'perfect standard' because 'being activist' required being 'super-active' and engaging in 'tireless commitment, selfless sacrifice, unparalleled devotion' (Bobel, 2007: 154). In this case, an activist identity was grounded in core values of rigour and humility rather than in involvement in specific actions. Brown and Pickerill (2009: 27) point out that this 'perfect standard' draws on gendered assumptions even though they stress that macho heroism related to daring acts during the participation of social action is not restricted to men (see also Hopgood, 2006; Houldey, 2022).

In contrast to the studies previously mentioned, Corrigall-Brown (2012) found that SCMs, who were leftist in ideology and had previously been involved in protest oriented SCOs, were more likely to identify as 'activists' and to stay involved. In contrast, those who had a negative view of activism rejected an activist identity despite engaging in exactly the same behaviour. Thus, while Bobel (2007) found that the label 'activist' was rejected because participants felt they did not deserve it, Corrigall-Brown (2012) observed that participants distanced themselves from it because they resented it.

Still another perspective is offered by Cortese (2015) who, based on interviews with LBGTQI+ movement participants, identified three types of activist identity: emphatics, demarcators, and reconcilers. *Emphatics* identified with an activist ideal-type, were deeply involved and often movement leaders setting the standard of activism in the organisation. *Demarcators* engaged in boundary-setting and distinguished between 'good activists' (themselves engaging in polite activism) and 'bad activists' (others engaging in radical, in-your-face activism). *Reconcilers* identified as activists, although they did not meet the criteria of the 'perfect standard' of high-level involvement. They had either only recently joined the movement, their activism had decreased or they perceived working in their current occupation (for example as teachers) as activism. Cortese (2015) refers to the latter group as *occupational activists*. The fluffy nature of the term activist justifies our use of the term SCMs and allows us to move beyond the notion of activism to consider varieties of participation in SCOs. Let us explain. As we argued in this chapter, SCMs might participate in SCOs continuously or intermittently, they might be paid staff members or unpaid volunteers. Some SCMs are creating SCOs that provide services, for example, a health food store. Other SCMs change mainstream organisations from within. We consider occupational activists a group of SCMs that are organising for change in mainstream organisations, for example by establishing Black studies programmes in universities. That does not make universities SCOs. However, taking into consideration SCMs in mainstream organisations, such as universities, allows us to make an important contribution to understanding the sustainability of organising for change over the life course.

Personal sustainability and (avoiding) burnout

How can SCMs sustain their participation in SCOs over the life course? What are the requirements for 'personal sustainability' (Cox, 2009; 2010) that are also important for the sustainability of SCOs? Paid and unpaid work in SCOs is physically, psychologically, physically, and financially stressful. Exhaustion, cynicism, and inefficacy are three key components of burnout (Maslach and Gomes, 2006). Exhaustion (the individual stress component) is experienced as being overwhelmed and drained; cynicism (the interpersonal component) is a response to exhaustion, initially self-protecting it undermines commitment to the cause; inefficacy (the self-evaluation component) is experienced as underachievement due to lacking resources and unachievable goals (Maslach and Gomes, 2006: 44). Thus, burnout results not only from vicarious post-traumatic stress, for example, when working with victims of abuse, but can also be triggered by the working conditions in SCOs, which are characterised by long working days, conflicts, and varied frustrations; in addition, SCOs often lack resources and recognition (Cox, 2010).

A study of unpaid SCMs who addressed social justice concerns in the context of school and studies, found that they experienced chronic psychological and mental health effects including chronic depression, stress, anxiety, and panic attacks, the decline of physical well-being as well as disillusionment and hopelessness (Gorski and Chen, 2015). Pursuing the 'perfect standard' identified by Bobel (2007), these SCMs developed a 'culture of martyrdom' (Gorski and Chen, 2015: 397) that prevented them from engaging in self-care (Houldey, 2022). These SCMs pursuing social justice felt that taking advantage of high-quality healthcare or taking time out to sustain themselves would undermine their activism. However, when they realised that burnout can lead to disengagement, some of the SCMs interviewed changed their attitude towards self-care and became interested in learning how to overcome the 'culture of martyrdom'.

Burnout is not only experienced by SCO volunteers but also by paid staff. Rodgers (2010) analysed the work culture and emotional context of Amnesty International, which is characterised by commitment, sacrifice and guilt. The normative expectations of selflessness that are reinforced and institutionalised in this human rights organisation result in high turnover of paid staff. Moreover, it is important to point out that pay for employment in SCOs is often poor and oftentimes precarious as it depends on unreliable funding through grants and donations (Eltanani, 2016).

It is common for (feminist) SCMs to work on short-term contracts or combine various part-time jobs or freelance work. After all, SCMs must make a living – they might work in a helping profession and volunteer in SCOs before they find paid employment in SCOs. Full-time activists who do not have a paid position in an SCO have to rely on savings, benefits, and the support of friends and family unless they have inherited wealth. Thus, those from privileged backgrounds will find it easier to volunteer than those who must provide for themselves and dependents. In this respect, it is important to consider class differences between SCMs (Valocchi, 2013). Notwithstanding international networks, recognition and prominence, SCMs' careers are often precarious (Newman, 2012; Faludi, 2013).

In order to prevent or overcome burnout, the imbalance between goals and resources to achieve them needs to be addressed. This can include shifting the focus of social change making, and to develop more realistic, pragmatic goals (Maslach and Gomes, 2006). Furthermore, engaging in mindfulness practices such as yoga, tai-chi, and meditation can help SCMs to deal with burnout and become more effective (Gorski, 2015). Achieving a balance through paying attention to personal needs, avoiding exhaustion from work, making time for reflection and play, and diversifying activities enables SCMs to avoid burnout and contributes to sustaining organising for change (Downton and Wehr, 1998: 543; Driscoll, 2020). However, the self-care practices in which SCMs engage vary with respect to access to resources and being able to take time off (Driscoll, 2020). In her study of feminist and women's right activists involved in online campaigning, Gleeson (2016) found that even though the two campaigners who worked on the campaign as paid part-time employees were in precarious positions, they remained far longer with the campaign than the unpaid campaigners. The paid campaigners avoided burnout since they were able to distance themselves from the campaign and work fewer hours. At the same time, the paid campaigners were highly identified with their work and reported that they spent more hours working than needed. Frantz's (2005) study of SCO staff also highlights how professionalism and social values were interrelated. Staff emphasised that they wanted to develop professionally in order to be better able to contribute to the realisation of the aims of the organisations for which they were working.

Social change making, paid or unpaid, has 'biographical consequences' (McAdam, 1989) for the private lives and professional choices of activists (which we will address also in Chapter 7 when we discuss outcomes of SCOs). Burnout is a risk both for volunteers as well as for staff in SCOs. In order to sustain activism, burnout needs to be avoided. There is a wide literature on 'work–life' balance, which discusses how employment and family can be reconciled (Eikof et al, 2007; Roberts, 2007). This literature has primarily addressed women's ability to combine work and care obligations. Roth (2016) suggests developing this further and consider how the involvement in SCOs can be reconciled with family and paid employment ('work-life-activism-balance'). Furthermore, shifting or boundary-crossing between different SCOs or different forms of paid and unpaid activism, might contribute to the sustainability of involvement in SCOs and the prevention of burnout. In the final section of this chapter we turn to professionalisation and paid participation in SCOs.

Professionalisation

As we have argued throughout the book, different strategies respond to and reflect different political contexts and different needs, values, and goals of SCOs and SCMs. It is important to keep in mind that radical outsider activism can have system-stabilising effects (Blühdorn, 2006), while occupational and academic organising for change can have significant negative career consequences and may include harassment and intimidation (Taylor and Raeburn, 1995; Ferber, 2018). Thus, high-risk social change making is not limited to direct action but can also include occupational and academic organising for change. Occupational organising for change occurs in paid employment in a range of occupations including radical social work (Lavalette, 2011; Turbett, 2014; Emejulu and Bassel, 2015; Jupp, 2022) and academia (Taylor and Raeburn, 1995; Askins, 2009; Brown and Pickerill, 2009; Kyle et al, 2011; Ferber, 2018; Shepherd, 2018; Mayer, 2020; Joseph and Connelly, 2021). Academic activism refers to academics who are involved in social change making and who reconcile their work as researchers and educators with their work as activists.

The latter can play a particular role in sustaining activism, although in the neo-liberal and managerial university, the spaces for academic organising for change are increasingly difficult to create and to defend (Crowther and Scandrett, 2016; Shepherd, 2018). Especially for those who successfully obtain permanent positions, academic positions can offer long-term activists paid employment that allows them to continue working with SCOs and SCMs as well as socialising new generations of SCMs while at the same time earning a wage that makes it possible to maintain a livelihood and perhaps sustain a family. It also offers spaces for SCMs who return to university for courses or a degree, which provide a space for reflection, learning, and networking (Kyle et al, 2011; Roth, 2015). Thus, the academy can support and sustain as well as legitimise and professionalise social change making (Kyle et al, 2011).

Shifting between different forms of organising for change over the life course can sustain SCMs and SCOs (Roth, 2016). SCMs gain experience in paid and unpaid work, which can be transferred from one sphere of activism to another. This includes learning processes as well as spill-over effects (Meyer and Whittier, 1994). Such shifts are also important to address or prevent burnout. For example, a gay rights SCM who had been involved in direct action and advocacy work demanding support for communities affected by HIV and AIDS might open a gay friendly health clinic, thus providing a service for one of the affected communities while making a living.

So far, only a few studies focus on those working in such professionalised SCOs (but see Frantz, 2005; Hopgood, 2006; Rodgers, 2010; Eltanani, 2016). These studies highlight the motivations of paid staff and their career opportunities as well as their working conditions, which include precariousness and burnout. In addition, the working lives of humanitarian and development workers have recently received more attention (Fechter, 2012; Harrison, 2013; Roth, 2015; Visser et al, 2016; Houldey, 2022). This research addresses the tensions, strains and contradictions experienced by paid staff members who have chosen highly demanding and potentially dangerous work (Fast, 2014). The commitment and devotion of paid staff in SCOs challenges a strict distinction between activism and professionalisation processes.

A qualified workforce in professionalised SMOs, the third sector and the aid industry is of interest not only for job satisfaction and career building of individual aid workers, but also for their employers, for donors, and for clients or beneficiaries (Richardson, 2006). Organisations seeking to promote the professionalisation of social change agents emphasise good leadership skills, the ability to write grant proposals and reports and represent the organisation. One important aspect of the professionalisation of humanitarian organisations concerns the debate around the creation of professional pathways. Furthermore, training represents a non-financial incentive that might contribute to employee motivation and lower staff turnover (Loquercio et al, 2006). However, SCOs do not necessarily have the resources to provide staff and volunteers with training opportunities. While some larger organisations can pay for the participation in shorter or longer training or university courses, smaller organisations are less able to support their staff and volunteers. Thus, SCMs themselves take on the responsibility to obtain further skills and knowledge, either as training on the job or through participating in university programmes or training courses (Roth, 2015).

Work in SCOs is as diverse as the SCO sector (see Chapter 1). Its workforce occupies a range of occupations and roles from formal professional positions such as fundraiser, human resources manager, nurse, or accountant, to jobs such as befriender, driver, or administrative assistant (NCVO, 2015). A large proportion of the work in SCOs, especially among the more professionalised ones, is paid, but the distinction between paid and unpaid workers is not always clear. One could say that some of the paid staff actually 'donate work' by working long hours and thus undertaking voluntary work for the same organisation (Baines, 2004; Almond and Kendall, 2000). In addition, some volunteers receive a nominal fee or stipend and therefore could be perceived as very low-paid workers (Taylor, 2015; Musick and Wilson, 2008). Furthermore, many of those providing aid in disaster zones for organisations like Oxfam, Save the Children or Doctors without Borders are low or unpaid 'volunteering professionals' and include doctors, engineers, logisticians and nurses (Shutt, 2012; Eltanani, 2016).

Across the sector, employees experience a broad range of working conditions (Taylor and Roth, 2019). Staff of SCOs are usually paid less than in the public and particularly the private sector. The fact that SCO staff earn less than in other sectors has been termed the 'third sector wage discount', but some studies indicate that the gap has been closing (Leete, 2001; Rutherford, 2015). Moreover, in a few international SCOs the executive staff salaries are comparable with the for-profit sector (Stroup, 2012). Due to the fact that SCOs are confronted with insecure funding arrangements, many contracts are part-time or fixed term (Almond and Kendall, 2000; Leete, 2006) and characterised by precarity (Standing, 2011; Kalleberg, 2009; 2011). Studies indicate that in the UK about 40 per cent of paid staff in the third sector have part-time contracts whereas 10 per cent have a temporary contract (Taylor and Roth, 2019). At the same time, staff in TSOs tend to be overqualified and underemployed, that is working fewer hours than they would like or in jobs that do not match their qualifications (Mirvis, 1992; Almond and Kendall, 2000; Clark and Wilding, 2011; NCVO, 2016). Moreover, outsourcing and austerity have resulted in the intensification and under-resourcing of SCOs that deliver public services (Baines, 2011; Damman et al, 2014). SCOs that rely primarily on unpaid volunteers and do not depend on state funding may be less affected by these changes.

Taylor and Roth (2019) illuminate some of what individuals find meaningful about their work in the voluntary sector. Studies found that staff report higher levels of job satisfaction than in other sectors despite lower wages (Benz, 2005; Borzaga and Depedri, 2005; Donegani et al, 2012). Low remuneration is argued to be offset by various symbolic rewards and the 'good glow' (Dean, 2020) that come from working for a greater good, helping those in need or promoting social justice (Onyx and Maclean, 1996; Borzaga and Tortia, 2006; Cunningham, 2011; Baines, 2011). It is not surprising that studies found that paid staff join those SCOs as workplaces that reflect their core values or beliefs (Rosso et al, 2010) including faith-based organisations (Wuthnow, 2004), political activist groups (Andrews, 2007), humanitarian organisations (Roth, 2015), or those that pursue social justice through social care (Baines, 2004; 2011). Similarly, unpaid volunteers hold a similar set of values, which motivates them to participate in SCOs (Musick and Wilson, 2008; Dempsey and Saunders, 2010). Nevertheless, some staff have joined SCOs by accident rather than because of their values or beliefs (Harrow and Mole, 2005; Taylor, 2005), while others have instrumental motivations (Musick and Wilson, 2008; Eliasoph, 2011; Lyons et al, 2012; Taylor, 2015).

Conclusions

In this chapter we have surveyed different forms of involvement, what motivates people to join SCOs, and how they sustain their involvement. We argued that a biographical perspective is particularly useful for understanding the variety of pathways that lead to SCMs' involvement in SCOs, for example how it is related to their careers and family lives. We also discussed what role gender, class, and ethnicity play for involvement in SCOs. We situated individuals within broader historical contexts by addressing political generations. The chapter addressed professionalisation processes and the role that they play for the sustainability of SCOs and SCMs. We argued that a nuanced perspective on professionalisation is necessary in order to better understand how social change making can be sustained at personal, organisational, and movement levels. This includes acknowledging the diversity of SCMs and SCOs as well as the shifts in historically variable contexts that shape political generations, and their intersections with life course of SCMs (Roth, 2016) and in the development of SCOs. We consider work in SCOs as meaningful work (Taylor and Roth, 2019) and call attention to burnout and how it can be prevented.

We considered how organisations recruit SCMs into high- and low-risk social change making. In this context, we noted the relationship between online and offline social change making, digital prefigurative politics, slacktivism, and clicktivism. We reviewed different theoretical perspectives (for example psychological, organisational) that seek to explain the recruitment of volunteers into organisations. We also discussed the recruitment of staff and the phenomenon of boundary-crossing (Lewis, 2008; Roth, 2015; Roth et al, 2023), that is changing between different causes as well as between different strategies of social change making.

Moreover, the composition of SCOs change over time as a result of volunteers and staff joining and leaving organisations. These changes have important consequences for organisational development, influencing goals and strategies. We therefore argue that the changing patterns of participation and the influx and turnover of members in social change SCOs matter both on the individual and on the organisational level. Furthermore, due to the transfer of SCMs from one organisation to another, patterns of participation have important consequences for coalition building, the creation of networks, and the diffusion of ideas and repertoires of action. We will discuss collaborations and coalitions as well as conflict and competition among SCOs in the next chapter.

6

Collaboration, Competition and Conflict

The Coalition of Labour Union Women (CLUW), which was formed in Chicago in 1974, to give voice to women in the male-dominated US labour movement (which we introduced in Chapter 1) is also a good case through which to introduce our chapter on the interaction between different SCOs. As we already noted, the founding members of the organisation came from a variety of backgrounds. Many had been long-standing trade union members, others came from the second-wave women's movement and wished to improve the working conditions of non-unionised women, some were also involved in the civil rights and student movements and other causes. What united them was the desire to improve women's working conditions, but founding members disagreed about the best strategy. Given the low unionisation rate of women and female-dominated sectors of the labour market, initially there was some debate whether this would be best achieved within the context of the trade unions or in an autonomous organisation. The view that CLUW would have more impact acting within the framework of the trade union federation AFL-CIO (American Federation of Labor and Congress of Industrial Organizations) prevailed. This decision meant that founding members decided that the best strategy of supporting (non)unionised women was from within the labour movement. In order to do this, they sought to unionise women who had not yet joined trade unions, bringing women into union leadership positions, and by adding women's issues on the agenda of trade unions. These efforts are characterised by collaboration with other organisations (trade unions, women's organisations) and conflict within the organisation. Through solving the internal conflicts, CLUW became a *bridging organisation* between the women's movement and the labour movement by framing 'women's issues' (day care, pay equity, sexual harassment, reproductive rights) as 'workers' issues' (pay, working conditions) and 'workers' issues' as 'women's issues' (Roth, 2003).

While CLUW represents a successful example of an SCO that was able to bridge women's and labour issues, this is not always the case. A strike of

132

day care workers (working in a female-dominated profession) in West Berlin in Germany in 1989 failed because the women on the picket line lacked the support of male public sector workers (for example, rubbish collectors), women involved in the autonomous feminist movement, and the female senators of the Berlin Senate. These potential allies did not recognise the demands of the striking day care workers who represented the low-paid public sector workers providing reproductive labour and thus supporting women in paid employment as relevant for their constituencies. The striking day care workers thus became victims of 'exclusionary solidarity' (Ferree and Roth, 1998). Thus, in this case, it was not possible to mobilise the support of male trade unionists or feminist supporters, which each defined solidarity narrowly focusing on their specific interests.

These two vignettes are illustrative of the central argument in this chapter. Without CLUW to bridge women's and labour organisations, 1970s US women's labour activism may have met the same fate as the West Berlin strike of day care workers. This chapter shows that the ways in which SCOs collaborate, compete, or conflict, or even do none of these things, shape social change making efforts, sometimes in minor ways, sometimes in profound ways. Throughout this book, we have been developing an interactionist approach (Roth, 2003; Fligstein and McAdam, 2012; Saunders, 2013; Jasper, 2015) to explain how SCMs and SCOs shape and are shaped by historical developments, institutional structures, and organisational cultures. In this chapter, we focus on some of the ways in which SCOs shape *one another* through different types of relationships. In this sense, the chapter uses a relational realism approach, focusing on the ways in which relationships between SCOs emerge, develop and dissolve as new experimental structures are experimented with, sometimes abandoned, and sometimes improved (Tilly and Goodin, 2006: 11). We draw on case studies from women's, environmental, and global justice SCOs and integrate different theoretical frameworks from subfields on varieties of SCO including intersectionality, organisational ecology, and institutional isomorphism to examine different relationships between SCOs. By using these concepts, we take heed of Bebbington's (2004) warning against ignorance of the social structures within which SCOs exist and which exist within SCOs. The reality of social change processes requires interaction across a diversity of actors across multiple scales and places.

Central to our argument is the idea that a range of different types of SCOs, varying in tactics and in their position on a continuum on the axes of local and transnational and ad hoc to professional, engage in multiple direct and indirect interactions including collaboration, competition, conflict, and indirect influence (Figure 6.1). These interactions are, themselves, shaped by the tactics, values and goals and resources of the SCOs involved in networks, which are situated within and shape as well as are shaped by the

Figure 6.1: Contact among social change organisations

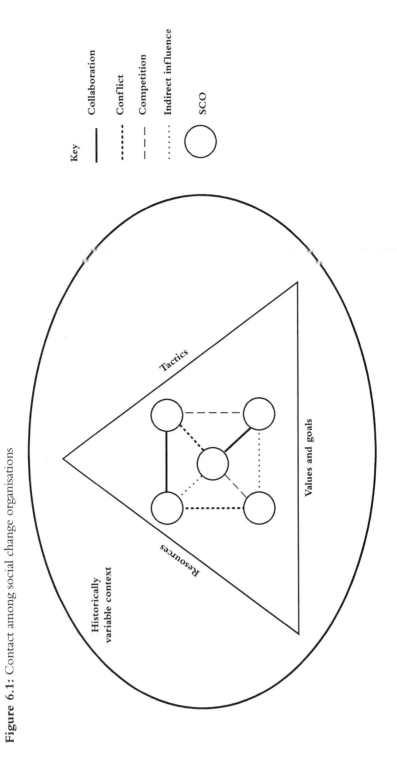

historically variable context. In the next chapter, we are going to examine the multifarious outcomes of such efforts.

This chapter is structured as follows: First, we briefly introduce the theoretical approaches that inform our analysis. Then we discuss the utility of these theories for understanding collaboration, competition, and conflict between SCOs and apply them also to transnational networking and online contexts. We acknowledge that, in addition to collaboration, competition, and conflict SCOs might simply ignore each other. Although we do not elaborate on this, we do recognise how they can indirectly influence one another in the absence of interaction.

Intersectionality, organisational ecology, institutional isomorphism

First, we use the notion of intersectionality (Crenshaw, 1991) as a starting point for understanding interaction among SCOs. Put simply, intersectionality refers to the fact that individuals and groups experience multiple forms of privilege and discrimination, which do not just add up but inform one another. For example, one's gender might result in advantages and disadvantages, but these differ for different racial–ethnic and/or socio-economic groups. This has, of course, significant implications for SCMs and scholars as it problematises what it means for an SCO to address gender inequality, class differences, or racial privilege, and other aspects of inequality. How SCOs address intersectional inequalities shapes patterns of interaction with other SCOs and SCMs. Furthermore, structural and political intersectionality need to be distinguished (Crenshaw, 1991). Structural intersectionality focuses on the effects of multiple subordination, for example how immigrant status and unemployment shape the experience of domestic violence. It can be experienced at the individual or group level; people can be, in multiple ways, disadvantaged or privileged, or disadvantaged in some and advantaged in other respects. Intersectional perspectives help us to better understand who is represented by and involved in SCOs and what consequences this has for the interactions among SCOs. Intersectional approaches allow us to better identify and address inequality and power relations within SCOs than approaches that focus only on one marker of inequality, for example race, class, or gender. This does not just concern who participates in an SCO, but also how the different members and groups shape SCO agendas and their choice of tactics. Thus, while structural intersectionality refers to experiences of privilege and disadvantage, political intersectionality refers to the strategies to acknowledge and address structural intersectionality. This means that political intersectionality acknowledges structural inequalities among SCMs and broader publics. SCOs that pursue political intersectionality recognise that it is impossible to focus on a single issue – for example, gender – without taking multiple levels of inequality and the ways in which they intersect into consideration. This affects how – for example – women's organisations mobilise: Inequalities among women can be addressed by pursuing equal representation of different groups of women with different concerns, forming caucuses, or engaging in coalitions in order to achieve political intersectionality (Roth, 2021).

Second, the organisational ecology approach (Hannan and Freeman, 1977) provides us with a more specific theoretical basis through which we can understand not only interactions among SCOs but also SCOs' reasons for avoiding interaction. These reasons may result in or be caused by competition or conflict. The organisational ecology approach is also useful in helping us to understand how SCOs might come to establish mutually beneficial – symbiotic – relations, and how they might consciously, among themselves, work out a division of labour that allows each to work in different ways for similar goals. Krause (2014), for example, analyses the 'global field' of humanitarian SCOs. SCOs in this field orient themselves towards and seek to differentiate themselves from one another.

We also use, third, the concept of institutional isomorphism, which posits that SCOs (in particular NGOs and VSOs) become increasingly similar as they engage more with the state (DiMaggio and Powell, 1983). This argument runs contra to the organisational ecology argument about differentiation of labour in a competitive field. In practice, though, institutional isomorphism is more differentiated than a blanket approach would suggest. The voluntary sector has been subject to the joint pressures of competition for funding and the need to collaborate to achieve success. Some grassroots voluntary sector organisations have had or anticipated negative experiences with collaborating to win grant competitions and have preferred to resist 'mission drift' (Meier and Meyer, 2016). We now turn to examine collaboration among SCOs, with particular emphasis on coalitions. We also consider the division of labour between different types of SCOs,

Collaboration

To illustrate the heterogeneity within and between SCOs, we begin by considering them through the lens of intersectionality. This lens reveals how the differences among SCOs' constituencies can make it challenging for SCOs to collaborate and invites us to look at the strategies they use to do so. All SCOs – even those that claim to focus on a single issue – are required to grapple with the concerns of a diversity of staff, volunteers, adherents, and bystanders that necessitate the bringing together of multiple interests and perspectives (Roth, 2021). It also means that SCOs need to confront and reflect on the fact that they might be exclusionary and include or privilege only a particular segment of society. This became very evident in

2020, when the increased media attention for BLM forced a wide range of organisations, including SCOs, to reflect on their membership, activities, and history. In addition to universities and other institutions, the National Trust (NT), a heritage and conservationist organisation in the UK, has started to address the fact that many of the stately homes in its ownership have been financed by profits derived from slave ownership and colonial exploitation (National Trust, 2020). Furthermore, the NT has responded by broadening its membership beyond its traditional White middle class constituency by adding new sites and activities that might make the organisation more attractive to BAME peoples and those less affluent (Harflett, 2014). Similarly, BLM has shed light on racial discrimination in development and humanitarian organisations (Benton, 2016; Martin de Almagro, 2018; Tegbaru, 2020; Khan, Dickson, and Sondarjee, 2023). Thus, racial – as well as gender and class – hierarchies play a role in national and international SCOs engaged in a wide range of issues.

When we think about SCOs that focus on women's, civil or gay rights, we might have an ideal typical constituency in mind. But an exclusive focus on any of gender, race, or sexuality overlooks that each individual (and group) is affected by multiple markers of difference, privilege and discrimination. In this sense, SCOs are also much less homogenous in their issue foci than they might at first appear. What do we mean by homogenous? In particular, we refer to the ways in which SCO sectors are given labels that suggest their focus is on a single issue. For instance, SCOs that work on women's issues are not just about women, but also about the intersecting concerns of labour, as we introduced in our opening vignettes, as well as class and race and other markers of privilege and discrimination. The same applies to civil rights or labour organisations (Roth, 2021), as well as environmental SCOs as we illustrated in the second vignette at the start of Chapter 1, about Jo, a transgender environmental SCM. The presence of multiple markers of difference is increasingly acknowledged by a variety of SCOs currently mobilising to address structural and political intersectionality (Milkman, 2017; Einwohner et al, 2021). Coalitions are one strategy to pursue political intersectionality. Thus, in contrast to Brooker and Meyer (2018), who consider intersectional coalitions as one subtype of coalitions, we argue that all coalitions need to be approached from an intersectional perspective.

Coalition building

A coalition brings together SCOs with different goals and constituencies. As we shall discuss, coalitions are more or less temporary, depending on their success at holding themselves together (Brooker and Meyer, 2018). Signing up to them does not necessarily involve a fundamental change to an SCO's belief system; however, this is a potential outcome as we discuss later. According to Diani (1995: 22), coalitions 'exhaust their function when their goal is achieved or it is clear that their goal is lost'. However, coalitions vary in their duration and might persist after they have achieved the goal that initially brought them together (Brooker and Meyer, 2018). A coalition might also be thought of as a way to bring together non-identical but at least weakly interlocking belief systems (Ferree and Miller, 1985). In other words, coalitions (sometimes) reach the lowest common denominator in terms of the goals they seek (Gerhards and Rucht, 1992; Corrigal-Brown and Meyer, 2010; B. Roth, 2010). Our discussion of coalitions proceeds in two ways. First, we discuss how coalitions – as a networking form bringing together SCOs with different goals and issues foci – represent a central form of political intersectionality (Bystydzienski and Schacht, 2001; Cole, 2008; Agustin and Roth, 2011). Second, we illustrate the reasons why coalitions are sometimes temporary, but can, at other times, endure or have lasting impacts on coalition members.

As a central form of political intersectionality (Cole, 2008), coalitions may bridge any combination of SCOs addressing class, gender, race, ethnicity, environmental or any other issue (Bystydzienski and Schacht, 2001). Coalitions crossing the class-divide require the work of bridge-builders (Rose, 2000) and bridging organisations (Roth, 2003), who are able to translate between different organisational cultures and values that characterise, for example, labour, peace, and environmental SCOs. Such coalition-building requires overcoming entrenched divisions and differences, for example, between working-class communities focusing on jobs and economic security, and middle-class SCMs supporting peace and environmental issues.

Such an alliance developed in Liverpool, UK, in the late 1990s. Dockside workers there were denied trade union representation, and, in 1996, formed a charter to protect their rights to decent working conditions. Women on the Waterfront formed shortly afterwards, consisting of female relatives of the workers who carried out media work and conducted candle-lit vigils in support of their male friends and relatives. The workers soon reached out to dockworkers in other countries and established an international steering committee to support each other in the conduct of 12-hour stoppages. By 1996, the dockworkers and Women on the Waterfront had joined an alliance with anti-roads protesters, Kurdish Groups and Reclaim the Streets (a group that reclaimed roads as public spaces – not to be confused with women's mobilisation to Reclaim the Night). The heyday of this alliance, in April 1997, was marked by a march of between 3,000 and 20,000 participants (depending on who you ask) for social justice, which united SCOs working on a diverse range of issues, not only workers' rights, women's rights and the environment, but also homelessness, asylum, and pensioners' rights (Rootes and Saunders, 2005).

Like the Liverpool Dockers' alliance, cross-class coalitions need to address the positionality of their constituencies who might include SCMs who are more and less financially well-off and those from different ethnic groups. Examining a cross-movement coalition in Boston in the US, Beamish and Luebbers (2009) identified four bridging processes, which included: cause affirmation, strategic deployment, exclusion, and the co-development of cross-movement commitments. Employing the previously mentioned bridging processes brought together groups from the environmental justice movement, peace, and anti-weapons proliferation movement, and allowed them to resolve tensions and maintain collaboration. This cross-movement coalition successfully stopped the construction of a federally funded, high security National Biocontainment Laboratory in a poor, largely African American inner-city neighbourhood (Beamisch and Luebbers, 2009). The core leaders of the environmental justice SCO were rooted in the housing projects of the Boston neighbourhood whereas White, middle-class activists from peace and anti-weapons proliferation SCOs came from other parts of Boston. The two groups differed in their preferences for tactics, and the significance of the planned laboratory, but were able to build trust and mutual co-commitment. Bridging processes involve taking the perspectives and interests of coalition partners into account, and necessitate being aware of differences in power and resources, especially in contexts characterised by inequality (Beamisch and Luebbers, 2009).

Furthermore, the framing of issues plays a central role for successful cross-class coalition building as demonstrated by the New Jersey Right-to Know Coalition, which mobilised against the use, storage, and transportation of toxic substances (Mayer et al, 2010). The coalition included health and safety activists from trade unions and a range of community and environmental organisations. Union activists thus broadened the frame from a workplace health issue to an issue of concern of the broader population. Such framing resonated with (middle-class) environmental SCMs. Both sides realised that they needed one another to strengthen their case and they successfully engaged in frame alignment – which means generating a diagnosis and prognosis of the issues that audiences can agree with (Benford and Snow, 2000) – and the bridging of different cultures of organising for change (Mayer et al, 2010: 764).

We have examined how intersectionality can be used as a political strategy to help develop and maintain coalitions, but why are SCO coalitions oftentimes temporary? When developing a coalition, the setting of goals needs to appeal to common sense social or political notions. Unfortunately, though, this may result in a somewhat uneasy coming together that challenges the identity of at least some of the SCOs involved (B. Roth, 2010: 112). Consequently, coalitions sometimes collapse because short-termism is built into their design (Saunders and Papadimitriou, 2012), because of ideological (Staggenborg 1986), or resource disputes, or repression (Krinsky and Reese, 2006). Gillham and Edwards (2011) report the downfall of the Mobilization for Global Justice Coalition (MGJC) in New York in 2001. The three sub-coalitions of the MGJC worked in advocacy, faith and anarchist/anti-imperialist fields. They each decided to go their own way to maintain legitimacy in the face of the 9/11 terrorist attacks. Here, an external shock resulted in coalition dissolution, but perhaps this would have happened sooner or later regardless of the 9/11 attacks due to ideological differences. Certainly, their highly differentiated responses to 9/11 would have made it difficult for them to continue to work together.

The Make Poverty History (MPH) coalition is another example of a temporary coalition. In 2005, MPH brought together 500 UK-based SCOs as diverse as autonomous direct-action networks and established humanitarian NGOs (such as Oxfam and Save the Children) with political parties (Saunders, 2008a; Saunders and Papadimitriou, 2012). It culminated in one of the largest demonstrations Scotland has ever known (approximately 225,000 people marched through the streets of Edinburgh) (Gorringe and Rosie, 2006). The diversity of MPH was impressive, bringing together many different types of organisations and spectacularly mobilising thousands of people. But its diversity and therefore the fragile nature of its interlocking relationships may have also been part of its downfall. Weak identity bonds make coalitions difficult to sustain. Although many organisations could sign up to the very broadly framed mantra to 'Make Poverty History' there were disagreements about the means through which that could be obtained (Rootes and Saunders, 2007; Saunders and Papadimitriou, 2012). The coalition existed as a formal entity for only a period of one year. However, even if some coalitions are short-lived this does not mean that they do not have legacy. MPH continues to exist in the imaginaries of many SCMs, who will have learned valuable lessons from the experience (Brooker and Meyer, 2018).

Luna (2010) also argues that coalitions can have a lasting impact beyond the existence of the coalition itself. She studied a coalition called March for Women's Lives in the US, which was organised by four mainstream feminist organisations (NOW, NARAL, Planned Parenthood, and the Feminist Majority Foundation). These organisations sought the endorsement of the march from SisterSong, an organisation of women of colour, with the aim of achieving political intersectionality. SisterSong demanded for the march to be renamed and the emphasis be shifted from 'reproductive rights' to 'reproductive justice'. Furthermore, the organisation asked for the inclusion of organisations of women of colour in the managing and steering committees. The involvement of SisterSong in the coalition thus resulted in a shift away from individual rights ('reproductive rights') to a broader social justice frame ('reproductive justice') as a result of political intersectionality. This means that shaping the agenda of coalitions members is thus an additional outcome of coalition participation.

Coalitions, then, need not be temporary. They are also understood as enduring alliances (see, for example, Van Dyke and McCammon, 2010; Brooker and Meyer, 2018). Coalitions encourage and facilitate the building of solidarity bonds, based on notions of equality, diversity, liberty, peace, and tolerance (Bandy and Smith, 2005). The building of solidarity along these lines is 'an active process of negotiating differences or creating identity' (Waterman, 2001: 234). Coalitions, such as the US–Polish coalition to stop Smithfield pork from entering the Polish meat industry (Juska and Edwards, 2005), are, in this view, seen as a stepping stone towards developing more enduring ties. For example, the Amazon Alliance lasted for 19 years and had strong emotional bonds and resource exchanges (Pieck, 2013).

Some transnational coalitions such as Peoples' Global Action (Wood 2005) and Occupy (Roth et al, 2014) are participant centred, developing careful mechanisms to be inclusive of all who are involved. Others are much more organisation centred (Cullen, 2005), and others still – like the European Social Forums were – are hybrid (della Porta, 2009; Santos, 2013). SCOs coalesce into different types of transnational (and national, regional and local) coalitions, differentiated from one another in terms of the extent to which they work across issues, such as labour, women's rights and environmental issues in campaigns against trade liberalisation (for example, Waterman, 2005), or on a single issue such as campaigns against child labour (Brooks, 2005). The SCOs engaged in these coalitions might make a choice to remain specifically focused, or they may realise how the issues they are working on intersects with others. In particular in protest camps, for example Greenham Common, Occupy, or Camps for Climate Action, coalitions not only engage in protest and advocacy, but also in service provision and prefigurative politics (Eschle and Bartlett, 2023; Eschle, 2023; Kavada, 2023). In fact, as Eschle (2023) and Kavada (2023) note, the reproductive labour that is performed in protest camps is not only often characterised by a gendered division of labour, but also frequently overlooked. Thus, more attention needs to be given to care work, reproduction, interdependence and vulnerability of SCMs (Houldey, 2022; Eschle, 2023; Kavada, 2023). This applies not only to protest camps, but also to the community programmes of the Black Panther Party in the late 1960s and early 1970s, which provided breakfast and other food programmes to poor communities, and mobilised resources from Black enterprises, thus forming unexpected coalitions (Potorti, 2017).

There is a long list of factors thought to facilitate (and which also, presumably, sustain) coalitions. These factors include a conducive socio-political environment (Barker, 2001 on the Polish Solidarność movement; Staggenborg, 1986); complementarity in ideology or identity (McCammon and Campbell, 2002; Cornfield and McCammon, 2010); the presence of individuals or organisations able to bring together diverse interests/organisational structures, known as bridging organisations (Roth, 2003) or bridge builders (Rose, 2000), shared grievances (Van Dyke and Soule, 2002; Van Dyke and McCammon, 2010; Saunders et al, 2016); similarity in organisational characteristics (Saunders, 2013); the presence of resources to commit to networking (Beamish and Lubbers, 2009: 648; especially for the voluntary sector, Milbourne, 2013); and weighing up trust benefit relations (Diani, 2015). But these factors are differentially distributed across coalitions at different scales and on different issues. On some issues in certain times and places *threats* might bring organisations together, on others at other times it is *opportunities* that bring them together (Staggenborg, 1980). Or it might be that the scale of the threat matters. For example, local threats are considered to bring together intra-sector coalitions, whereas broader threats facilitate cross-sector coalitions (Van Dyke, 2003; Brooker and Meyer, 2018).

The factors that represent barriers or opportunities to transnational coalitions tend to be very similar to the list of factors that constrain or encourage local/national coalitions (Young, 1992). They include presence and support of international organisations with capacity to kick-start the networking, well-established national movements, and foreign allies that have similarities, capacity for communicating regularly, institutions or corporations open to change, conducive economic conditions, the absence of war and mass public dissent (Bandy and Smith, 2005). Additional factors at the transnational level might concern the need to carefully (a) respect national autonomy (resonant of service providing SCOs' concerns for local autonomy) (Brooks, 2005) and (b) negotiate cultural differences in the building of solidarity networks (Smith and Bandy, 2005).

The internet has made it easier for transnational coalitions to form under very similar conditions to local or national coalitions, but it is important to note that ICT also matter for national and local coalitions. Cammaerts (2005) studied the role of ICT in each of: the Association for Progressive Communications (APC), an umbrella organisation; Labour Start, a portal organisation (an intermediary); ATTAC,[1] a platform organisation (a platform space designed for interaction); and in Indymedia, an internet-based activists' news site. The internet allows for horizontal networks of communications within and across countries. It makes it possible for volunteers to do much of the work of developing shared identities and goals. ICT allow unequal organisations to engage as relatively equal partners in transnational exchanges because they are low cost, flexible and allow for almost instant communication over significant distances (Cammaerts, 2005). However, we want to remind readers of digital inequality, which concerns access to devices, storage space, data, and the knowledge to take advantage of the affordances of ICT and familiarity with data privacy and security practices and regulations.

Although ICT have made the formation of transnational coalitions easier, we wish to stress that coalition formation is nothing new. SCOs have – for centuries now – participated in coalitions. Based on an examination of Protestant and Catholic organisations since the 16th century, Stamatov (2010) reminds us that transnational coalitions and networks have existed for a long time. Furthermore, SCOs that constituted the International Women's movement and the women's peace movement formed transnational networks during the first wave of feminist mobilisation at the end of the 19th century. Organisations like the International Council of Women (founded in 1888), the International Woman Suffrage Alliance (founded in 1904), and the International Committee of Women for Permanent Peace (founded in 1915), which later adopted the name Women's International League for Peace and Freedom (WILPF), included members from all continents, religions, political affiliations, and occupations (Rupp, 1994). However, the organisations were dominated by European and 'neo-European' women and the official languages were English, French, and German. Although the organisations sought to widen participation through providing financial support and travel grants, the collective identity and basis for solidarity focused on motherhood (excluding involuntarily childless and voluntarily childfree women) and the organisations experienced tensions between national and international identity (Rupp, 1994). Additional examples for transnational networks and exchanges include the connections between the Communist International and Black and colonial liberation struggles following the Russian Revolution (Featherstone and Høgsbjerg, 2021). Furthermore, Slate (2012) examined the relationships and exchanges between leaders of the Indian independence movement and the American civil rights movement. This illustrates not only that transnational collaborations do not depend on the internet, but stresses also the importance of exchanges between individuals, which are loosely facilitated by SCOs. Nevertheless, nowadays ICT and social media play a crucial role for the creation and maintenance of coalitions. SCOs do, of course, not only collaborate – online, offline, or both – they also compete with each other as we discuss in the next section.

Competition

While SCOs come together in networks and support each other in coalitions despite differences, they might also compete despite sharing common interests. How does competition for resources shape the relationships between SCOs? Especially when resources are scarce and when SCOs depend on funding to carry out their activities, they need to come up with strategies to attract support in a competitive field. Many SCOs engage in fundraising campaigns tailored to their distinctive approach. As Dean (2020) points out, supporting charities is not only crucial for SCOs who raise necessary funding, it also bestows 'symbolic power' on the donors. The professionalisation of fundraising campaigns has led to charges of the corporatisation of activism, as professional SCOs compete to raise money from alternative sources such as concerts, wristbands, and other products (Dauvergne and Lebaron, 2014). The competition for resources has made it normal to now think it possible to help achieve social justice or environmental protection by buying a product (Moore, 2008; Dauvergne and Lebaron, 2014).

Competition for scarce resources matters particularly for service-providing SCOs who have high expenses carrying out their work, for example for salaries, access to space, and equipment. In the context of neo-liberalism, services have been more and more transferred from the public sector to the private and third sectors. Many service-providing SCOs therefore apply for grants to carry out their activities (Watkins et al, 2012). However, historically a 'mixed economy of welfare' always existed though under varying conditions and with more or less state support (Harris and Bridgen, 2007) and is thus not unique to neo-liberalism. In the UK, as elsewhere, the voluntary sector has been under threat from shrinking public sector budgets, competitive frameworks, and burdensome administrative reporting requirements (Jupp, 2022). Local service providing SCOs, often with significant community experience, have often lost out on contracts that have been awarded to larger, professional organisations that are seen to simplify service provision and cut costs (Vangen and Huxham, 2003). Threats to the voluntary sector have been recognised by central government, and mergers and cooperative cross-sector partnerships have been encouraged (Rees et al, 2012).

Smaller service providing SCOs have lost out in multiple ways. Compared to their more professional and resource-rich counterparts, they have less time to invest in networking and fewer staff to help shape funding bids that accurately reflect their organisations' true remit. They also have less power than larger organisations to dictate the terms of collaboration and are sometimes included tokenistically on funding bids to allow bigger organisations to tick the 'community involvement' box on grant applications (Milbourne, 2013). Although such collaboration can sometimes work well for all parties, the process of uneven collaboration has also led to jealousy, mission drift, and resistance. Thus, some grassroots service providing SCOs have consciously tried to maintain their autonomy, protecting their own community-specific knowledge and skills, and choosing to work independently of other organisations (Milbourne, 2013). The voluntary sector might go through peaks and troughs in line with changes to funding regimes at the country level, but, overall, the number of SCOs is thought to be proliferating. The organisational ecology approach is useful for understanding why there are so many different types of organisations and how they co-exist through a series of different types of relationships.

According to Hannan and Freeman (1977), the overall pattern of organisational diversity in an organisational field is the result of competitive and co-operative interdependencies that determine whether or not each independent organisation will survive. If the organisation survives, then the next question to ask is whether it will prosper. Organisations are more likely to prosper when they can 'find niches to protect themselves against competition' (Aldrich, 1999: 43). Competition will occur, it is suggested, when the presence of one organisation has an adverse effect upon another. This competition is pure when both organisations suffer. The analogy of a predator-prey relationship is used to describe the situation that occurs when competition results in benefit to one party, but sufferance to the other.

Symbiosis is the term used to describe the situation where two organisations can co-exist to mutual benefit. Symbiosis often occurs when the interdependence of two organisations is based on mutual need. One example of symbiosis is the radical flank effect. A radical flank is the part of the SCO sector that has more radical goals and actions, and which can make the demands of more reformist organisations appear more acceptable (Freeman, 1975). The radical flank effect was systematically explored by Haines (1984), who charted the development and successes of the civil rights movement in the US, noting that moderate organisations performed better once the more radical wing emerged. Both the demands and strategies of more reformist groups look more reasonable to policy makers when more radical alternatives are present. In turn, the presence of reformist groups benefits radical groups; their slow or incremental progress motivates other SCMs to demand quicker and faster change with more daring strategies. This notion puts flesh on the bones of the argument that we made in the Introduction to this book. We noted that although NGOisation (Lang, 2013; Stroup and Wong, 2017) might lead a professional organisation to make compromises, such compromises can result in important broader repercussions in the SCO sector and wider society. While NGOisation might take the sting out the tail of individual organisations, it will not necessarily set back social change processes because of the actions and reactions it generates among other SCOs and the legislative and cultural outcomes that we will discuss in the next chapter.

Organisations that are more specialised (that is, are in a niche) may therefore be freer from competition and be able to work in collaborative, even symbiotic relationships, with others. Some of the more enduring coalitions we discussed earlier did consist of very differentiated organisations.

This may have sustained relationships, but, in the end, ideological clashes or changes in the socio-political environment saw even some of the more enduring coalitions fall apart. On the contrary, if there is overlap between organisational niches, competition is likely to be the result. If the overlap impinges on a greater proportion of the relative niche area of one organisation than another, that group with the largest impingement is likely to feel the competition more intensely than the other.

McPherson (1983) used a similar methodology to investigate the niche overlap between SCOs engaged in voluntary work and reported the unsurprising finding that voluntary organisations serving youths and the elderly have very little niche overlap as far as age of members were concerned. This co-exists alongside both types of organisations being free from competition with one another. This social ecology approach also resonates with Milbourne's (2013) stories about SCMs in smaller service providing SCOs feeling that their toes had been trodden on as larger organisations trampled over their niches and won contracts for what used to be the work of locally embedded organisations. Thus, 'smart application skills' (the term used by a Youth Centre worker interviewed by Milbourne [2013] to describe how larger organisations unfairly win contracts) have resulted in predator–prey relationships and feelings of dismay among more vulnerable and poorly resourced, but well-connected and knowledgeable, local groups.

Hannan and Freeman (1977) anticipated that a 'blooming' sector of organisations would result in differentiation. However, institutional isomorphism seems to counter that notion. Institutional isomorphism happens when the rules and requirements for the conduct of SCOs lead them to behave in similar ways (DiMaggio and Powell, 1983). As grants become more specific and the voluntary sector becomes more controlled by audit trails and performance management, organisations might lose their individual characteristics. If this were true, it would have significant ramifications for competition among voluntary sector organisations. Organisations that are barely differentiated will intensely compete to fill the same niche. But it might be 'jumping the gun' to panic about this. While SCOs working in the voluntary sector might have a tendency to become isomorphic, just as some protest-focused SCOs presumably have a tendency to institutionalise (Michels, 1911; van der Heijden, 1997) these are, by no means, guaranteed universal responses to the pressures of responding to the state. Evidence suggests that processes of institutionalisation of organisations are differentiated across different organisations even if network relations might reduce institutional autonomy (Oliver, 1991). Despite a tendency to institutionalise, particularly in the NGO sector, isomorphism is restricted by path dependencies and differences in the historically variable contexts in which SCOs operate. In this context, path dependency refers to resistance to change to fit in with institutional requirements. It can include commitment to the founding principles of the organisation, and the degree of entrenchment in pre-existing routines. More commitment and more entrenchment act as barriers to change, as do internal political struggles and leadership determination to deliver or be principled. The resource environment, such as employee turnover and the existing presence of mechanisms to maintain financial stability also constrain isomorphism (Ramanth, 2009), perhaps because they provide organisations with the ability to maintain their niche.

Organisational ecology and related theories do not provide us with a foolproof plan for determining the extent of competition between organisations. This stems from the fact that the focus is not on interactions between organisations, but more on determining the likelihood of organisational survival and adaptations to competition – much like its ancestor discipline of population ecology. One specific weakness is that it does not allow us to predict the type of competition that will occur as a result of niche overlap. What is especially missing is any convincing theoretical explanation for how a niche overlap can just as easily result in either cooperative or non-cooperative symbiosis as it can in competition. Ironically, the conditions that create competition (that is, similar organisational modes, issues, ideologies and repertoires) are suggested by other scholars to be the very same factors that actually create amicable conditions for cooperation.

Hannan and Freeman (1989: 103) admit that competition is hard to observe because it is often indirect. And here is an empirical problem. As a researcher, how do you know if you have identified all of the dimensions of the social environment that impact upon competition rates? Although they admit that the choice of dimensions of niche to analyse is an important question to address, Hannan and Freeman seem unwilling or unable to expand upon how the problem is best solved. We think that in-depth, longitudinal, and inductive research is an important part of the answer to this puzzle. Competition can sometimes result in conflict. If competition is more common across organisations that are similar, we might also anticipate conflict among such actors. Intuitively, though, we would be more likely to expect conflict between SCOs that differ in their ideologies, goals, strategies, and tactics.

Conflict

Indeed, conflict can emerge across organisations relatively similar in their goals even when they are making a serious attempt to collaborate. In this section of the chapter, we will discuss two types of conflict. First, we address conflict among SCOs with similar goals or infighting (Ghaziani and Kretschmer, 2018). We will draw particularly on examples of organisations that pursue women's rights and gender equality. In the second part of this section, we will discuss the conflicts between SCOs that oppose each other.

Conflicts among potential allies

Women's movements are well known for controversy and coalition (Ferree and Hess, 2004). These conflicts include the dominance of White heterosexual middle-class cis-women and associated questions about the inclusion of working-class women, women of colour, and lesbians – to name only a few conflicts. As discussed previously, the concept of intersectionality has been introduced to acknowledge the positionality of multiply marginalised groups and acknowledge the participation of women of colour, in a variety of social movements and SCOs. Conflicts concerning the inclusion of women of colour still persist as the debates around the Women's March on Washington (WMW) shows. The march took place in January 2017, one day after the poorly attended inauguration of Donald Trump as the 45th president of the United States. On that day, about 4 million people participated in Washington DC and other cities in the largest demonstration in the history of the US. Moreover, the march was accompanied by many similar protests around the world (Boon et al, 2017). Although the WMW has been lauded for its efforts to mobilise a wide range of participants, it has also been criticised for failing to be truly inclusive. It began as a Facebook group called for a 'Million Women March' (Boon et al, 2017: 5). But after the call went viral it was criticised for the lack of racial diversity among its organisers as well as the appropriation of the name[2] (Gokariksel and Smith, 2017: 632). Subsequently, the protest event was renamed the Women's March on Washington, invoking the famous civil rights march on Washington in 1963. Conscious and successful efforts were made to include prominent SCMs representing a wide range of communities and emphasising diversity (Boon et al, 2017: 5). The WMW provides a good example of the difficulties of, and the need for, mobilising diverse constituencies and crafting solidarities across difference. Put differently, it is a good example of the need for and the challenges of achieving political intersectionality.

Similarly, there are many accounts of the disappointments and misunderstandings that occurred when East European women and American and West European women first came together after the end of the Cold War (as we addressed in Chapter 2). The literature on East–West debates over the concept of feminism, the resistance to feminism, and the lack of feminist consciousness in the former socialist countries, is extensive (Einhorn, 1993; Havelkova, 1997; Ghodsee, 2004; Einhorn, 2006; Slavova, 2006; Funk, 2007). One reason that feminism was rejected in the former socialist countries was because it was associated with communism (Einhorn, 1993). The socialist legacy generated an (at least initial) aversion among women activists and the public at large to quotas or other positive measures to achieve gender equality (Choluj and Neusüss, 2004). Feminism was also rejected as a Western import that did not take into consideration the different experiences of women in the former socialist countries (Siklova, 1997; Ghodsee, 2004).

Thus, feminism was considered unnecessary (Sloat, 2005) and was not just controversial, but stigmatised (Gal and Kligman, 2000: 98). Slavova (2006) explains Eastern women's resistance to Western feminist ideas and practices with four aspects: the presumed universality of feminist goals and methods; the liberal equal rights agenda emphasising 'sameness' rather than 'difference' of men and women; the fact that the role of patriarchy in communism had not been analysed by Western feminists; and the alleged easy alliance between feminism and Marxism. While Slavova (2006) finds fault with liberal and Marxist feminism, Ghodsee (2004) criticises Western cultural feminism for overlooking the heterogeneity of women's interests and exporting 'feminism-by-design' to the former socialist countries. What unites these assessments is that, although they address different branches of 'Western feminism', they tend to represent Western feminism as monolithic, overlooking tensions and debates between Western feminists.

'Eastern' feminism was grounded in the different experiences of women in socialist and post-socialist societies that, as Slavova (2006) points out, echo the frustration of women from the Global South at the UN world women's conferences as they felt their perspectives were (initially) not addressed. Both, women from the Global South as well as Eastern European women challenged feminist demands that reflected the interests of women in the Global North. However, as we have already noted, Western feminism is not monolithic and needs to consider the interests of poor and working-class women, racialised women, and sexual minorities. Accustomed to a double burden (homemakers and breadwinners), Eastern European women were concerned with issues of social justice and expressed solidarity with men. Given the lack of civil and political rights under socialism, women felt primarily oppressed as citizens, not as women. Because dissident movements emerged around kitchen tables, the private sphere was political, and the political significance of the public–private boundary was not the same as in the West (Miethe, 2000; Watson, 2000; Einhorn and Sever, 2003). Feminisms mirror the experiences in different systems and societies. Such variations need to be acknowledged in efforts to develop transnational feminism. In addition, anti-gender movements emerged in CEE, which seek to defend family values and reject gender ideology, LGBTQIA+ rights and reproductive rights. Such anti-gender movements emerged also in other parts of the world. However, in the CEE countries conservative governments and the Catholic and Orthodox churches criticise 'EU-imperialism' that forced the candidate countries to adopt gender equality and LGBTQIA+ rights (Graff and Korolczuk, 2021).

Women's SCOs continue to discuss and negotiate majority and minority positions, which can result in a re-framing of issues to broaden the agenda (Luna, 2010; Agustin and Roth, 2011; Bygnes, 2012). Furthermore, Staggenborg (1986) examined how conflict arose among anti-abortion organisations who pursued the same issue. This was due to differential participation in and commitment to coalition work, unequal allocation of resources and decisions to continue to work on lobbying that was too expensive for organisations within the coalition to maintain on their own, rather than because their organisations were sharing a niche. A current conflict concerns the 'TERF-Wars' (Pearce et al, 2020). Whether this is a conflict among feminists is itself a contested issue. TERF stands for 'Trans-Exclusionary Radical Feminists' and the conflict concerns the inclusion or exclusion of trans-women as 'women' – in general, but in particular in 'women only' spaces. Issues that are raised include whether trans-women might pose a threat to cis-women and girls, and whether trans-women have benefited from male privilege at some point in their lives. However, trans-women are at a high risk of being victims of violence, especially those from disadvantaged backgrounds.

Conflicts (or infighting) within SCOs and among potential allies are not necessarily destructive; they can also be productive as they clarify the identities, strategies and goals of inevitably heterogeneous constituencies of SCOs (Ghaziani and Kretschmer, 2018), and thus contribute to achieving political intersectionality.

Conflicts between opposed SCOs

Unsurprisingly, conflicts do not just occur among SCOs that – despite differences – share similar goals, overall. Rather, we call attention to the conflictual relationships between opposing SCOs, for example those that promote social justice and those that are reactionary. One prominent fault line is the conflict between, on the one hand, leftist and anti-fascist organisations, and, on the other hand, fascist and right-wing organisations. As we discussed in Chapter 2, such conflicts have existed since the 1930s when fascism emerged in various industrialising societies in Europe and beyond. Although fascism was defeated in World War II, fascist groups continued to be active in the second half of the 20th century (Virchow, 2017); thus, they existed in Europe and the US long before the Great Recession of 2007/2008. Although contemporary far-right groups in the US and Europe differ to some extent (Blee, 2017), it is important to emphasise the similarities between right-wing SCOs in Europe and the US that share anti-feminist, anti-immigrant, homophobic attitudes and seek to 'take back' the country in the name of White citizens (Bhambra, 2017a, 2017b; Bobo, 2017; Narayan, 2017). Such claims are especially problematic when supported by descendants of those who have engaged in settler colonialism (Morgensen, 2011).

Such new right SCOs engage in 'othering'; this means that they emphasise traditional gender roles and gender binaries. This is expressed in anti-gender sentiments that need to be distinguished from the 'TERF-wars' mentioned earlier. Furthermore, they tend to exclude ethnic minorities, immigrants, and minority religious groups. However, various right-wing groups including the Front National or the English Defence League have recruited migrants and ethnic minorities (Scrinzi, 2015; Pilkington, 2016). Ferree (2020) argues that gender serves as 'glue' for these efforts to defend masculinities, which feel threatened by the gains of women, sexual and ethnic minorities. Similarly, Kováts (2018) argues that right-wing SCOs represent a 'culturalist response to structural crises'. They react against the 'neoliberal consensus' (Mouffe, 2014) by attacking human rights, gender and LGBTQIA+ equality legislation and discourse. The Catholic Church plays a crucial role for the emergence of anti-gender movements (Kuhar and Paternotte, 2017, see, also, Chapter 2).

While right-wing populist SCOs respond to the outcomes (see Chapter 7) of progressive social justice movements, they are countered by progressive movements representing broad coalitions of anti-fascist, pro-feminist, and pro-LGBTQIA+ SCOs in both the US and Europe. In the US, a variety of protest groups formed immediately after Trump won the presidency, including the WMW that we discussed previously. This protest – the largest in the history of the US – was accompanied by many similar protests around the world (Boon et al, 2017). In addition, SCOs organised many other events to protest against the Trump administration including BLM, Earth Day, the March for Science, and airport immigration rallies. These initiatives made significant use of social media to facilitate both online and offline organising for change (Boon et al, 2017). In addition, Indivisible, an SCOs against right-wing populism, directly borrowed tactics of the Tea Party to mobilise grassroots support (Deckman, 2017; B. Roth, 2018). The Indivisible Guide, written by three former Democratic congressional staffers provided practical support to set up local groups to became active in their area, for example in town hall meetings, and put pressure on state Senators and US House members. In March 2017, about 6,000 verified groups were active across the US (Boone et al, 2017: 9). The 'Resistance', bringing together a broad range of left-leaning, progressive groups united in an Anti-Trump Surge (Meyer and Tarrow, 2018; Fisher, 2019) represents a good example of a counter-movement against US right-wing populism. Counter-movements can be considered an outcome of SCOs that are shaping and are shaped by historically variable contexts and are thus contributing to social change.

Conclusions

SCOs are part of the historically variable context that shapes them and that they are trying to shape by employing various strategies. In order to understand social change making efforts, it is therefore important to understand how SCOs relate to and interact with each other. In this chapter, we have reviewed the ways in which SCOs collaborate, compete or conflict (or do none of these things). In particular, we have used the lens of political intersectionality to illustrate how SCOs can work with, and through, difference to form enduring alliances. The need to achieve political intersectionality has been learned the hard way by many SCOs and SCMs. Markers of difference have led SCMs from minority or less privileged backgrounds to feel marginalised and this has caused conflicts (Emejulu and Bassel, 2023). Such conflicts have important ramifications for organising for change. On the one hand, there emerge conscious efforts to avoid marginalisation; and on the other hand, new SCOs emerge to fill gaps left by their forebears. Competitive environments for SCOs have similar ramifications. Where resources (for example, new members or money) are scarce, organisational ecology predicts competition will ensue. A result is that organisations may find their demise, or will instead need to adapt, finding themselves a niche and a differentiated selling point. Our interactionist approach to the study of SCOs recognises the importance of failures as well as successes. Both shape social change making processes. Only by learning about the difficulties of bringing different constituencies together, or through learning about the implications of competitive social environments, can SCOs begin to work out strategies for redressing the problems.

The examination of these relationships builds on earlier chapters, in which we examined different strategies of pursuing social change, which shape resource needs and opportunities to participate. We note that that the relationship between outsider and insider activism is of political interest with respect to the ability to create alliances and mobilise resources (Glasius and Ishkanian, 2014). Different strategies enable a division of labour that facilitates cooperation and allows competition and conflict between different SCOs to be overcome. The collaboration between actors with preferences for different tactics and strategies relies on brokers who have gained experience and are respected in different political contexts. They can mediate between various spheres of activism; insider SCOs and SCMs can provide access, legitimacy, and financial resources whereas their outsider counterparts are less constrained to be accountable and therefore can be more critical and engage in disruptive protest events. For insider SCOs, coalition forming may be constrained by upward accountability.

In order to examine collaborative, competitive, and conflictual relationships among SCOs we have drawn together as yet separate literatures. From the literature on advocacy and protest focused SCOs, we developed a richer understanding of the notion of coalition building, by merging this with social movement scholars' recent focus on intersectionality. To understand competition, we used the notion of 'organisational ecology' from organisational studies that has been disproportionately applied to voluntary organisations. The merging of these literatures allows us to make one thing especially clear; that is the important point that SCOs never act in isolation (even if they choose to ignore each other). Moreover, conflicts between SCOs can lead to new coalitions, whereas SCOs with similar goals might collaborate as well as compete. Moreover, SCOs also complement each other – more moderate organisations benefit from the 'radical flank' effect, whereas SCOs that engage in 'outsider activism' gain from allies who are active inside organisations. This means that SCOs that perform different strategies are not necessarily antagonistic but engage in overt or covert divisions of labour. In the next chapter, we turn to the outcomes of SCOs.

7

Outcomes of Social Change Making

In 2016, the British green transport activist John Stewart won the Sheila McKechnie Foundation Long-Term Achievement Award for excellence in environmental campaigning. Prior to this, in 2011, he came top of the list of the UK's most effective environmentalists as judged by *The Independent* newspaper. When we interviewed Stewart in 2001 and again in 2004 he already had an impressive track record of what we might call 'success' within a range of environmental SCOs.

Stewart began his environmental SCM career working with a local transport group in Lambeth, London, which sought to make public transport fares fairer. This group became institutionalised and obtained council funding to deliver services to make public transport policy greener. This led to Stewart's involvement in campaigns against road building in the 1980s. By the late 1980s this work had expanded to coordinating a London-wide network called All London Against the Road Menace (ALARM), which had around 250 local groups. To stop NIMBYism (that is, not-in-my-backyard tendencies), all grassroots groups signing up to this network were asked to pledge to agree to the principle of 'no more new roads in London', which prevented groups from pitting themselves against each other, thus preventing conflict and competition among groups pursuing the same goals. In 1990, UK transport minister Cecil Parkinson dropped all of the road schemes planned for London. Stewart told us that – if the anti-roads campaigns of the late 1980s had not been successful – Clapham Common (a significant green space in London) would now be a spaghetti junction of roads full of traffic. After this success, the network turned to help other national anti-road groups struggling to fight what had been dubbed the UK government's largest road building scheme since the Romans (Saunders, 2013). It morphed into ALARM-UK, with around 300 groups across the country. The network engaged in non-violent direct action and again deemed itself successful. Stewart told us:

'ALARM-UK felt like they had done their job. In 1989, the whole of the British Transport policy was "for" roads. By 1997, 10 years later, road building was still there … but on a much smaller scale, and public transport schemes were being proposed … which would have been inconceivable 10–15 years ago.' (Stewart in interview, May 2001)

Subsequently, Stewart shifted to anti-aviation campaigning, initially with an organisation called Heathrow and Community Action Network (HACAN) Clearskies. The group has been active in campaigning for clear skies, to cease night flights that disrupt local residents' sleep patterns and to halt new runway development. Stewart was also founder member and chair of Airport Watch, which has used the same non-NIMBY approach against airport expansion as did ALARM-UK, although it has been less obviously successfully. Stewart's work on aviation has, however, had significant impacts on public discourse. In 2007, the British Airports Authority (BAA) attempted to put an injunction on all SCMs associated with Airport Watch to prevent a Camp for Climate Action in the vicinity of Heathrow Airport. As this was an umbrella group, it would have affected thousands of campaigners. In court, the injunction was revealed untenable and was restricted to just a handful of prominent campaigners, including Stewart. BAA effectively scored an own-goal, raising awareness of the Camp for Climate Action and helping it to successfully mobilise thousands of SCMs.

We have opened this chapter with this vignette of John Stewart's involvement in a range of SCOs because his work neatly illustrates the ways in which the outcomes of SCOs are diverse. SCOs influence and are influenced by the lives of individuals engaged in them, who consequently come to reflect on and participate in different forms of organising for change. SCOs also influence the ways in which other SCOs develop, as well as contribute to broader social change processes. SCMs like Stewart broker between different SCOs and thus contribute to the interaction between organisations with different aims and strategies. In Stewart's case, successful outcomes on roads campaigning led, in the first instance to expanding a regional network to a national one, and, in a second case to switching to a different issue. There are apparent (although difficult to prove) policy successes, as well as significant mobilisation gains. Stewart's work has also had profound effects on his own life.

In this chapter, after explaining why we talk about 'outcomes' rather than 'success', we examine three broad categories of SCO 'outcomes' (Staggenborg, 1995): first we discuss institutional and political outcomes, including mobilisation outcomes; next we turn to socio-cultural outcomes; and finally, we address individual outcomes (those outcomes that affect the biographies of individual SCMs as well as beneficiaries through the provision of goods and services). We endeavour to show – as in the case of the work of John Stewart – how the different outcomes are intertwined, but also how they reflect the goals and strategies of particular SCOs, and the context in which they are operating. Thus, we are fully aware that it is problematic to attribute an outcome to an individual SCO. Instead – as this book argues – we argue that it is important to see the impact that SCOs and SCMs have in a broader context that includes the interaction between SCOs that we have examined in the previous chapter. Indeed, relational realism, the ontology that shaped the last chapter, posits that actions, interactions, and reactions are what shapes social change outcomes. Furthermore, we argue that SCOs oftentimes achieve more than one outcome and show how different types of outcomes are related to one another in further sets of actions, interactions, and reactions.

The variety of SCO outcomes we examine showcase the diversity of the intended and unintended outcomes of SCOs and the interplay among them. We illustrate the interplay among different SCO outcomes in Figure 7.1 The different outcomes of SCOs are shaped by a variety of SCOs working with a range of tactics. The outcomes, in turn, reflect back on the tactics available to and preferred by SCOs. Of course, this is also mediated by the historically variable context that impacts SCOs, and that SCOs impact. We argue that the conditions for achieving outcomes depend on the chain of outcomes across the different categories and their repercussions as much as it does on the external environment in which SCOs reside.

Outcomes rather than success

It is important to us to use the term 'outcomes' rather than 'success', not only because it is difficult to operationalise the term 'success' but also because the concept of 'outcomes' is more inclusive. Success at what? At forming (and sustaining) an organisation? At generating public support? At raising awareness? At achieving a goal? If so, a goal of which magnitude? In contrast to the more inclusive term outcomes, the much narrower term 'success' usually assumes a straightforward, linear, relationship between SCO goals, SCO tactics, and goal attainment.

The problems associated with assuming a linear relationship between intended goals and success (or failure) are threefold. First, SCOs often have unintended outcomes that are not strictly related to their goals – some positive and some negative (Meyer, 2021). Second, any supposed linear relationship does injustice to SCOs with programmatic goals that are harder to obtain. SCOs with programmatic goals have a wide range of outcomes, even if they are not able to achieve social change to the degree they would wish. Scholars of feminist SCOs were among the first to point out that horizontal, participatory radical feminist organisations' apparent lack of

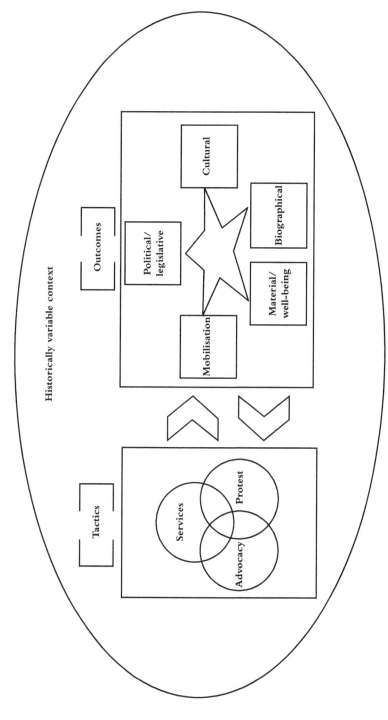

Figure 7.1: The outcomes of SCOs' tactics

success at achieving their objectives could not be fairly compared to the apparent successes of SCOs seeking small policy changes (see Staggenborg, 1995: 345). For example, radical feminists' demands to restructure society and abolish patriarchy make success on programmatic terms less achievable than, say, getting a policy through parliament that seeks to encourage gender parity among political representatives. But this does not make the former de facto unsuccessful because of the wide range of other possible outcomes, whether this is service provision for people in need or long-lasting impact on the SCMs involved in radical politics.

Third, it is difficult to ascertain whether the obtainment of goals is a direct result of SCO action, or if there are other exogenous factors at work (Giugni, 1999). For example, ALARM-UK, which we mentioned in the opening vignette of this chapter, may have exaggerated its role in generating its alleged successes because it may not have accounted for a wide range of other factors that helped determine the scaling down of the UK's road building scheme, including treasury cuts and EU rulings about the necessity for Environmental Impact Assessments (Robinson, 2000). For similar reasons, Bosi et al (2016) use the term 'consequences' rather than outcomes. Even when we use the notion of 'outcomes' rather than 'success', it remains challenging to work out what is and is not an SCO outcome. Just in the study of SCOs that focus on protest alone, 'the field lacks a consensual definition of, or classification of ... outcomes' (Earl 2004: 509). We unpick these issues further in our discussion of different types of SCO outcomes.

One of the first studies on the 'success' of protest-focused SCOs was Gamson's (1975, revised and updated in 1990) *The Strategy of Social Protest*. He later altered his state-centric view of the success of SCOs by adding cultural outcomes, but was initially pre-occupied with 'new advantages', which means winning some specific policy gains, and 'acceptance'. Acceptance – in a US-specific context – refers to being accepted as a legitimate political actor with the standing to testify before Congress. Gamson's (1975) work has been criticised for being too narrowly focused; acceptance, for instance, can achieve little if the concerns of the SCO are marginalised. Moreover, acceptance could be conceived of as a form of failure for three reasons: it might lead to co-option (Piven and Cloward, 1977) resulting in 'vanilla victories' (Stroup and Wong, 2017); 'new advantages' might lead to undesirable outcomes; and other unintended but positive outcomes might occur that were not among the SCO's original aims (Amenta and Caren, 2004: 464). Moreover, there are deeper levels of acceptance than testifying to Congress, such as sitting on agenda setting round tables, providing committee evidence, and contributing to Senate hearings and meetings. We now turn to discuss policy, legislative and institutional outcomes in more depth.

Policy, legislative and institutional outcomes

Policy and legislative changes are among the most obvious and most discussed outcomes of SCOs because even cultural goals often require some sort of state action (Amenta and Caren, 2004: 461). Furthermore, SCOs that focus on the provision of goods and services – which we will discuss later – are at the mercy of the policy context within which they find themselves and to which they must either adhere, or challenge; and which they may indirectly impact even if only through their existence.

Many SCOs aim directly to challenge policy decisions and to change legislation. Political and legislative changes range from seeking to change a regime type itself, to influencing the minutiae of a policy proposal; or from implementing a policy to helping with the delivery of a small part of a broader policy package. All of these forms of change interact sometimes iteratively and sometimes in positive feedback cycles, challenging the ways in which SCOs work. As we alluded to in Chapter 2, SCOs significantly contribute to democratisation processes (for example, the Solidarity movement Solidarność in Poland), including extending suffrage (for example, to women and ethnic minorities). The work of SCOs has also contributed to decriminalisation of homosexuality and legalisation of gay marriage. Sometimes, SCOs directly seek to modify policy; at other times they do so indirectly through influencing public awareness and media coverage. Sometimes, still, they do so even more indirectly by providing services that inadvertently raise awareness of policy failure (for example, food banks and soup kitchens).

We illustrate the difficulties of focusing just on policy outcomes with the example of a well-known environmental SCO, Friends of the Earth (see Saunders, 2013). Friends of the Earth has been hailed a policy entrepreneur for the 'critical role' that it played in persuading the UK government to adopt the 2008 Climate Change Act (2008) (Carter and Childs, 2018). Between 2005 and 2008 it organised an impressive multi-level campaign known as 'The Big Ask'. It mobilised its local group members to write and collect letters and/or sign postcards to their Members of Parliament, secured celebrity endorsement, undertook online (video) campaigning, worked on festival outreach, and joined a significant coalition that staged large-scale street demonstrations in central London. Towards the end of this campaign effort, the UK government agreed to sign up to a 50 per cent reduction of greenhouse gas emissions by 2050 compared to a 1990 baseline; with interim targets along the way, and this was legislated in the Climate Change Act (2008). Since 2019, there has been a Target Amendment Act to aspire to achieve a 100 per cent reduction of emissions by 2050. We might consider this case to be a SCO 'success story'; however, the obvious changes we can observe are just the tip of the iceberg of the multiple, rich and sometimes even unintended outcomes that SCOs can have. Let us unpack this some more.

The fact that The Big Ask campaign in the UK happened in the run up to an observable policy change is sometimes taken as evidence that the 2008 Climate Change Act was an outcome of Friends of the Earth's campaigning (Lorenzoni and Benson, 2014; Carter and Childs, 2018; Friends of the Earth, nd). However, there is a 'black box' problem (Giugni, 1999; Earl, 2000) in knowing exactly what was the cause of the government's decision to implement the Climate Change Act (2008). Was the cause, or set of causes, directly due to the work of the SCO (in Giugni's 1999 terms, was it 'internal' to it?). Or was it because the SCO found itself within a favourable political environment (that was 'external' to it)? Or was it due to other factors still? And what caused the 2019 target revision? Probably not the earlier campaign. External and alternative explanations seem just as plausible for the Friends of the Earth case as the internal one. There were multiple coterminous actions that took place, which helped to encourage the government to introduce the Climate Act into the Queen's Speech. Around the same time as the Big Ask campaign was active, for example, the *Stern Review* was released. This report argued that the cost of mitigating climate change then (in 2006) would be cheaper than waiting for its worsening effects to hit us and deal with the problem later. Also, it was around the same time that the UK Conservative government under David Cameron rebranded itself as an environmentally friendly party with promises of the 'Greenest Government Ever' and there was a peak in the coverage of climate change in national newspapers (Saunders et al, 2018). These are just a few factors that influenced the government among multiple ones. Indeed, literature about policy outcomes of SCOs often overlooks the importance of other actors and events that lead to policy change such as the media, public opinion, the electoral cycle, and party systems (Amenta, 2003; Green and Jennings, 2017). This makes our approach, focused on varieties of SCO that engage in different strategies, and have more or less far-reaching goals, so important.

This brief story about Friends of the Earth's Big Ask Campaign is a facile account of the outcomes of SCOs not only because of the difficulty to know what caused the outcome, but also because of its focus almost exclusively on policy success (Nulman, 2016). Such a narrow view of SCO outcomes is restrictive. Just as there are many different SCOs with complementary or conflicting aims and strategies, there are also many outcomes of SCOs. Even those that focus on policy change have other important outcomes that must not be overlooked. Bringing this back to our Friends of the Earth case, we can appreciate how focusing on policy achievement sidelines the effects that the campaign might have had on those involved in it (individual outcomes), on the wider SCO sector (mobilisation outcomes), and upon broader public attitudes (institutional and cultural outcomes). We might relate this to the range of outcomes of environmental movements Rucht (1999) identified. Although environmental movements' ultimate goal of halting environmental degradation has clearly not been achieved, many other intended and unintended outcomes have been. Environmental movements have shaped attitudes and behaviours, altered public opinion, sparked the development of a new sustainability oriented industrial sector, grown the numbers of activists and organisations, become professional, generated international interest, set agendas, and supported Green parties (which, in turn, has furthered the environmental agenda) (Rucht, 1999). Further sets of actions and reactions have ensued. Some SCOs have reacted to the apparent co-optation of green political parties (for example, German Green Party members who are SCMs); and ecological products are bemoaned by some as status symbols rather than meaningful political participation that can prevent the dual environmental and climate crises (for example, *Ethical Consumer*).

Similarly, Bernstein's (2003) research on the 'success' of lesbian and gay SCOs challenges the notion that success straightforwardly equates with policy outcomes. Between 1961 and 1977, 18 US states reversed sodomy laws; but between 1986 and 1991 none did (Bernstein, 2003). At face value, the earlier period might appear to have more concrete outcomes than the later one. However, the legislated changes in the earlier period did not prevent gay men from being arrested for disorderly conduct or vagrancy when looking for partners. Moving away from the 'only-behind-closed-doors' mentality, which finds gay relationships acceptable only if they are kept in the closet, required broader cultural shifts that were obtained in the latter period as gay sex gradually became more socially acceptable (Bernstein 2003). Importantly, the decriminalisation of homosexuality lowered the risk of getting involved in SCOs promoting the rights of sexual minorities.

Other times, still, the relationship between SCOs and policy making is even more intertwined. This is particularly the case for SCOs that engage in service provision, that have been considered to be an important part of civil society in the UK since Tony Blair's premiership in the 1990s. Service providing SCOs were given policy initiatives as part of his government's strategic plan to position New Labour as supporting neither the market (the remit of Conservatives) or the state (the remit of 'old' Labour) (Kendall, 2000). Voluntary organisations have also been invited into state partnerships under the Big Society agenda (in the mid-2000s by the Conservative–Liberal coalition following a Labour government). Thus, significant policy changes have been implemented to facilitate the important work of third sector SCOs in politics and in society. But can this be said to be an outcome of this type of SCO? Policy changes facilitating SCOs as partners in policy and governance are the result of synergistic interactions between the state and SCOs. They are, in part, an outcome of the valuable work undertaken by SCOs in the voluntary sector (as John Stewart's Lambeth-based transport group that we mentioned in the opening vignette illustrates) while also being an outcome of deliberate neo-liberal attempts to shrink the role of the state. This also applies to international NGOs, which have grown tremendously while the budgets of bilateral aid organisations have decreased (Watkins et al, 2012).

Another important lesson that we can learn from the literature on the policy outcomes of SCOs is that they are closely interrelated with other types of outcomes, such as political culture, public attitudes, and media coverage. Sometimes SCOs contribute to policy *as well as* having partial responsibility for altering political culture more broadly. European anti-nuclear SCOs, for example, have been credited with helping to shift away from an international aggressive security policy (Meyer, 1999). For Meyer (1999: 202) 'failure to bring about central demands does not demonstrate lack of effect; rather, it suggests a more complicated process of exercising influence: one involving short-term marginal impact and long-term changes in political culture'.

Political culture is also closely related to public attitudes. According to Burnstein (1999), interest organisations (a term he uses as an amalgam of SMOs and interest groups, because, like us, he finds distinctions between them to be unhelpful) tend to have little effect on policy when it is clear what the majority of citizens think about a public issue. Instead, he suggests that their policy influence is indirectly achieved through the vehicle of shaping public attitudes. The effects of SCOs on public policy, broader cultural shifts and individual participants are interdependent (Meyer and Whitter, 1994). Our reference to a study in 1994 indicates that this is not an entirely novel argument, but what is novel in our account is the ways in which varieties of SCO, including those in advocacy, protest, *and* service provision generate, together, dynamic circumstances that create interdependent shifts for individuals, society, culture, and policy together. Institutional outcomes are an important dimension of political change.

Institutional outcomes

We distinguish two types of institutional outcomes. One concerns the effects of SCOs on governmental institutions; the other one concerns the effects of SCOs on institutions outside of the polity. Note, however, that this is not a simple dichotomy and that we consider institutions to also be part of socio-cultural currents (mentioned previously). Effects on governmental institutions have knock-on effects on other institutions and vice versa.

Women's SCOs provide a good vehicle through which to think about changes to governmental institutions. As we discussed in Chapter 3, women who were excluded from political rights appropriated the organisational form of the 'club' and invented lobbying to influence political change (Clemens, 1993). Similarly, Skocpol (1992) examined the role of disenfranchised women in contributing to the emergence of the welfare state in the US. As we have illustrated through our own research, women did not automatically gain equal political representation after they secured the vote (Roth and Saunders, 2019; 2020). The number of women who stand for election and the numbers of female legislators might be interdependent outcomes of feminist organising for change (Gelb and Hart, 1999), while at the same time the presence of female role models in mainstream politics impacts the shape and form of feminists' social change making activities (Roth and Saunders, 2019). Over time, expectations regarding gender equal representation changed, as Paxton et al (2006) demonstrate in a historical and comparative perspective. Between 1893 and 1945 women fought for the right to vote. After 1945 women's right to vote was widely taken for granted and newly sovereign states tended to incorporate that right at a basic level. Around 1970 – during the second wave of the feminist movement – the pressure to incorporate women increased and gender quotas or benchmarks were introduced. In addition, governments started to establish equality offices and at the UN World Women's Conference in Beijing in 1995, gender mainstreaming was adopted. The number of women in office has a broader set of repercussions for SCOs. Our own comparison of women's political participation in Sweden and the UK suggests that stronger representation of women in parliament is a factor that might encourage Swedish women to take to the streets in protest more so than their British counterparts (Roth and Saunders, 2019), illustrating the complex relationship between individual and institutional outcomes. As Katzenstein (1990: 28) states 'gender consciousness emerges from, is negotiated in, is recreated out of, and in turn acts upon political institutions'.

Partly in response to women's SCOs, higher proportions of women have entered the workplace since the 1970s. Since the 1980s, they have come to recognise themselves as more equal partners than they had been previously. How this manifests within institutions appears to be highly context dependent. Katzenstein (1990) studied the unobtrusive mobilisation of women in the US military and the Catholic Church, seeking to change organisations from within (see also Valiente, 2017 for feminist mobilisation in the Catholic Church in Spain). Organisations with recruitment problems might actually benefit from the efforts to be inclusionary, that is admitting previously marginalised or excluded groups such as women, racial and sexual minorities. This applies to the Catholic Church whose image has suffered from various abuse scandals as well as national militaries. For example, in 2018, the UK military opened up all ranks to women and increased its efforts to recruit women and ethnic minorities. The inclusion of women, the opening up of state militaries to gays and lesbians, and their involvement in peacekeeping have resulted in a re-gendering of militaries (Duncanson, 2015; Duncanson and Woodward, 2016). In the year 2000, the UN adopted Security Resolution 1325 to acknowledge the disproportionate impact of wars and conflicts on women and girls, and to ensure the inclusion of women among peacekeeping missions (Shepherd, 2011). The involvement of women in political institutions and the subsequent transformation of these institutions has been described as 'state feminism' (Stetson and Mazur, 1995; Eisenstein, 1996; Kantola, 2010). More recently a shift from 'state feminism' to 'market feminism', which reflects neo-liberalism, has been noted (Kantola and Squires, 2012). Institutional outcomes affect mobilisation outcomes, which we now discuss.

Mobilisation outcomes

According to Staggenborg (1995: 341), 'the category of mobilization outcomes focuses on organizational successes and the ability to carry out collective action'. These days, many SCOs have details of their successes on their webpages, used as a tool to mobilise financial supporters, donations, and volunteers, further illustrating interdependencies between different types of SCO outcomes. As we learned from Chapter 4, resources are crucial for an SCO to function. One successful outcome of an SCO, therefore, is its ability to sustain itself, also known as organisational survival (Gross and Etzoni, 1985) or organisational maintenance (Diani and Donati, 1999). This incorporates not only effective financial management, but also good communication with potential service users or donors and reputation management. As noted earlier, sexual abuse tainted the image of the Catholic Church, but it has also damaged the reputation of humanitarian SCOs (Dean, 2020; Dickson, 2023). SCOs must effectively balance resource inputs, including volunteer time, expenditures, and the cost for users and beneficiaries (Kendall and Knapp, 2000). A positive mobilisation outcome is the ability to mobilise an appropriate number of SCMs.

Positive mobilisation outcomes matter not only at the organisational level, but also for broader SCO sectors. The ideas and actions of SCOs can diffuse to other organisations, sectors, and countries, sustaining broader social change action, and also social change itself. To give some examples: the movement tactic of reclaiming the streets – re-appropriating roads for parties – to resist car culture and capitalism spread from the UK to most of the Western world at the height of the global justice movement (della Porta, 2007). Similarly, the tactic of occupying squares to find democratic solutions to the 2008 financial crisis spread from Wall Street to almost all the corners of the globe (*Social Movement Studies* 2012, Special issue (11/3–4) on Occupy!; Eschle and Bartlett, 2023). Even if there is not diffusion of tactics across countries, SCOs can sometimes have an impact on the policies of other countries as is common in transnational advocacy networks (Keck and Sikkink, 1998). A movement might gain a policy advantage in its own country, which can have a knock-on effect in terms of shaping international norms and persuading other countries to follow suit. In West Germany, for example, demands of anti-nuclear SCOs were relatively quickly integrated into policy. The West German government was then able to press the US and the North Atlantic Treaty Organization (NATO) for a stronger arms control policy (Meyer, 1999).

It is also important to mention that successes of SCOs can be demobilising for other SCOs (as we discussed in Chapter 6). Winning a competitive contract might be a successful outcome for the contract winner, but it might displace smaller local SCOs familiar with localised expertise that might be better suited to the work but are unable to compete (Milbourne, 2013). Moreover, the actions of an SCO might backfire – innocent bystanders could get caught up in active movement repression and/or their actions might result in restrictions on the material rights of others (Amenta and Young, 1999).

SCOs work together to iteratively create broad outcomes. For example, della Porta (1999) discusses the left libertarian movements of the 1960s–80s, noting how their shifting identity frames moved from being highly politicised (liberals opposed to conservatism), to Manichaean (good opposed to evil) to pragmatic. This coincided with public framings of the movements as initially negative – viewing them as a menace or terrorists, then as the socially marginal and finally as acceptable and normalised forms of political engagement. SCOs can also be important for triggering new waves of protest, or other related SCOs. The SCOs active in the West in the 1960s, for example, reinvigorated older organisations working on issues such as women's rights and the environment. Women SCOs developed links between patriarchy and other issues, as well as spawned other related movements related to the issues associated with LGBTQIA+ and child sex abuse (Whittier, 2004). SCOs can influence future generations of SCOs through 'organizational seeding' (Raeburn, 2004) via SCMs entering new caucuses, through organisational networks, by adjusting the balance of collaboration, competition and conflict as discussed in the previous chapter and through their role in shaping changes in an overall SCO sector (Whittier, 2004).

In the US, the struggle for the Equal Rights Amendment (ERA) (in the 1970s and 1980s) was facilitated by the sustained mobilisation of the National Women's Party (1945–60) (Taylor, 1989; Taylor and Rupp, 1990). The campaign for the ERA ultimately failed due to the counter-mobilisation (Mansbridge, 1986). Nevertheless, the increased number of women elected to public office in the 1970s was an indirect mobilisation outcome of women organising for the ERA and broader change. It was only after a few 'self-starters' had been elected to public office, that women's SCOs devoted direct resources to helping others; but without the cause of women's rights perhaps the self-starters would not have even got as far as they did (Staggenborg, 1989). Not only moderate groups, also radical women's SCOs like the Chicago Women's Liberation Union (CWLU[1]) struggled to survive – being mired with difficulties related to resources, mobilising new activists and internal conflicts. Nevertheless, the CWLU was part of a broader social SCO community and was later able to successfully mobilise many women to join anti-abortion actions (Staggenborg, 1995).

Mobilisation outcomes, then, refer to outcomes that have repercussions for the sustainment of organisational activity or of a broader SCO sector. In a hostile political environment, abeyance structures might sustain an SCO, but an SCO may also stay active through shifting its focus onto broader cultural outcomes, individual identity change, or through seeking to target non-state actors. In the previous chapters, we have highlighted that individuals participating in SCOs tend to participate in multiple SCOs simultaneously and successively, or dip in and out of participating in different SCOs, and thus contribute to coalition building and the diffusion of strategies. Our emphasis on the meso- (or organisational) level is not intended to belittle the role of individual activists in shaping mobilisation outcomes. We return to discuss individual outcomes after first considering socio-cultural outcomes.

Socio-cultural outcomes

We build on Eyerman and Barretta's (1996) 'production of culture' approach to understand the cultural effects of SCOs, showcasing the ways in which SCOs are co-producers of social change. They form in a particular socio-cultural context and also help to generate new socio-cultural contexts. Eyerman and Barretta (1996) recognise that a folk song is not a stand-alone cultural artefact, but is 'explained in relation to a social organization of production, distribution, and recognition' (Eyerman and Barretta, 1996: 504). Thus, our account of the cultural outcomes of SCOs is focused both on changing attitudes about rights and wrongs in society in general (gender, sexuality, climate change and so on), as well as the take up, spread, and usage of cultural artefacts. This combination of changes to attitudes, beliefs, actions, identities, and material culture is collectively known as 'cultural collective benefits' (Amenta and Young, 1999). We first look at changes in broader public attitudes.

Common sense understanding has changed significantly regarding issues such as slavery (d'Anjou, 1996), gender (Whittier, 2004; Pearce et al, 2020; Mackay, 2021), and sexuality (Bernstein, 2003; Ayoub, 2016) at least partly due to the efforts of SCOs. Thus, in the case of cultural outcomes, success has been achieved when the mainstream media adopt new ways of thinking about issues that have been promulgated by SCOs and these come to filtrate common understandings of, and moral positions in relation to, an issue – often causing a backlash and thus being the impetus for the formation of further SCOs. Gamson (1990) calls this type of outcome a 'cultural advantage'. Let us now examine some cultural advantages.

Gender attitudes in society changed markedly *after* (but not straightforwardly simply because of) women's SCOs, particularly in relation to access to abortion, economic equality, and domestic violence (Gelb and Hart, 1999), even if there is still some way to go. In the early 1990s, many women reported supporting the women's movement and claimed that their lives had been improved by it. On International Women's Day in 2023, a YouGov poll showed that although only 33 per cent of the population of the UK would call themselves feminists, 85 per cent thought that women and men should 'have equal rights and status in society, and be treated equally in every way' (YouGov, 2023).

An examination of award-winning children's stories in the 1970s found that female characters were hardly developed at all, which indicated a cultural belief that girls have less value than boys (Weitzman et al, 1972). In a more up-to-date study into the 2000s, Clarke, et al (2003: 446) conclude that since the 1960s, 'increasing visibility of female characters ... may reflect decreases in the degree of conflict over such roles since then'. But bias against female characters has not declined straightforwardly over time. Overall, recent studies found that female characters are still underrepresented, and gender stereotypes prevail (Hamilton et al, 2006; Lindsay, 2023). Portrayals of African Americans in children's stories follow similar patterns: Black children have appeared less frequently in children's books when civil rights activism was most active (Pescosolida et al, 1997). Racial and ethnic minorities still tend to be underrepresented and stereotyped in the media (Tuchachinsky, 2015). However, Stamps (2020) notes a shift from unfavourable to positive Black male characters in scripted television programmes. Furthermore, Billard and Gross (2020) found that LGBTQ media representation has improved over time, although they note that more work needs to be done to represent transgender issues. Their historical overview highlights the importance of media for the LGBTQIA+ community which preceded changes in mainstream media.

Stories that normalise LGBTQIA+ people, women and people of colour could, in one sense, be seen as important cultural outcomes of movements. This signals some improvements in society for those marginalised by their sexuality, gender, ethnicity, or skin colour. The need for SCOs to take racism seriously was one outcome of the recent BLM movement, which also encouraged SCOs working on other issues to find adaptive ways to mount public protests during COVID-19 lockdowns. Awareness of White privilege and the need to redress forms of entrenched racism are two outcomes of the ongoing struggle to ensure that Black lives really do matter. As mentioned in the introduction to our book, after the brutal death of George Floyd on 25 May 2020 in Minneapolis, Minnesota, the BLM protest went global (Shahin et al, 2021). In the UK, in addition to police brutality (Joseph-Salisbury et al, 2021), the disproportionate death rates of BAME people who are overrepresented among hospital staff, public transport, and other high risk (and often low paid) occupations have been noted (Otu et al, 2020). The cultural shame felt over the UK's colonial past is illustrated in resistance to the scandalous treatment of the Windrush generation (Goodfellow, 2019) and the victims of the Grenfell Fire tragedy (a block of flats home to predominantly BAME people and known to be a fire hazard, which burned to the ground), as well as statue toppling mobilisations (Moody, 2021) and calls for museum repatriation (Lonetree, 2021). Subsequently, many other institutions, including universities and corporations, documented solidarity with BLM (regardless of the underrepresentation of BAME in these organisations, especially in leadership positions).

As we have discussed in the previous chapter, SCOs directly and indirectly make a difference to each other as well as many other institutions. For example, there are calls to change the culture of humanitarian SCOs, which have been criticised for being too top-down, too imperialist, and too out-of-touch (Khan et al, 2023). SCOs also influence institutions such as medicine, art, science, law, and education. Good examples are the establishing of institutes and degrees on gender and Queer studies, environmental studies (which might or might not address environmental justice), Black studies, post-colonial studies, disability studies, and many other programmes that put social change on the agenda. Moreover, many universities pride themselves in their strategies that focus on 'changing the world for the better' through their research and teaching. SCOs and SCMs might choose to intervene to change the institutional regimes guiding work in these fields. In so doing, they might challenge any one or all three of: the rules and assumptions, the personnel and activities, and the subjects addressed by institutions. In the late 1960s and early 1970s, for example, activists in the US sought to challenge the scientific institutions providing laboratory research that supported the military–science complex (Moore, 1999). Their efforts coalesced with broader cultural and institutional shifts that resulted in new ways of doing science. Within ten years all of the major and most of the minor scientific institutions in the US changed from being exclusive professional associations to public interest institutions that took citizens' concerns seriously and directly communicated its results with the public. More recently, the Tate (an important art museum with sites in Cornwall, Liverpool, and London) has been challenged with creative acts of protest by activists requesting that the gallery moves 'Beyond BP', in a series of protests against the oil giant BP's sponsorship (Memou, 2017). BP is considered to be a climate villain for its role in contributing to greenhouse gas emissions. Following the protests, BP ended its 26-year sponsorship.[2]

Cultural outcomes are closely linked with individual outcomes: changing someone's biography through participation in SCOs might lead them to develop new values and ideals. There is a conceptual space for outcomes that fit between biographical outcomes (for individuals) and cultural change (for broader swathes of the public); and that is in relation to cultural outcomes for a community of activists. Saunders (2008b; 2013), for example, describes how radical environmentalists came to adopt similar cultural traits such as veganism, a casual clothing style, dreadlocks and shunning car use. Similarly, Salt and Layzell (1985) document how the wives of UK striking miners adopted a more unisex clothing style. Cultural changes are also reflected in the lives of individuals, as we now examine.

Individual-level outcomes of SCOs

Individual outcomes refer to the effect that SCOs have on individual people. We note two complementing types of individual outcomes: the effects of participation on individual SCMs, which we refer to as *internal*; and the effects on individuals who receive goods or services provided by SCOs, which we regard as *external*. We suggest that the internal and external are complementary because sometimes SCMs are the beneficiaries of their own actions, that is in mutual aid and self-help SCOs and will therefore receive both internal and external benefits simultaneously.

Internal individual-level outcomes of SCOs

We argue that the biographical consequences of participation in SCOs must be considered using an intersectional approach, which recognises the ways in which different aspects of privilege and discrimination intersect in shaping participation as well as the effects of movement participation on biographies (see Roth and Saunders, 2022). In Chapter 3, we introduced high- and low-costs and -risks of activism (McAdam, 1989). The ways in which costs and risks are attributed and the potential consequences of the performance of different forms of social change making tactics affect individuals very differently depending hugely on their socio-demographics. For example, African American participants in the US civil rights movements faced significantly higher costs and risks than their White counterparts, including the risk of being lynched. Furthermore, Black protesters attract more police attention than their White counterparts and during the COVID-19 pandemic faced not only police brutality, but also the risk of infection (Njoku et al, 2021). Less dangerous, but still a barrier to equal participation, economic background also matters: Sugarman (1967) argued that the costs of volunteering in SCOs to enhance career development are much higher for people from working class backgrounds who cannot afford to defer their gratification. The career benefits of volunteering and low-paid internships provide advantages to people who can afford to defer their gratification given that that volunteering is associated with career advancement (Wilson and Musick, 2003) and that those involved in formal volunteering tend to earn more than those who are not involved (Li et al, 2008).

Our call to use an intersectional approach is important because many studies on the biographical consequences of participation in SCOs are somewhat outdated and limited in their focus on left-libertarian movements whose primary participants have been White and middle class. This drastically overlooks the diversity of potential individual level outcomes. For example, based on a review of 57 studies comparing participants and non-participants in SCOs that engage in protest, Vestergren et al (2017) identify six different 'objective' psychological/biographical outcomes of such SCOs. Note that Vestergren et al (2017) did not consciously bias their study towards left-libertarian movements, but most of the literature that they reviewed focuses on SCOs of this ilk. The six objective outcomes that Vestergren and colleagues (2017) noted are: (1) marital status, (2) parenting, (3) other social relationships, (4) career and work–life balance differences, (5) continued involvement, and (6) consumer behaviour. Briefly put, this extensive body of literature finds that SCMs who have participated in left-libertarian movements are generally thought to marry later or not at all (McAdam, 1989; Franz and McClelland, 1994; McAdam, 1999; Shriver et al, 2003). They seem more likely to avoid parenting or have children later (Dunham and Bengtson, 1997; Sherkat and Blocker, 1997; McAdam, 1999). They develop tightly knit friendship groups at the expense of out-group relations (Shriver et al, 2003; Saunders, 2008b), start their careers later and often end up in creative, social, or morally oriented jobs (Fendrich and Tarleau, 1973; Braungart and Braungart, 1990; Sherkat and Blocker, 1997; Fillieule, 2015). They often continue to be involved in progressive causes throughout their lives (Drury et al, 2003) and often do this through changes to their lifestyle (Vestergren et al, 2017).

Based on our intersectional approach we argue that it is inappropriate to attempt to generalise these findings across varieties of SCO and SCO sectors (Roth and Saunders, 2022; Roth et al, 2023). We argue that generalisation is not appropriate because socio-cultural norms vary across time and space; different causes and varieties of SCO attract different classes of SCMs; and SCMs have their own biographical backgrounds, individual life courses and positionalities that react in different ways to participation. It especially difficult to generalise across people who are 'boundary crossers' (Roth et al, 2023), that is individuals who move from one cause or variety of SCO to another, or who are engaged in more than one form of social change making simultaneously. No two boundary crossers will be identical. Only a deep biographical approach can properly trace who does what, when and with what consequences.

In relation to time and space, for example, marriage rates and parenthood may vary across countries, as well as among members of faith-based third sector organisations, trade unions, feminist, or LGBTQIA+ SCOs. Overall, in many countries, marriage rates have dropped in recent decades and having children out of wedlock is now much more accepted than 50 years ago (Perelli-Harris et al, 2017) – arguably a cultural outcome of the women's and counter-cultural SCOs of the 1960s and 1970s. McAdam (1999) similarly found that some of the biographical effects of SCO involvement are less profound when we control for changes in culture over time. He discovered that as postponement of transition into the adult life course became increasingly commonplace, left-wing activism became less important as predictor for it.

In relation to time, it is also important to consider generational and cohort effects. The individual outcomes of varieties of SCO likely differ due to generational effects – those period effects that are thought to condition political attitudes (for example Mannheim, 1952, see Chapter 5). Also important are micro-cohort effects – the difference that quite subtle shifts in the external culture over a one to two year period can have on political socialisation (Whittier, 1997). Enduring outcomes of SCOs differ for individuals depending on the social, political and cultural conditioning that stems from micro-cohort effects. These nuances are tempered by the extent to which older generations share skills and knowledge with newer generations. Thus, the review of studies that investigate biographical outcomes needs to keep in mind that some of these results are historical, concern different generations, and do not apply to all (contemporary) SCOs.

In relation to different causes and varieties of SCO, studies of volunteering and humanitarianism come to different conclusions than those on left-libertarian movements. Recent studies of members of third sector organisations find that married people with children are *more likely* to participate in formal volunteering than those who are single and are not parents (Nesbit, 2017). As we have discussed in Chapter 5, parenthood and employment can be reasons to get involved in SCOs. Unsurprisingly, the gendered division of labour in the private sphere affects volunteering (Einolf and Philbrick, 2014; Parry et al, 2021). Some SCOs, in particular humanitarian NGOs, are 'greedy organisations' that make it difficult to maintain relationships (Roth, 2015), whereas aid workers in relationships are more likely not to stay involved in humanitarianism (Korff et al, 2015). Those involved in formal volunteering are more likely to be employed and volunteering contributes to career advancement (Wilson and Musick, 2003).

For SCMs working in the humanitarian field, the experience, and the particular set of skills that such work engenders, means that it 'may be even more difficult' leaving humanitarian organising for change 'than entering it' (Roth, 2015: 160). Despite the difficulties they face in leaving humanitarian social change making, they adopt a professional flexibility that emerges from the near ubiquity of being employed on short-term contracts.

Further education, for example diplomas or other postgraduate degrees, allow humanitarian professionals not only to gain additional knowledge and credentials, but also to build networks and to reflect on the paradoxes and dilemmas of aid work (Roth, 2015).

Similarly to those engaged in other forms of SCOs (Saunders et al, 2012), the structural availability (being in the right place at the right time) of people working in the humanitarian field helps them remain involved by securing new contracts (Roth, 2015). Another similarity that can be found across SCO varieties is that local SCMs tend to 'generalise' to participate in campaigns on broader issues (Saunders, 2013), just as those who 'stick plasters' (Jupp, 2022) on wounds through service provision become subversive humanitarians (Vandevoordt and Verschraegen, 2019, see our Introduction) and conservationists can become subversive environmentalists (see Chapter 1).

In relation to boundary crossing, we note that feminist SCMs have varied their participation from different modes of participation as the movement has institutionalised: increasingly, participating in everyday resistance and 'the politics of associationalism'. Staggenborg (1995) points to the plethora of grassroots initiatives and caucuses that are women-led and feminist motivated – an important mobilisation outcome. Our own research on the Occupy movement (Roth et al, 2014) illustrated how many of the SCMs present were in a transitional phase of their life course and/or had become disillusioned with more mainstream or radical SCOs.

In addition to the six 'objective' changes, Vestergren et al (2017) identify 13 more 'subjective' individual level outcomes of participation in SCOs. Among the most important of these are identity, sustained commitment (see Chapter 5), well-being, and skill development. In our own work (Roth and Saunders, forthcoming), we see factors like empowerment, identity development, consciousness raising, senses of pride, and cognitive liberation (that is believing that one's actions can make a difference, McAdam, 1989) as important in shaping how biographical consequences play out. Without these factors present, we would expect little self-transformation. For example, individuals' sense of 'self' changes through participation only when new senses of collective identity are generated (Roth, 2000; Saunders, 2008b; Feigenbaum, 2010; Mackay, 2023; Roth and Saunders, forthcoming). SCMs' identities are reimagined partly through changing assessments of the legitimacy of the actions of in-groups and out-groups. For example, SCMs who engage in protest can come to distrust police (Drury and Reicher, 2000), institutions or even other SCOs (Saunders, 2008b), while establishing a firmer belief that they are, or had been, doing the right thing (Adamek and Lewis, 1975), just as fundraisers might become disillusioned and seek to engage in radical action (Fisher, 2006).

It is likely that different types of biographical outcomes of SCO participation affect each other. For example, the values that SCMs come to adopt affect their moral choices, which in turn affects their life choices – such as finding socially progressive or at least morally benign employment. Some professions are purposefully chosen by people who are inclined towards social change making. For example, teachers, social workers, lawyers, and a range of other professionals engage in 'occupational activism' (Valocchi, 2013; Gorski and Chen, 2015; Shepherd, 2018; Mayer, 2020).

There are doubtless many types of SCO participation, but a consequence of most is that SCMs gain 'pleasure and enjoyment' from them (Roberts and Devine, 2004: 281). One reason for this is that individuals benefit from helping others (Dolan et al, 2008). Formal volunteering is especially useful for older people who may be seeking an identity or relief from loneliness (Pinquarty and Sorensen, 2001), for instance after retiring from their job, or losing a significant life friend or partner (Greenfield and Marks, 2004; Harflett, 2014). Plagnol and Huppert (2010) found that formal volunteering is associated with the following positive outcomes; self-rated health, meeting people, engaging in social activities, attending religious meetings, as well as the cultural values of benevolence, universalism, hedonism, and achievement. It is, however, difficult to understand whether volunteering has these outcomes or if it is these characteristics that lead people to volunteer in the first place. True to our own interactionist and constructivist approach, studies that have used panel data to get a handle on causality have found that the causality can go both ways: happier people are more likely to volunteer; and volunteers are more likely to be happy (Meier and Stutzer, 2008). Evidence from the Americans' Changing Lives two-wave panel survey (House, 1995) finds that volunteers are more likely to have the preconditions of, not only happiness, but also 'life satisfaction, self-esteem, sense of control over life, physical health and depression', and that well-being is enhanced by voluntary work (Thoits and Hewitt, 2001: 115).

Addiction, mental and physical health conditions, victimisation, sexuality, body shape, and childlessness are just some of the causes that have are supported by mutual aid and self-help SCOs, wherein members support one another. Many self-help SCOs used to function as 'pen pal' networks (Taylor and Leitz, 2010) but today are often online groups. Clearly the benefits of mutual aid and self-help SCOs are multiple because SCMs are the beneficiaries of their own action.

However, while the participation in SCOs can have many positive outcomes for SCMs, it is important to keep in mind that there are also negative outcomes as the growing body on activist research documents. Burnout is not only linked to a high workload in SCOs (for example, Houldey, 2022; Tavarez, 2022), regardless of whether this work is paid or unpaid. Moreover, activists also suffer from sexism and racism within SCOs (Gorski, 2019; Ahia and Johnson, 2023; Eschle and Bartlett, 2023).

Emejulu and Bassel (2020) describe the 'politics of exhaustion' experienced by women of colour who fight against austerity and racism and feel marginalised by White anti-racist activists. Experiences of discrimination and marginalisation within progressive activist spaces can result in new SCOs and thus mobilisation outcomes (see, for example, Emejulu and Sobande, 2019; Emejulu and Bassel, 2023). In turn, privileged – for example White and/or middle-class – SCMs need to be aware of power differences, and listen and create space for change makers who feel marginalised and silenced. We now discuss the individual outcomes for external beneficiaries.

External individual outcomes of SCOs

In this section we discuss the achievements of SCOs involved in the delivery of goods and services, notwithstanding that engagement in such organisations can also have profound impacts on the individual SCMs who engage in them. While some SCOs improve people's lives through their fights for social justice through political, legislative, and institutional channels, other SCOs directly provide services and training themselves instead of asking the government to make changes. They might even hold government contracts to engage in this work. Larger organisations provide accounts of how many beneficiaries they have reached and what they were able to deliver in glossy annual reports. However, even small SCOs can have significant impacts.

We would like to illustrate this by turning to the organically grown network Cornwall Cloth Masks, which emerged in spring 2020 at the beginning of the COVID-19 pandemic in the southwest of the UK. Within only a few months, the 700 volunteers in the loosely connected network produced over 5,000 masks that they distributed to local community workers to help prevent the spread of COVID-19. The visible outcomes were significant and multifarious. The many masks that were produced provided protection and reassurance for thousands of individuals, reduced stress, and depression for those in need of personal protective equipment and the experience was doubtless an empowering and life-affirming activity for those involved.

Other SCOs produce not goods but services. These services might be in relation to healthcare, social care, housing, and education (Clarke et al, 2000; Hills et al, 2002). Larger, merged, voluntary sector agencies – such as healthcare providers or housing associations – have quite specific remits and therefore more targeted outcomes than community-based providers, which work more holistically across a range of welfare fields (Hoggett et al, 2009). There are two main types of effectiveness for SCOs that focus primarily on services and goods. These are outputs that are intermediate – for example, the volume of goods and services produced and the quality of those goods – and those that are final – the 'actual impacts on service users or 'external communities, depending on context' (Kendall and Knapp, 2000: 122). Such outcomes require careful monitoring and reporting. In some situations, a better outcome is a larger quantity of a service or output, in others, the quality of the output is key – depending on the services or goods provided by the SCO.

Some of the goods and services provided by international SCOs engaged in humanitarianism and development include medical assistance, education, food, and shelter. There are SCOs with a single purpose and others that are multi-mandated. The globally active multi-mandated SCO Save the Children focuses on children's lives and fighting for children's rights. In its annual report from 2019, Save the Children reported that it had supported 38.7 million children and 29.1 adults across 117 countries, including 9.5 million children and 8 million adults in 130 humanitarian emergency responses across 55 countries (Save the Children, 2019).

One of the most famous contemporary SCOs is Médecins Sans Frontières, which is responding to humanitarian crises. MSF combines the provision of medical care with the duty to bear witness (Davey, 2015). Among the outcomes of MSF are its exposures of abuse, forgotten crises, and inadequacies of the aid system. Not all MSF sections are operational – that is involved in delivering services overseas. Some (for example, MSF-USA, MSF-Germany, MSF-UK) are involved in fundraising, advocacy, public education, and volunteer recruitment. The non-operational sections have the outcome of supporting the operational sections (Stroup, 2012). The achievements of MSF have been recognised through it being awarded the Nobel Peace Prize in 1999.

Islamic Relief is the largest Islamic humanitarian NGO operational around the world. Its service provision resembles in many respects the activities of the secular SCOs with which it cooperates. It generates some outcomes specifically tailored to Islamic humanitarian values, such as provision of food packages and ritually slaughtered meat during holidays. This addresses not only the religious needs of beneficiaries, but also of donors (Petersen, 2012; Tomalin, 2012).

These well-known international SCOs have been termed 'behemoths', which have been contrasted with countless small SCOs known as 'butterflies' (Swidler and Watkins, 2017). The scope of operations and outcomes vary. Smaller SCOs, which might only include a few founding members, concentrate on one village, orphanage, or school, and may focus on one issue only. Yet they can still be hugely impactful – for example, a health professional who specialises on a particular disease or health problem might provide highly valuable and efficient care (Swidler and Watkins, 2017). While aid organisations receive much praise, there is also an extensive criticism of what humanitarian organisations actually achieve, the extent to which they are following the principle to 'do no harm', or are actually extending conflicts, whether the provision of aid leads to inequalities in communities, or whether aid is culturally appropriate. Thus, rigorous assessments of the impact of aid are needed (Koddenbrock, 2016; Swidler and Watkins, 2017).

The effort to improve aid has resulted in professionalisation processes, which we have discussed in earlier chapters. Whether these professionalisation processes have actually improved outcomes by making aid better is another question. Thus, although the efforts of SCOs to provide humanitarian aid and contribute to development are well-intentioned, it is not always clear whether these contributions address needs and whether it reaches the beneficiaries – a term used to refer to recipients of aid – most in need. However, a closer look at the decision-making processes of humanitarian NGOs raises the question what role 'needs' play in operational and resource allocation decision-making. Koddenbrock (2016) identifies a range of decision-making factors which include organisational identity; changing programme priorities; national differences; being present in the appropriate number of countries (not too many, not too few), donor preferences, media attention; and security conditions. This suggests that humanitarian agencies produce projects that are 'relatively independent of beneficiaries' needs and preferences' (Krause, 2014: 4). Swidler and Watkins (2017) describe the intersecting projections of donors, brokers, and aid recipients as 'fevered imaginations' (p 19), while Dean (2020) points to the 'good glow' associated with benevolence, and Khan et al (2023) point out the dark sides of 'White saviorism'. Overall, we can begin to see how the provision of goods and services have broader repercussions: on the lives of those in receipt of goods and services; on the ability of SCOs to sustain themselves; and on broader SCO sectors; all of which take place in close interaction with the historically variable context.

A sub-set the SCOs that mix the production of goods with advocacy work are the bureaucratised and professional SCOs that have been dubbed 'protest businesses' (Jordan and Maloney, 1997). These are established hierarchically organised organisations that have a strategic and pragmatic approach to campaigning. A key feature of protest businesses is that they tend not to involve their adherents in campaigning but rather use them to raise funds through direct-debit memberships. An indirect – but nonetheless still important – outcome for such organisations is in the provision of selective incentives (Olson, 1965) such as the car bumper sticker, the monthly newsletter, or the 'adoption' of a mascot. These outcomes matter because they can provide solidary incentives (Hildreth, 1994) to physically distant and otherwise disengaged supporters. The production of selective incentives as a set of goods matter as an SCO outcome in their own right, but also in relation to mobilisation outcomes; the incentives they provide to individual members/donors are able to keep SCOs well-resourced to allow them to continue their professional functions. For example, language courses for migrants enable them to participate in SCOs and put them in networks of relations that facilitate structural availability (Costanza-Chock, 2014). These mobilisation outcomes might be more beneficial for the SCOs (and SCMs) than beneficiaries by facilitating the infrastructure and maintenance of SCOs.

Conclusions

Throughout our book we have investigated how SCOs and SCMs contribute to social change. We have illustrated the depth and diversity of SCOs' outcomes throughout society at a number of levels that are interrelated: the polity, broader society, and culture, as well as SCOs and individuals, and illuminated some of the complex interactions between and among these levels. We chose to classify the outcomes of SCOs as policy/legislative, institutional, mobilisation, socio-cultural, and individual as a heuristic device more so than as a strict taxonomy. The reason for this is because of our own recognition that the impacts of SCOs are spread across, between, and among all of these different sub-categories at multiple levels, especially so given that SCOs collaborate (see Chapter 6).

One challenge of assessing the outcomes of SCOs has been the difficulty of ascertaining whether the attainment of an SCO's goal is a direct result of SCO action, or if there are other exogenous factors at work. To get this right involves tracing causal mechanisms between the actions of SCOs and the outcomes it is important to engage in longitudinal studies, which is not always possible. Giugni (1999) suggests a way around this problem. He thinks that we should begin by making a list of the plausible consequences of movements, look for what may have caused those consequences and reconstruct causal patterns over a number of cases. A methodologically sound discussion of the outcomes of SCOs necessitates in-depth understanding of multiple factors internal and external to SCOs and broader SCO sectors to understand what really did lead to the outcome that SCOs have been credited with. Similarly, in assessing the outputs of a service- or goods-focused SCO, one would need to compare a matched town or city that does not have the SCO to one that does to understand whether there have been improvements over a set of particular dimensions over a relevant timeslot (Kendall and Knapp, 2000: 123; see also Bardsley et al, 2019 for a matched case and control field experiment that sought to understand if a community based initiative to save energy helped households in a local community to reduce their energy demand). Such measurements, Kendall and Knapp (2000: 123) warn 'need to be carefully designed and are often expensive to collect'. Similarly, ratings of the satisfaction from end-users of SCO produced services and goods must come from carefully thought through survey work.

It is the entanglement of different types of outcomes of varieties of SCO, which work across many issue sectors with multiple strategies, that makes them so difficult to study. Our book addresses this challenge by surveying the strategies of a wide range of varying SCOs in historically variable contexts.

We encourage scholars to take a holistic, longitudinal, and mixed methods approach to the study of SCO outcomes. We acknowledge that given the complexity of SCOs' outcomes this is hard to achieve given the word limits of journal articles or the short time frame of funded research projects. This results in rather piecemeal studies of outcomes that might be better studied in book-length treatments. Perhaps the most important lesson for those trying to research SCO outcomes is the need for careful design of longitudinal studies that are able to compare outcomes to a specific benchmark prior to efforts to organise change, and which are aware of, and account for, complex sets of actions and interactions across historically variable contexts, SCOs and SCMs. This requires very careful historical analysis, combined with well-designed life history and panel survey research.

Conclusions: Organising for Change

Throughout the book we have argued that SCOs are as much shaped by historically variable contexts as they in turn shape this context in interaction with other SCOs. Recognising SCOs as co-creators of social change invites us to consider together temporality, interaction, and the variety of forms of SCOs, and to do so within the broader historically variable context. The factors that allow SCOs and SCMs to secure social change vary across time and place. Thinking in this way alerts us to the magnitude and complexity of disentangling SCO outcomes – on each other, on SCMs, on policy, on legislation, on institutions and on culture as well as in relation to broader social, economic, cultural, and technological contexts at multiple (local, national, and international) levels over time. We therefore stress the value of our holistic approach, which encourages us to think realistically about the very real challenges of accurately tracing the outcomes of SCOs back to the source or sources from which they originated.

It is, nonetheless, important to recognise how an outcome in one sphere (for example, cultural or biographical) might set on course some chain reactions in different spheres (for example, political or material). Indeed, this is probably one reason why existing work on the outcomes of SCOs is currently unclear about the precise mechanisms through which outcomes are secured. This is part of the beauty of our approach: a simple, linear, theory of 'organising for social change' would do injustice to the multiple processes at play within and among SCOs and their broader historically variable context. A holistic account of the outcomes of organising for change must recognise how individual, SCO-sector, socio-cultural, and socio-political outcomes come to shape one another in usually unpredictable ways.

Throughout this book we have examined varieties of SCO and a range of intersecting classes of SCMs. What are the lessons learned and what are the implications of our intervention? In this, our concluding, chapter we first highlight the relevance of our work to the circumstances we find ourselves in at the beginning of the 2020s. Then we discuss the three key themes that our book raises about the role of SCOs and SCMs in social change processes. These relate to temporality, interaction among SCOs, and the varieties of organising for change. Then we discuss how the general lessons from each chapter form a holistic understanding of the role of SCOs and SCMs in social change processes. We build a composite diagram to illustrate this holistic approach. Finally, we outline how SCMs might benefit from our book and sketch out avenues for future research that are opened up by our work.

Implications of our work for current times

The current epoch signals concern about the future of humanity globally and the prospects for democracy in many countries. Not too long ago, in the US, Donald Trump gathered public support to question the outcome of a free and fair election – and will undoubtedly do so again, should he again run for office. Similarly, Jair Bolsonaro in Brazil challenged his election defeat. In Hungary, Victor Orban's project for illiberal democracy meets regular opposition in the streets. In Germany, far-right movements and parties vehemently oppose immigration to the horror of those who welcome displaced refugees. In the UK, while the decision to leave the EU has been taken, there continue to be irresolvable disagreements about the impact this decision has and how it should be implemented. Rising costs of living and falling wages have caused strike action in many countries, but trade unions face legal restrictions and in some countries striking workers are confronted with police brutality. The BLM movement stresses the urgency to undo persistent racial inequalities. Progress towards gender equality are under attack and need to be defended. More and more SCOs and SCMs recognise the necessity to form intersectional coalitions to achieve social justice. Meanwhile, the actions of democratic governments on climate change are falling short of the requirements to prevent catastrophic climate change, which puts humans and many other species under severe threat. Frightfully, global emissions are rising while the climate bomb is ticking. The threat of climate change explains a surge in youth activism by Fridays for Future and the framing of climate change as an existential threat by Extinction Rebellion and the Aufstand der letzten Generation (Uprising of the Last Generation). If democracies do not deal with climate change, protest may turn disruptive. The future looks bleak if we add to this list of woes a set of concerns about the democratic implications of SCOs. As we mentioned in Chapter 2, it is somewhat disconcerting that billionaire philanthropists are shaping the world through their funding schemes as much as governments. Moreover, others have criticised the lack of systemic criticism from pragmatic NGOs, which could be taken to imply that they are handmaidens of governments that are shifting to the right.

Our book is a reminder not to be completely beset by such woes. This is not to say that social change is not worth fighting for. On the contrary! The struggle for progressive causes is real, and each and every one of us is beholden to act in accordance with our values. However, our historical perspective shows how social change comes and goes in waves. A shift to the right will likely spark a new wave of social change that will shift the political zeitgeist leftwards. As we noted earlier, SCOs are 'making' (Blee, 2012) and 'mending' (Hendricks et al, 2020) democracy, even though some might be thought to undermine and threaten it. Thus, democracy needs to be constantly defended, strengthened, and extended.

In the current context, our work is also a reminder of the need to take a more nuanced approach to thinking through what SCOs do and how they do it. Just as they are more than the sum of the types of activity they engage in, they are also not to be pigeon-holed into categories on the basis of where they sit on a continuum of reformism to radicalism. One suggestion in existing literature is that the dark side of pragmatic NGOs (in Swidler and Watkins', 2017 words, 'behemoths') is somewhat off-set by grassroots activism (in Swidler and Watkin's, 2017 words, 'butterflies'). However, some grassroots right-wing organisations such as the Proud Boys – a male only US-based neo-fascist far-right organisation – pose a significant threat to democracy. Moreover, well-meaning climate activists (Extinction Rebellion in the UK) blocking public transport might unintentionally undermine their cause by hindering precarious workers from reaching their work places and making them vulnerable to lay-offs. Although institutionalised large-scale NGOs might make compromises, most of them do not undermine democracy in comparable ways. Green parties that end up in government coalitions may support, as well as undermine, environmental SCOs and SCMs, and thus disappoint their constituencies. Viewing the broad range of actions that SCOs undertake, in direct and indirect interaction with each other using a historical approach, puts these concerns into perspective.

At the time of writing this book, a worldwide energy crisis, rising prices, the Ukraine war, and the earthquake in Turkey and Syria dominate the news. The ongoing COVID-19 pandemic still impacts relationships between SCOs, the state, and transnational organisations. Our approach to the study of SCOs reminds us of the ways in which the contemporary socio-political climate resonates with the historical patterns of association between the state and SCOs and of SCOs challenging the state (see Chapter 2). In the COVID-19 era, some SCOs provide support to individuals and communities in need and thus complement state action. At the same time, other SCOs protest against measures of the state, while transnational organisations seek to promote mutually supportive responses. COVID-19 has also changed the way in which SCOs work and communicate with members, beneficiaries, and each other by accelerated the use of ICT. We await to see how these dynamics have affected the medium- to long-term strategies, resources, coalitions, and people involved in the SCO sector. We recognise that frustration might result in radicalisation processes. We now turn to the three core themes of our book.

Temporality

Our first theme is about the importance of time. We argue that scholars need to consider temporality at the macro-, meso-, and micro-levels in order to understand how SCOs emerge and how they transform. At the macro-level, this means the study of SCOs requires a historical perspective, which incorporates contextualisation within the broader social and political environment in which SCOs pursue different goals with varying strategies and resources. We have shown how political and gender regimes matter for both the demands of SCOs and the ways in which they are pursued. Temporality also matters at the meso- or organisational level. Not every newly formed SCO survives. Those that persist might change over time for a number of reasons that include: responding to a turnover of staff or members; a change in the historically variable context; as a response to demands from donors; as a result of the actions of competitor SCOs; or because they succeeded in achieving one of their goals. Other important changes include the professionalisation and NGOisation of SCOs, and the merging of two or more SCOs.

We also need to consider temporality at the micro- or individual level to understand the ways in which the involvement of SCMs in SCOs is embedded in everyday life and changes over the life course. SCMs life circumstances can draw them in to, as well as draw them out of, social change making activities. The life course approach also invites us to think about the ways in which SCMs can be simultaneously and/or consecutively, continuously, or intermittently, involved in different types of SCOs that pursue different types of tactics and strategies. Thus, it is important to understand that SCOs and SCMs are not static, but constantly responding to internal and external changes. Thus, processes of social change to which SCOs and SCMs contribute are not linear, but complex systems of circumstances, actions, interactions, and reactions.

It is also important, at this juncture, to discuss the rise of internet use and its effects on SCOs. On a macro level, the internet shapes society at large (witness significant shifts towards online banking and online shopping, for instance). At the meso-level, it has altered the ways in which SCOs act (they are able to reach each other and their members much more efficiently and have found new ways to raise funds), and it has also afforded individuals new ways to hear about and get engaged in organising for change. We include the internet in our discussion of temporality because the internet has shrunk the world, through an acceleration of existing processes of time-space-compression (Harvey, 1999). However, our historical account shows that the internet has not created a dramatic shift in the practices of SCOs. Transnational coalitions previously formed in the absence of social media networks, and SCOs still communicated en masse through newsletters sent through the post. While the speed and reach of communications have changed, there is, nonetheless, remarkable continuity in social change processes over time.

SCO interaction

A historical and biographical approach to SCOs and SCMs leads us to our second key theme – about the importance of interaction between SCOs. We have discussed different relationships between SCOs – collaboration, competition, conflict, and indirect influence, as well as the role of SCMs as boundary crossers and therefore brokers. This means, of course, that each SCO can have different relationships with other SCOs. These might be collaborative and competitive with some like-minded SCOs, but conflictual or indirect influence with those that pursue different goals and interests. We therefore urge scholars to focus not just on the differences between different types of SCOs but on the relationships between them. This relational approach, as Diani (2015) argues, invites the study of organisational fields as opposed to organisational types. Bringing together our ideas of temporality and interaction highlights the importance of paying attention to dynamics and interactions at various levels, which shape and are shaped by SCOs and SCMs in historically variable contexts.

When we view professionalised SCOs as one possible form of social change making nested within a broader ecology of SCOs and SCMs, their compromises and lack of systemic critique of the state appear less damaging to democracy than Stroup and Wong (2017) have implied. The entire SCO sector does not succumb to compromises just because some have done so. In fact, we see a division of labour between SCOs that pursue service provision, advocacy, and protest, which represent different forms of organising for change. We therefore also argue that it makes sense to perceive distinctions between insider activism and outsider activism on a continuum rather than as categorically distinct. Insiders are pragmatic and willing to compromise with a variety of stakeholders to achieve incremental change, to shape the social and political agenda or to provide crucial services that are otherwise missing. Outsiders are more radical and uncompromising. However, as we have stressed throughout the book, over the course of their life course, SCMs might simultaneously or successively, continuously or after a break, be engaged in insider and outsider activism. Moreover, SCOs that engage in outsider activism might interact with those engaged in insider activism. While the pragmatism of insider organisations, and the hands-on aid they provide, can – from a more radical perspective, especially if treated in isolation – be seen as stabilising the status quo, insider organisations also provide a stepping stone for further change. Multiple baby steps eventually add up to giant steps. We also know that radical change – with respect to women's political rights, civil rights legislation, or the legalisation of homosexuality, as well as environmental, and human rights issues – requires ongoing commitment to implement and institutionalise legal change. But we are deeply convinced that to bring about or resist social change, a combination of different strategies, which include pressure from above *and* below – political sandwiching – is required. The polite or gentle pressure from insider SCOs, which have a seat at the table and access to a variety of resources, including media recognition, representation in commissions, and financial support from a variety of donors, can provide an opening for the uncompromising but resource poor outsider SCOs. Indeed, the same organisation might adopt a multi-pronged approach, which Friends of Earth is doing quite well. It has been long established that the radical flank effect (Haines, 1984) enables moderate organisations to be more radical than they might ordinarily be, simply by virtue of being more moderate than their more radical counterparts who make their claims and actions appear more reasonable. Moreover, it is important to keep in mind that, in the view of some SCOs and SCMs, some causes such as climate change, defending democracy, eradicating discrimination and violence including human rights violations, are so urgent that they do not feel that any compromise would be justified. Indeed, many threads of social change that have historically delivered significant outcomes – including the suffragettes, civil rights struggles, and campaigns against the poll tax in Britain – have included elements of violent organising for change, notwithstanding the moral challenges of deploying violence and the fact that it can sometimes backfire (Malm 2021). Thus, we need to remember that the relationship between insider and outsider SCOs might not always be collaborative, it can also be conflictual as Stroup and Wong (2017) show. But such conflicts might also help lead towards progressive outcomes.

Varieties of organising for change

This brings us to our third theme, which emphasises the varieties of organising for change. By recognising the importance of temporality and the interaction of SCOs we seek to highlight that a tactic – such as protest, advocacy, or service delivery – in itself does not, and cannot, tell us the whole story about how change is achieved. Marches and protest can be ritualistic and might be more important to maintain a radical identity of those participating in a protest event than actually achieving change, even if indirect outcomes occur. Similarly, language or computer skills courses might at first glance seem unpolitical, but in fact lead to politicisation process and the development of leadership skills. This means that one strategy can have multiple outcomes, immediately or in the long run. Service provision, for example in addition to addressing a need, can also result in political socialisation and mobilisation of so-called beneficiaries, as well as bring about cultural and perhaps even legislative change by changing people's attitudes andputting issues on to the agenda. Recognising the multi-fold outcomes of SCOs and SCMs necessitates a need to pay more attention to the variety of activities undertaken by SCOs and how they unfold over time and through interactions. The recognition of varieties of change making requires the integration of social movement studies, third sector studies and the study of NGOs in humanitarian, development, and human rights studies. We summarise the varieties of SCO in Table 8.1.

Table 8.1: Varieties of social change organisation

Type of strategies	Type of resource needed	Who provides it?	Accountable to whom?
Education (for migrants and other disadvantaged groups)	• (un)paid trainers • training material • (cyber) Space	• individual donations and membership dues • private (large) grant • public (large) grant	• beneficiaries • members/ individual donors • foundation • government/UN agency/EU
Legal advice (for migrants and other disadvantaged groups)	• (un)paid legal experts • (cyber)space	• individual donations and membership dues • private (large) grant • public (large) grant	• beneficiaries • members/ individual donors • foundation • government/UN agency/EU
Healthcare (for disadvantaged groups, also for medical issues that are not yet recognised and/or treated by healthcare providers)	• (un)paid healthcare providers • medicine and PPE • space with equipment	• individual donations and membership dues • private (large) grant • public (large) grant	• beneficiaries • members/ individual donors • foundation • government/UN agency/EU
Humanitarian relief (could be provided domestically or internationally)	• (un)paid experts • (un)paid aid workers • travel resources • equipment • space	• individual donations and membership dues • private (large) grant • public (large) grant	• beneficiaries • members/ individual donors • foundation • government/UN agency/EU

(continued)

Table 8.1: Varieties of social change organisation (continued)

Type of strategies	Type of resource needed	Who provides it?	Accountable to whom?
Economic assistance (wide range of technical assistance, also education, training, domestically or overseas)	• (un)paid experts • (un)paid aid workers • travel resources • equipment • budget to pay local staff • space	• individual donations and membership dues • private (large) grant • public (large) grant	• beneficiaries • members/ individual donors • foundation • government/UN agency/EU
Advocacy (concerning all kinds of human rights, equality, environmental issues)	• (un)paid experts • activists • media access • representation in commissions • legitimacy • budget for travel, equipment, (cyber) space	• individual donations and membership dues • donations from allies	• beneficiaries • members/ individual donors • allies
Lobbying (again, all kinds of issues)	• (un)paid experts • activists • access to policy makers • legitimacy • budget for travel, equipment, (cyber) space	• individual donations and membership dues • donations from allies	• beneficiaries • members/ individual donors • allies
Protest (again, all kinds of issues)	• mobilisation expertise • speakers • protesters • budget for stage, posters • (social) media access	• self-funded by protesters • donations from allies	• beneficiaries • members/ individual donors • allies

A holistic approach to SCOs

We conclude that a holistic approach to organising for change, which considers various levels, is needed. At the individual level, we examined how SCMs get involved in SCOs, how their participation unfolds over the lifetime, and what impact this participation has on the SCMs themselves as well as for other individuals and groups. At the organisational level, we examined different types of organisations that mobilise a variety of resources, engage in a wide range of tactics and strategies, and interact with other

Figure 8.1: Social change makers, social change organisations and social change

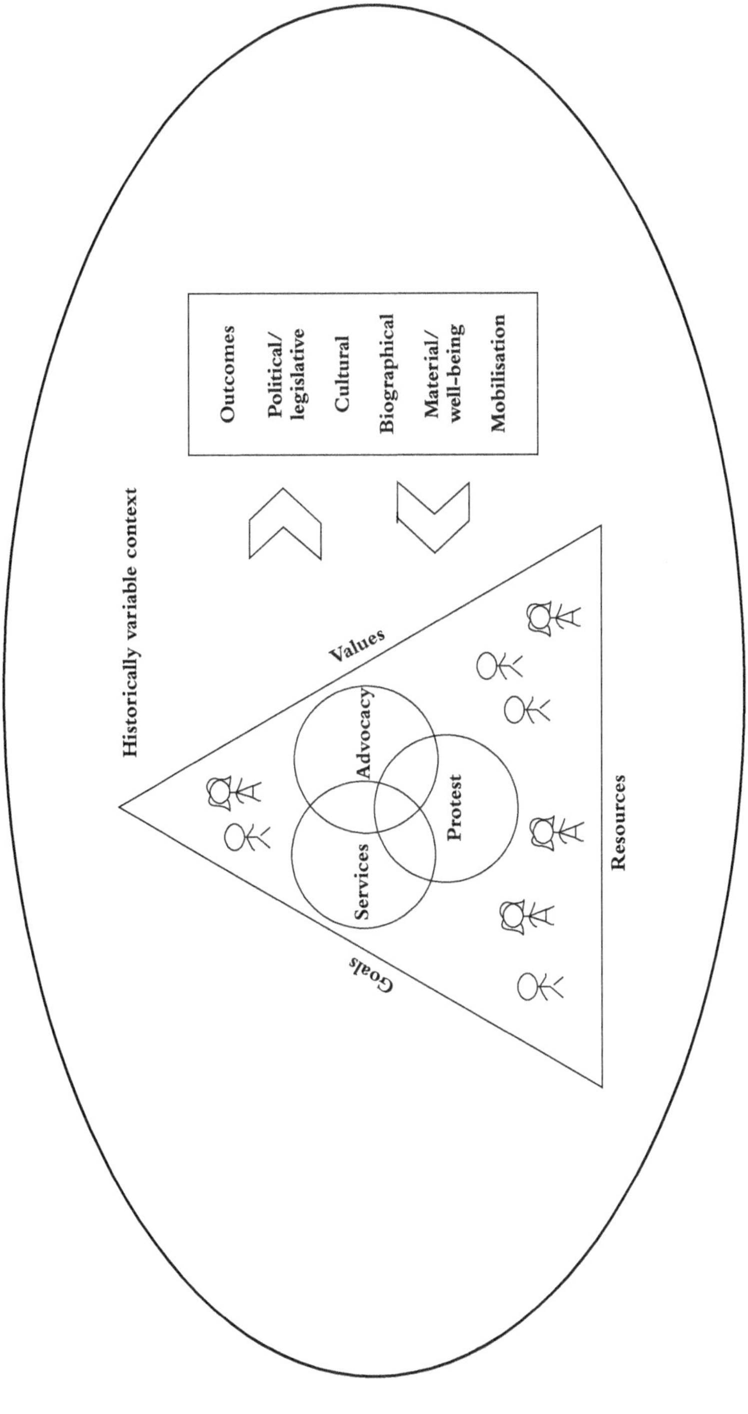

SCOs in a collaborative, competitive or conflicting way. At the national and international levels, we considered how historically variable context shape and are shaped by SCOs and SCMs. We summarise our approach in Figure 8.1.

The triangle symbolises the goals, values and resources that shape the tactics and networking of SCOs. The Venn-diagram of services, advocacy and protest represents overlapping tactics as well as networking of SCOs and SCMs. Note that contact between SCOs can be collaborative, competitive, conflictual, or indirect. SCMs, represented by the stick people, at different stages of their life course, get involved in a range of tactics and take on different roles within SCOs that have a variety of network links. Indeed, some of the network links among SCOs are brokered by the SCMs themselves. SCMs, SCOs, networks, and tactics – shaped by resources, goals and values – have outcomes that in turn shape SCMs, SCOs, networks, and tactics. These processes exist within broader historically variable contexts, which influence and are influenced by these processes for social change. This represents a very basic summary of our way of viewing the context and processes of organising for social change.

Inspiring social change makers

We posit that it is important to take the dilemmas that SCMs and SCOs face seriously. While we believe that it is important to critically interrogate the trade-offs and unanticipated consequences of the choices about resources and strategies that SCMs and SCOs in ever changing contexts face, we seek to avoid criticism, which might be disempowering. Instead, we argue that constructive critiques can, also, of course, help big NGOs to improve their accountability and transparency. We propose that our nuanced arguments about social change as processes of interaction have three major benefits for SCMs. First, we think it is helpful to consider that in order to collaborate, compromises are often needed and underpin successful coalitions. This might involve 'agreeing to disagree'. Second, we hope that our historical and biographical perspective has demonstrated that a shift or overlap between different forms of organising for change contributes to the sustainability of change making both at the individual and organisational levels. Thus, our approach might help SCMs to accept why it is that they feel the need to shift from one form of organising for change to another over the course of their lives. There need not be an identity crisis, a feeling of letting the side down, or of bailing out. Finally, we hope that our approach highlights the ways in which different approaches oriented towards social change are helpful. We show how difficult it can be to anticipate the outcomes of various strategies. Immediate aid in a situation of need might result in long-term politicisation and mobilisation processes. On the other hand, those demanding structural change might find satisfaction in more short-term immediate projects. We urge SCMs to reflect on outcomes rather than success and consider 'failures' as learning opportunities. The outcomes of social change making are always manifold, complex, and dynamic. In order to avoid sexism, racism, and other forms of discrimination within SCOs it is important not only to focus on the greater good but on the interaction with other SCMs. Only then will social change making be empowering for SCMs and their collaborators and beneficiaries. Just as there is no such thing as a free gift (Chapter 4), there is also no such thing as a perfect strategy for social change.

Future research

So where do we go from here? Our book is an invitation to open up dialogue between scholars of different disciplines and SCMs engaged in a variety of causes. We emphasise that service provision can be political and radical. It might complement or underpin contentious politics. We also note that insider activism might be just as important for bringing about significant change as outsider activism. At the same time, we believe that all of these strategies have risks and limits. Therefore, it is important that they complement each other – including both collaborative as well as conflictive relationships. In our broad historical survey of various causes, we have scratched the surface. We hope that social movement scholars, third sector researchers, and students of NGOs will find our approach useful and inspiring. We encourage social movement scholars to extend their research beyond protest events and see how protest events are related to other forms of organising for change. We encourage third sector researchers to make use of the concepts developed by social movement researchers and pay more attention to the political consequences of volunteering. We also advocate for more longitudinal studies on the consequences of SCMs' involvement in SCOs to supplement the fine scholarship on the activists of the 1960s and 1970s. To do this work will require in-depth historical and comparative studies on the emergence and development of SCOs in different historical and political contexts.

APPENDIX

Our Projects

1. Volunteering in the male life course (1988–90)

Around 1988, Silke joined a project on 'Socialisation in Retirement' as research assistant. The project, funded by the Deutsche Forschungsgemeinschaft (DFG, the German equivalent of the UK's Economic and Social Research Council [ESRC]), was led by Martin Kohli. It aimed to understand how retired men cope with the loss of paid work to structure their everyday lives. Five groups of men aged 60 and older, some of them still pursuing paid work as part-time workers or self-employed men, were contrasted to different groups of volunteers. Silke was responsible for interviewing volunteers in the Rote Kreutz (Red Cross) and the Arbeiter Samariter Bund (Labour Samaritans' Union, a first aid organisation associated with the labour movement). The ten life history interviews she conducted revealed that the men started to volunteer in their youth or mid-life, not in their retirement. Subsequently, she examined the role of volunteering in the male life course in her masters' dissertation, carrying out ten additional interviews with young and middle-aged men. She found that volunteering provided stabilisation throughout the life course, especially crises times, such as unemployment or divorce. Silke's master's dissertation also examined the significance of voluntary organisations in modernisation processes. Work on the project has informed our thinking about the necessity of understanding paid and unpaid work in a life course perspective and to consider voluntary organisations as shaped by and contributing to social change.

2. The Coalition of Labor Union Women (CLUW) in the US (1994–97)

Silke's next project was her PhD thesis, funded by the Hans Böckler Stiftung (the research foundation of the German Trade Union Federation) and the University of Connecticut. Silke was interested to investigate the challenges of women to get involved and assume leadership positions in bureaucratic organisations. Trade unions had for a long time been male-dominated although this changed due to de-industrialisation and the higher involvement of women in the paid labour force. The Coalition of Labor Union Women (CLUW) presented an excellent case study to study efforts of women to change trade unions. Moreover, she developed the concept of *bridging organisations* that connect different social movements (labour, women, civil rights). Silke employed an intersectional analysis (without using that term), looking at the intersection of race, class, and gender, and how it shaped conflicts and solidarity within CLUW and the organisations with which CLUW interacted. Between 1994 and 1996, Silke conducted over 80 interviews (including life- history interviews) with members of CLUW and its collaborators. She also conducted a survey among the membership resulting in over 500 responses (response rate 25 per cent). CLUW is featured in various vignettes and chapters in the book. This project allowed Silke to study social change at intersecting micro-, meso- and macro-levels. We feature CLUW in vignettes in Chapter 1 and Chapter 6.

3. Day care strike in West Berlin of 1989 (1997–98)

Silke and Myra Marx Ferree (her PhD supervisor) were intrigued by a strike of day care workers that took place in West Berlin in the fall and winter of 1989 (about the time the Berlin Wall came down). Based on an analysis of newspaper articles and documents of the union documenting the strike action, they developed the notion of 'exclusionary solidarity'. They wanted to explain why the female day care workers where not supported by the male-dominated trade unions, the autonomous feminist movement of West Berlin and the female dominated Senate (the city government of West Berlin). This lack of support might seem surprising, given that day care workers represent a group of low-paid public sector workers (a concern of trade unions) and enable women in paid employment to go to work (a concern of feminists). This work informs Chapter 6 of *Organising for Change*.

4. Transformation of Environmental Activism (2000–2001)

The Transformation of Environmental Activism Project, coordinated by Christopher Rootes, was a pan-European comparison of environmental activism from the 1970s to early 2000s, funded by the European Commission FP7. It sought to investigate the changing character of environmental activism. At the time, it was the largest systematic comparison of environmental activism in Western Europe. After completing her master's thesis, Clare was involved as a research assistant on the project, responsible for understanding the character of environmental movements in south east London. She conducted a survey of southeast London-based environmental organisations, did case analysis on protests against the channel tunnel rail link and interviewed around 40 activists, including John Stewart who features in our Chapter 7 vignette. The project also revealed the ways in which not-in-my-back yard activists can stop infighting when they work together to build coalitions, as we discuss in Chapter 6 of *Organising for Change*.

5. Competition, collaboration and conflict in London's environmental networks (2001–2004)

This project was Clare's PhD thesis, funded by the ESRC. She sought to investigate the traction of social movement theory in understanding the collaboration, competition, and conflict between and among environmental organisations in the UK (with a special focus on northwest and southeast London). She conducted a survey of over 200 local environmental organisations, 40 in-depth interviews with key SCMs and participant observation in three environmental organisations (one conservationist, one reformist and one radical). She concluded that it was more helpful to conceive of the organisations she surveyed as a 'network' rather than a movement. The study, therefore, contributed to our understanding of SCOs as being part of sets of actions, interactions, and reactions, and to Chapter 6 in particular.

6. Paradoxes of aid work: biographies and careers or people in aid (2004–13)

This project carried out by Silke focused on the biographies and careers of 'people working in aid', by which we mean volunteers and paid staff working for non-governmental, multi- and bi-lateral organisations engaged in human rights work, development cooperation and humanitarian relief. The project was funded with grants from the University of Pennsylvania and the University of Southampton. Silke conducted biographical interviews with current and former aid workers were primarily in London, New York and Geneva, as well as via Skype. The aim of the project was to understand what drew people to aid work and how they experienced their work. Over 50 interviews with women and men of different age groups and nationalities were conducted to explore the 'paradoxes of aid work', which are based on and perpetuate global inequalities at multiple levels. This work informs our thinking about different ways of organising for change, professionalisation processes, accountability and outcomes which we discuss in Chapters 3, 4 and 7 of *Organising for Change*.

7. Democracy in Europe and the Mobilization of Society (2004–2008)

The DEMOS: Democracy in Europe and Mobilization of Society project was funded by the European Directorate General for Research (FP7) and coordinated by Donatella della Porta. Clare was a research associate who worked intensively on the UK case, supervised by Christopher Rootes. The project compared the democratic principles and practices of global justice organisations across seven European countries, also including a team that examined transnational organisations. The project used combined methodologies of document analysis (including of websites), organisational surveys, European Social Forum participant surveys, and participant observation in global justice organisations. During this project, Clare learned a great deal about global justice movements and about how movements make decisions. These insights inform Chapters 3 and 6. For more information about the project, see the website: https://cosmos.sns.it/projects/demos-democracy-in-europe-and-the-mobilization-of-society/.

8. The impact of European Union enlargement on Eastern European women's NGOs and East–West collaboration (2005–2007)

After organising a conference on 'Gender Politics in the Expanding European Union' (University of Pennsylvania, 2005), Silke worked on a project that sought to assess the impact of EU enlargement on women and women's NGOs in Poland, Hungary, the Czech Republic, and Slovenia. The data and methods included document analysis, observations at conferences, and 13 interviews carried out via telephone and e-mail with experts and activists from Poland, the Czech Republic, Slovenia, Hungary, Croatia, and Germany. We draw on this work in the opening vignette of Chapter 2 and Chapter 6, among other chapters of *Organising for Change*.

9. Friends of the Earth International (2005–2007)

The Friends of the Earth International: Negotiating a North–South identity project was funded by the UK Economic and Social Research Council (award number RES-155-25-0008) and coordinated by Brian Doherty. Clare worked as research assistant – designing the survey and analysing the findings. The project aimed to understand how the different national organisations within Friends of the Earth International worked together and how they overcame tensions in relation to environmental and social justice priorities. The research design consisted of a network survey of Friends of the Earth International organisations (n=71) (for which Clare was responsible) alongside participant observation in meetings, document analysis and interviews. The work informs our analysis in Chapter 6, which seeks to understand the ways in which organisations collaborate, compete and conflict.

10. Caught in the Act of Protest: Contextualising Contestation Project (2009–12)

The Caught in the Act of Protest: Contextualising Contestation Project was a multi-country project, coordinated by Bert Klandermans and Stefaan Walgrave. It was administered by the European Science Foundation, but the national funding agencies funded the country-specific contributions. Clare was principal investigator for the ESRC funded UK case, working with Christopher Rootes, Maria Grasso, Cristiana Olcese, Stephan Price and Emily Rainsford. The project represents the first attempt to robustly and systematically survey street demonstrators. During the course of the project, we surveyed participants in over 80 street demonstrations, and the number of demonstrations surveyed using the methodology continues to grow. As part of the project, we conducted a survey of Occupy London participants and did biographical interviews with 12 activists. Silke helped to coordinate the Occupy part of the project, including conducting interviews and analysing the data. We learned a great deal about pathways to recruitment into protest and factors that sustain involvement and multiple memberships in SCOs. For more information about the project, see our project website: https://www. protestsurvey.eu/. Our vignette of Jo (in Chapter 2) is based some of the people Clare met during this project while surveying climate change demonstrators. Chapter 5 opens with a vignette of Mike, a participant in Occupy London.

11. Surveying people working in aid, assessing skills and experiences: a pilot study (2011–12)

Given the limited availability of representative data on aid workers, the goal of this study was to adapt the Caught in the Act of Protest (see Caught in the Act of Protest: Contextualising Contestation Project, described earlier) methodology to humanitarian workers. Silke and Clare worked together with Lucy Jordan on this project that measured the demographic characteristics of aid workers and experiences and attitudes towards aid work. In Tanzania, where we recruited participants through on-site sampling, 233 respondents engaged with our short face-to-face survey, but only 24 (10 per cent) also filled out the longer web-based survey. We were able to recruit 24 participants for the web-based survey through a training course. The on-site research, carried out in Tanzania, clearly demonstrated that differences in online-access matter. International aid workers had much better internet access than local staff, which impacted on their participation of the web-based survey. This project informs our work on the need to consider digital inequality when discussing the affordances of ICT.

12. How citizens participate in politics (POLPART) (2014–18)

The POLPART project was the outcome of a European Research Council Advanced Investigator Award, won by Bert Klandermans. Clare was principal investigator for the UK case. The work was an attempt to understand why people decide to either not participate in politics at all, to participate in electoral politics only, to participate in protest politics only or to participate in both. The team engaged in meta survey analysis, experimental survey vignettes and conducted nine focus groups in several countries (including Argentina and Chile). The project informs our analysis in Chapter 5. For more information about the project, see our project website: http://www.polpart.org/.

13. Designing a sensibility for sustainable clothing (2018–20)

This project, funded by the UK Arts and Humanities Research Council, worked with small groups of people in making, mending, and modifying clothes to see whether it encouraged them to adopt more pro-environmental ways of thinking, feeling and acting. Clare worked with Fiona Hackney (Manchester Metropolitan University), Irene Griffin (Falmouth University), Joanie Willett (University of Exeter), Katie Hill (University of Wolverhampton) and Anjia Barbieri (University of Exeter) on this project. Fiona had previously written about 'quiet activism' – forms of activism that take place out of the limelight, away from obvious acts of protest and often in the home. We came to realise that making and mending clothes is a form of quiet activism, which shapes both practices and social norms. This project informs *Organising for Change* through its emphasis on less directly obvious forms of organising for change. This is part of the reason why we conceive of SCMs broadly: as engaging in quiet activism, prefigurative practices and other types of action often mistakenly not considered to be political.

14. Military veterans in disaster relief (2018–19)

Based on her research on humanitarians, Silke became interested in former military personnel joining disaster relief organisations. In 2017, she participated in a training event of a disaster relief organisation that brought together military veterans and other civilians. In 2018 and 2019, Silke conducted interviews with staff (nine), volunteers (seven), and interns (six) of this organisation. Some of the interview participants were military veterans, some were enrolled in or had completed humanitarian studies programmes. The organisation was engaged in domestic and international disaster relief. In addition to the interviews, Silke also attended staff meetings and participated in several training events, each lasting several days. She also explored the necessity of carrying out a digital ethnography alongside traditional ethnography, given that the interaction of members of the organisations took place as much online and offline. The ethnography was interrupted by the COVID-19 pandemic and, at the time of writing, it is unclear whether it will be resumed. The work informs our thinking in *Organising for Change* by stressing the importance of considering the hybridity of online and offline interaction in SCOs.

15. A new climate movement? (October 2019)

This project, funded by the Centre for Sustainable Prosperity, was led by Clare in collaboration with Brian Doherty and Graeme Hayes. We conducted a representative survey of those who participated in the October 2019 Extinction Rebellion protests. The project taught us a lot about the types of people who participate in Extinction Rebellion surveys, including their organisational memberships and past histories of protesting. The work, therefore, informs our analysis in *Organising for Change* on the need for a biographical approach.

Notes

Introduction

[1] We use not-for-profit and non-profit interchangeably depending on whether we are referring to US-English or UK-English scholars.

[2] Cis-gender refers to the correspondence between the gender identity as male or female and the sexed body. (Note that sex differences are socially agreed upon and thus socially constructed.) Trans-gender in contrast refers to 'a range of gender experiences, subjectivities and presentations that fall across, between or beyond stable categories of "man" and "woman"' (Hines, 2010: 1).

[3] Sojourner Truth (ca. 1797–1883) escaped slavery and fought against slavery and for women's rights (Zackodnik, 2004).

Chapter 2

[1] https://www.humandignitytrust.org/, last accessed 4 April 2023.

[2] Please note that throughout the text, we sometimes refer to LGBTQIA+ and sometimes to LGBT. These inconsistencies are due to the fact that the way in which organisations and publications refer to LGBTQIA+ issues has changed over time. We follow the practices of the organisations and publications we are citing.

[3] https://www.rowntreesociety.org.uk/news/statement-on-rowntree-colonial-histories/; https://www.leverhulme.ac.uk/history-trust, last accessed 22 September 2023.

[4] UNIFEM stands for United National Development Fund for Women and is part of UN Women.

Chapter 3

[1] However, see Rossdale (2019) for a nuanced discussion of militarised masculinities and militarised desire in the context of anti-militarist activism.

Chapter 4

[1] https://www.msf.org/reports-and-finances, last accessed 4 April 2023.

[2] https://www.msf.org/reports-and-finances, last accessed 4 April 2023.

[3] https://www.msf.org/reports-and-finances, last accessed 4 April 2023.

Chapter 6

[1] ATTAC stands for Association pour la Taxation des Transactions financieres et l'Aide aux Citoyens (Association for the Taxation of financial Transactions and Aid to Citizens) https://www.attac.org/, last accessed 22 September 2023.

[2] The concern was that Million Women March would appropriate the name of the 'Million Men March' a march of African American men and boys to protest against police brutality

and discrimination. See https://www.theguardian.com/us-news/2015/oct/10/million-man-march-20-years-later-anniversary, last accessed 22 September 2023.

Chapter 7

[1] The Chicago Women's Liberation Union (CWLU) was a radical feminist organisation and should not be confused with the Coalition of Labor Union Women (CLUW), an organisation of trade union women.

References

Aall, P., Miltenberger, D.T. and Weiss, G. (2000) *Guide to IGOs, NGOs, and the military in peace and relief operations*, Washington DC: United States Peace Department.

Abrams, M. (1959) 'Social change in modern Britain', *The Political Quarterly*, 30(2): 149–56.

Acker, J. (1990) 'Hierarchies, jobs, bodies: A theory of gendered organizations', *Gender & Society*, 4(2): 139–58.

Adamek, R. and Lewis, J. (1975) 'Social control violence and radicalization: Behavioural data', *Social Problems*, 22: 663–74.

Adams, T.M. (2007) 'The mixed moral economy of welfare: European perspectives', in B. Harris and P. Bridgen (eds) *Charity and mutual aid in Europe and North America*, Abington: Routledge, pp 43–66.

Agustin, L.R. and Roth, S. (2011) 'Minority inclusion, self-representation and coalition-building: The participation of minority women', in A.E. Woodward, J.M. Bonvin and M. Renom (eds) *European women's networks. Transforming gendered well-being in Europe: The impact of social movements*, Farnham: Ashgate, pp 231–47.

Ahia, M. and Johnson, K. (2023) 'The Puʻu we planted: (Re)birthing refuge at Mauna Kea[1]', in C. Eschle, and A. Bartlett (eds) *Feminism and protest camps*, Bristol: Bristol University Press, pp 37–60.

Aldrich, H. (1999) *Organizations evolving*, London: Sage.

Alexander, J.C. and Giesen, B. (1987) 'From reduction to linkage: The long view of the micro-macro link', in J.C. Alexander, B. Giesen, R. Muench, and N.J. Smelser (eds) *The micro-macro link*, Berkeley, CA: University of California Press, pp 1–42.

Allotey, P., Ravidran, T.S. and Sathivelu, V. (2021) 'Trends in abortion policies in low- and middle-income countries', *Annual Review of Public Health*, 24: 505–18.

Almeida, P.D. (2009) 'Social movements, political parties, and electoral triumph in El Salvador', *NACLA Report on the Americas*, 42(6): 16–21.

Almond, S. and Kendall, J. (2000) 'Taking the employees' perspective seriously: An initial United Kingdom cross-sectoral comparison', *Nonprofit and Voluntary Sector Quarterly*, 29(2): 205–31.

Amenta, E. (2003) 'What we know about the development of social policy: Comparative and historical research in comparative and historical Perspective', in D. Rueschemeyer and J. Mahoney (eds) *Comparative and historical analysis*, New York: Cambridge University Press, pp 91–130.

Amenta, E. and Caren, N. (2004) 'The legislative, organizational and beneficiary consequences of state-oriented challengers', in D.A. Snow, S.A. Soule and H. Kriesi (eds) *The Blackwell companion to social movements*, Oxford: Blackwell, pp 461–88.

Amenta, E. and Young, M.P. (1999) 'Making an impact: Conceptual and methodological implications of the collective goods criterion', in M. Giugni, D. McAdam, and C. Tilly (eds) *How social movements matter*, Minneapolis, MN: University of Minnesota Press, pp 22–41.

Ancelovici, M. (2021) 'Conceptualizing the context of collective action: an introduction', *Social Movement Studies*, 20(2): 125–138.

Andreassen, T.A., Ereit, E. and Legrad, S. (2014) 'The making of "Professional Amateurs": Professionalizing the voluntary work of service user representatives', *Acta Sociologia*, 57(4): 325–40.

Andrews, M. (2007) *Shaping history: Narratives of political change*, Cambridge: Cambridge University Press.

Anheier, H.K. and Toepler S. (1997) 'Philanthropic foundations: An international perspective', *Administrative Science Quarterly*, 42(2): 3–23.

Armstrong, E.A. and Bernstein, M. (2008) 'Culture, power, and institutions: A multi-institutional politics approach to social movements', *Sociological Theory*, 26(1): 74–99.

Arnold, G. (1995) 'Dilemmas of feminist coalitions: Collective identity and strategic effectiveness', in M.M. Ferree and P.Y. Martin (eds) *Feminist organizations: Harvest of the new women's movement*, Philadelphia, PA: Temple University Press, pp 276–290.

Askins, K. (2009) '"That's just what I do": Placing emotion in academic activism', *Emotion, Space and Society*, 2(1): 4–13.

Atkinson, A. (1991) *Principles of political ecology*, London: Belhaven Press.

Averett, K.H. (2016) 'The gender buffet: LGBTQ parents resisting heteronormativity', *Gender & Society*, 30(2): 189–212.

Ayoub, P.M. (2016) *When states come out. Europe's sexual minorities and the politics of visibility*, Cambridge: Cambridge University Press.

Baines, D. (2004) 'Caring for nothing: Work, organization and unwaged labour in social services', *Work, Employment and Society*, 18(2): 267–95.

Baines, D. (2011) 'Restructuring and labour processes under marketisation: A Canadian perspective', in I. Cunningham, and P. James (eds) *Voluntary organisations and publics service delivery*, New York and Abingdon: Routledge, pp 168–84.

Bandy, J. and Smith, J. (eds) (2005) *Coalitions across borders: Transnational protest and the neoliberal order*, Lanham, MD: Rowman and Littlefield.

Bardsley, N., Büchs, M., James, P., Papafragkou, A., Rushby, T., Saunders, C., et al (2019) 'Domestic thermal upgrades, community action and energy saving: A three-year experimental study of prosperous households', *Energy Policy*, 127: 475–85.

Barker, C. (2001) 'Fear, laughter and collective power: The making of Solidarity at the Lenin Shipyard in Gdansk, Poland, August 1980', in J. Goodwin, J.M. Jasper and F. Polletta (eds) *Passionate politics: Emotions and social movements*, Chicago, IL: University of Chicago Press, pp 175–94.

Barker, C., Cox, L., Krinsky, J. and Nilsen, A.G. (2013) *Marxism and social movements*, London: Brill.

Barnes, S.H., Kaase, M., Allerbeck, K.R., Farah, B.J., Heunks, F., Inglehart, R., Jennings, M.K., et al. (1979) *Political action: Mass participation in five Western democracies*, Beverly Hills, CA: Sage.

Barnett, M. (2011) *Empire of humanity: A history of humanitarianism*, Ithaca, NY: Cornell University Press.

Barnett, M. and Stein, J.G. (2012) *Sacred aid: Faith and humanitarianism*, Oxford: Oxford University Press.

Bassel, L. and Emejulu, A. (2017) *Minority women and austerity: Survival and resistance in France and Britain*, Bristol: Policy Press.

Baughan, E. and Fiori, J. (2015) 'Save the Children, the humanitarian project, and the politics of solidarity: Reviving Dorothy Buxton's vision', *Disasters*, 39(s2): s129–45.

Bawole, J.N. and Langnel, Z. (2016) 'Downward accountability of NGOs in community project planning in Ghana', *Development in Practice*, 26(7): 920–32.

Bayat, A. (2010) *Life as politics: How ordinary people change the Middle East*, Amsterdam: Amsterdam University Press.

Beamish, T.B. and Luebbers, A.J. (2009) 'Alliance building across social movements: Bridging difference in a peace and justice coalition', *Social Problems*, 56(4): 647–76.

Bebbington, A. (2004) 'NGOs and uneven development: Geographies of development intervention', *Progress in Human Geography*, 28(6): 725–45.

Bell, S.E. and Braun, Y.A. (2010) 'Coal, identity, and the gendering of environmental justice activism in central Appalachia', *Gender & Society*, 24(6): 794–813.

Benford, R.D. and Snow, D.A. (2000) 'Framing processes and social movements: An overview and assessment', *Annual Review of Sociology*, 26: 611–39.

Bennett, W. (2003) 'Communicating global activism', *Information, Communication & Society*, 6(2): 143–68.

Bennett, W.L. and Segerberg, A. (2012) 'The logic of connective action: Digital media and the personalization of contentious politics', *Information, Communication & Society*, 15(5): 739–68.

Benson, M. and Rochon, T.R. (2004) 'Interpersonal trust and the magnitude of protest: A micro and macro level approach', *Comparative Political Studies*, 37(4): 435–57.

Benton, A. (2016) 'African expatriates and race in the anthropology of humanitarianism', *Critical African Studies*, 8(3): 266–77.

Benz, M. (2005) 'Not for the profit, but for the satisfaction? Evidence on worker well-being in non-profit firms', *Kyklos*, 58(2): 155–76.

Bernstein, M. (2003) 'Nothing ventured, nothing gained? Conceptualizing social movement "success" in the lesbian and gay movement', *Sociological Perspectives*, 46(3): 353–79.

Berry, M.E. and Lak, M. (2021) 'Women's rights after the war: On gender interventions and enduring hierarchies', *Annual Review of Social Science*, 17: 459–81.

Bhambra, G.K. (2014) *Connected sociologies*, London and New York: Bloomsbury.

Bhambra, G.K. (2017a) 'Brexit, Trump, and "methodological whiteness". On the misrecognition of race and class', *The British Journal of Sociology*, 68: S214–32.

Bhambra, G.K. (2017b) 'The current crisis of Europe: Refugees, colonialism, and the limits of cosmopolitanism', *European Law Journal*, 23(5): 395–405.

Bhati, A. and Eikenberry, A.M. (2016) 'Faces of the needy: The portrayal of destitute children in the fundraising campaigns of NGOs in India', *International Journal of Nonprofit and Voluntary Sector Marketing*, 21(1): 31–42.

Billard, T.J. and Gross, L. (2020) 'LGBTQ politics in media and culture', *Oxford Research Encyclopedia of Politics*. Available at: https://doi.org/10.1093/acrefore/9780190228637.013.1263, last accessed 1 April 2023.

Billis, D. (2010) *Hybrid organizations and the third sector. Challenges for practice, theory and policy*, Basingstoke: Palgrave MacMillan.

Bitzan, R. (2017) 'Research on gender and the far right in Germany since 1990: Developments, findings, and future prospects', in M. Köttig, R. Bitzan and A. Pető (eds) *Gender and far-right politics in Europe*, London: Palgrave, pp 65–78.

Black, M. (1991) *Cause for our times: Oxfam – the first 50 years*, Oxford: Oxfam.

Blee, K.M. (2012) *Democracy in the making: How activist groups form*, Oxford: Oxford University Press.

Blee, K.M. (2017) 'Similarities/differences in gender and far-right politics in Europe and the USA', in M. Köttig, R. Bitzan and A. Pető (eds) *Gender and far-right politics in Europe*, Cham: Springer, pp 191–204.

Blühdorn, I. (2006) 'Self-experience in the theme park of radical action? Social movements and political articulation in the late-modern condition', *European Journal of Social Theory*, 9(1): 23–42.

Bobel, C. (2007) '"I'm not an activist, though I've done a lot of it": Doing activism, being activist and the "perfect standard" in a contemporary movement', *Social Movement Studies*, 6(2): 147–59.

Bobo, L.D. (2017) 'Racism in Trump's America: Reflections on culture, sociology, and the 2016 US presidential election', *The British Journal of Sociology*, 68: S85–S104.

Bocking-Welch, A. (2018) *British civic society at the end of empire*, Manchester: Manchester University Press.

Boon, G.M., Secci, J. and Gallan, L.M. (2017) 'Resistance: Active and creative political protest strategies', *American Behavioral Scientist*, 62(3): 353–74.

Borgonovi, F. (2008) 'Doing well by doing good: The relationship between formal volunteering and self-reported health and happiness', *Social Science & Medicine*, 66(11): 2321–34.

Born, D. (2019) 'Bearing witness? Polar bears as icons for climate change communication in National Geographic', *Environmental Communication*, 13(5): 649–63.

Borzaga, C. and Depedri, S. (2005) 'Interpersonal relations and job satisfaction: Some empirical results in social and community care services', in B. Gui and R. Sugden (eds) *Economics and social interaction: Accounting for interpersonal relations*, Cambridge: Cambridge University Press, pp 132–53.

Borzaga, C. and Tortia, E. (2006) 'Worker motivations, job satisfaction, and loyalty in public and nonprofit social services', *Nonprofit and Voluntary Sector Quarterly*, 35(2): 225–48.

Bosi, L., Giugni, M. and Uba, K. (2016) *The consequences of social movements.* Cambridge: Cambridge University Press.

Bourdieu, P. and Wacquant, L.J.D. (1992) *An invitation to reflexive sociology*, Cambridge: Polity Press.

Brandsen, T. and Pestoff, V. (2006) 'Co-production, the third sector and the delivery of public services: An introduction', *Public Management Review*, 8(4): 493–501.

Braungart, R.G. and Braungart, M.M. (1990) 'Youth movements in the 1980s: A global perspective', *International Sociology*, 5(2): 157–81.

Brescia, R. (2020) *The future of change: How technology shapes social revolutions*, Ithaca, NY: Cornell University Press.

Briggs, A. and McCartney, A. (2011) *Toynbee Hall: The first hundred years*, London: Routledge.

Brooker, M.E. and Meyer, D.S. (2018) 'Coalitions and the organization of collective action', in D.A. Snow, S.A. Soule, H. Kriesi and H.J. McCammon (eds) *The Wiley Blackwell companion to social movements*, Chichester, UK/Hoboken, NJ: Wiley, pp 252–68. Available at: https://doi.org/10.1002/9781119168577.

Brooks, E. (2005) 'Transnational campaigns against child labor: The garment industry in Bangladesh', in J. Bandy and J. Smith, (eds) *Coalitions across borders: Transnational protest and the neoliberal order*, Lanham, MD: Rowman and Littlefield, pp 121–40.

Brown, G. and Pickerill, J. (2009) 'Space for emotion in the spaces of activism', *Emotion, Space and Society*, 2(1): 24–35.

Browne, K. and Bakshi, L. (2013) 'Insider activists: The fraught possibilities of LGBT activisms within', *Geoforum*, 49: 253–62.

Bruegel, I. and Kean, H. (1995) 'The moment of municipal feminism: Gender and class in 1980s local government', *Critical Social Policy*, 15(44–5): 147–69.

Buchanan-Smith, M. (2003) *How the Sphere Project came into being: A case study of policy-making in the humanitarian aid sector and the relative influence of research*, London: Overseas Development Institute. Available at: https://odi.org/en/publications/how-the-sphere-project-came-into-being-a-case-study-of-policy-making-in-the-humanitarian-aid-sector-and-the-relative-influence-of-research/ last accessed 28 August 2023.

Buckingham, S. (2004) 'Ecofeminism in the twenty-first century', *The Geographical Journal*, 170(2): 146–54.

Budabin, A.C. and Richey, L.A. (2021) *Batman saves the Congo: How celebrities disrupt the politics of development*, Minneapolis, MN: University of Minnesota Press.

Bullard, R.D. (1990) *Dumping in Dixie: Race, class and environmental quality*, London: Routledge.

Bunnage, L.A. (2014) 'Social movement engagement over the long haul: Understanding activist retention', *Sociology Compass*, 8(4): 433–45.

Burke, J.M. (1989) 'Freemasonry, friendship and noblewomen: The role of the secret society in bringing enlightenment thought to pre-revolutionary women elites', *History of European Ideas*, 10(3): 283–93.

Burnard, T., Damousi, J. and Lester, A. (2022) 'Introduction-selective humanity: Three centuries of Anglophone humanitarianism, empire and transnationalism', in T. Burnard, J. Damousi, and A. Lester (eds) *Humanitarianism, empire and transnationalism, 1760–1995*, Manchester: Manchester University Press, pp 1–34.

Burnstein, P. (1999) 'Social movements and public policy', in M. Giugni, D. McAdam, and C. Tilly (eds) *How social movements matter*, Minneapolis, MN: University of Minnesota Press, pp 3–21.

Bursens, P. (1997) 'Environmental interest representation in Belgium and the EU: Professionalization and division of labour within a multi-level governance setting', *Environmental Politics*, 6(4): 51–75.

Bygnes, S. (2012) '"We are in complete agreement": The diversity issue, disagreement and change in the European Women's Lobby', *Social Movement Studies*, 12(2): 199–213.

Bystydzienski, J.M. and Schacht, S.P. (2001) *Forging radical alliances across difference: Coalition politics for the new millennium*, Lanham, MD: Rowman and Littlefield.

Cammaerts, B. (2005) 'ICT usage among transnational social movements in the networked society: To organise, to mobilise and to debate', in R. Silverstone (ed) *Media, technology, and everyday life in Europe: From information to communication*, Aldershot: Ashgate, pp 53–72.

Carroll, W.K. and Sapinski, J.P. (2015) 'Transnational alternative policy groups in global civil society: Enablers of post-capitalist alternatives or carriers of NGOization?', *Critical Sociology*, 43(6): 875–892.

Carson, R. (1962) *Silent spring*, New York: Houghton Mifflin.

Carter, N. and Childs, M. (2018) 'Friends of the Earth as a policy entrepreneur: 'The Big Ask' campaign for a UK Climate Change Act', *Environmental Politics*, 27(6): 994–1013.

Casquete, J. (2006) 'The power of demonstrations', *Social Movement Studies*, 5(1): 45–60.

Catton Jr, W.R., and Dunlap, R.E. (1978) 'Environmental sociology: A new paradigm', *The American Sociologist*, 13(1): 41–9.

Catton Jr, W.R. and Dunlap, R.E. (1980) 'A new ecological paradigm for post-exuberant sociology', *American Behavioral Scientist*, 24(1): 15–47.

Cheshmehzangi, A. (2021) 'Vulnerability of the UK's BAME communities during COVID-19: The review of public health and socio-economic inequalities', *Journal of Human Behavior in the Social Environment*, 2:172–88.

Chetkovich, C.A. and Kunreuther, F. (2006) *From the ground up: Grassroots organizations making social change*, Ithaca, NY: Cornell University Press.

Chevée, A. (2022) 'Mutual aid in North London during the Covid-19 pandemic', *Social Movement Studies*, 21(4): 413–419.

Choluj, B., and Neusüss, C. (2004) 'EU Enlargement in 2004. East-West priorities and perspectives from women inside and outside the EU' Discussion Paper written with support from the United Nations Development Fund for Women. Available at: http://blog.claudia-neusu ess.com/uploads/Neusuess-Choluj-UNIFEM-neuPaper.pdf, last accessed 1 April 2023.

Choudry, A. (2015) *Learning activism: The intellectual life of contemporary social movements*, Toronto: University of Toronto Press.

Chouliaraki, L. (2006) *The spectatorship of suffering*, London: Sage.

Clark, B. (2002) 'The Indigenous environmental movement in the United States', *Organization and Environment*, 15(4): 410–42.

Clark, J. and Wilding, K. (2011) 'Trends in voluntary sector employment', in I. Cunningham and P. James (eds) *Voluntary organisations and public service delivery*, Abingdon: Routledge.

Clarke, J., Gewirtz, S. and E. McLaughlin (2000) 'Reinventing the welfare state', in J. Clarke, S. Gewirtz and E. McLaughlin (eds) *New managerialism: New welfare?*, London: Sage Publications, pp 1–26.

Clarke, R. (2004) *Pioneers of conservation: The Selborne Society and the Royal SPB*, Selborne: Selborne Society.

Clarke, R., Guilmain, J., Saucier, P.K. and Tavarez, J. (2003) 'Two steps forward, one step back: The presence of female characters and gender stereotyping in award-winning picture books between the 1930s and the 1960s', *Sex Roles*, 49(9/10): 439–49.

Clayton, J., Donavan, C., and Merchant, J. (2016) 'Distancing and limited resourcefulness: Third sector provision under austerity localism in the North East of England', *Urban Studies*, 53(4): 723–40.

Clemens, E.S. (1993) 'Organizational repertoires and institutional change: Women's groups and the transformation of US politics: 1890–1920', *American Journal of Sociology*, 98(4): 755–98.

Clemens, E.S. and Guthrie, D. (2011) *Politics and partnerships: The role of voluntary associations in America's political past and present*, Chicago, IL: University of Chicago Press.

Clemens, E.S. and Minkoff, D.C. (2007) 'Beyond the iron law: Rethinking the place of organizations in social movement research', in D.A. Snow, S.A. Soule and H.P. Kriesi (eds) *The Blackwell companion to social movements*, Oxford: Blackwell, pp 155–70.

Clément, G. (2017) 'Activism and environmentalism in British rock music: The case of Radiohead', *Revue Française de Civilisation Britannique/ French Journal of British Studies*, 22(XXII–3).

Clifford, D. and Backus, P. (2010) 'Are big charities becoming increasingly dominant? Tracking charitable income growth 1997–2008 by initial size', Third Sector Research Centre and Centre for Charitable Giving and Philanthropy Working Paper 38. Available at: https://www.birmingham. ac.uk/Documents/college-social-sciences/social-policy/tsrc/working-pap ers/briefing-paper-38.pdf, last accessed 1 April 2023.

Clifford, D., Rajme, G. and Mohan, J. (2010) 'How dependent is the third sector on public funding? Evidence from the National Survey of Third Sector Organisations', TSRC Working Paper 45. Available at: https://www.birmingham.ac.uk/Documents/college-social-sciences/ social-policy/tsrc/working-papers/working-paper-45.pdf, last accessed 1 April 2023.

Cole, E.R. (2008) 'Coalitions as a model for intersectionality: From practice to theory', *Sex Roles*, 59: 443–53.

Cooke, B. (2003) 'A new continuity with colonial administration: Participation in development management', *Third World Quarterly*, 24(1): 47–61.

Cornfield, D.B. and McCammon, H.J (eds) (2010) *Labor revitalization: Global perspectives and new initiatives (research in the sociology of work, vol. 11)*, Bingley: Emerald Group Publishing Limited.

Corrigall-Brown, C. (2012) *Patterns of protest: Trajectories of participation in social movements*, Stanford, CA: Stanford University Press.

Corrigall-Brown, C. and Meyer, D.S. (2010) 'The prehistory of a coalition: The role of social ties in win without war', in N. Van Dyke and H.J. McCammon (eds) *Strategic alliances: Coalition building and social movements*, Minneapolis, MN: University of Minnesota Press, pp 3–21.

Cortese, D.K. (2015) 'I'm a "good" activist you're a "bad" activist, and everything I do is activism: Parsing the different types of "activist" identities in LGBTQ organizing', *Interface: A Journal for and about Social Movements*, 7(1): 215–46.

Costanza-Chock, S. (2003) 'Mapping the repertoire of electronic contention', in A. Opel and D. Pompper (eds) *Representing resistance: Media, civil disobedience and the global justice movement*, London: Praeger, pp 173–91.

Costanza-Chock, S. (2012) 'Mic check! Media cultures and the Occupy movement', *Social Movement Studies*, 11(3–4): 375–85.

Costanza-Chock, S. (2014) *Out of the shadows, into the streets! Transmedia organizing and the immigrant rights movement*, Cambridge, MA: MIT Press.

Coule, T.M., Dodge, J. and Eikenberry, A.M. (2022) 'Toward a typology of critical nonprofit studies: A literature review', *Nonprofit and Voluntary Sector Quarterly*, 51(3): 478–506.

Cox, L. (2009) '"Hearts with one purpose alone"? Thinking personal sustainability in social movements', *Emotion, Space and Society*, 2(1): 52–61.

Cox, L. (2010) 'How do we keep going? Activist burnout and personal sustainability in social movements?', Fourteenth International Conference on Alternative Futures and Popular Protest, Manchester Metropolitan University.

Cox, L. and Nilsen, A.G. (2007) 'Social movements research and the 'movement of movements': Studying resistance to neoliberal globalisation', *Sociology Compass*, 1(2): 424–42.

Cox, L. and Nilsen, A.G. (2014) *We make our own history: Marxism and social movements in the twilight of neoliberalism*, London: Pluto Press.

Crack, A.M. (2014) 'Reversing the telescope: Evaluating NGO peer regulation initiatives', *Journal of International Development*, 28(1): 40–56.

Craddock, E. (2021) *Living against austerity: A feminist investigation of doing activism and being activist*, Bristol: Bristol University Press.

Crenshaw, K. (1991) 'Mapping the margins: Intersectionality, identity, politics and violence against women of color', *Stanford Law Review*, 43: 1241–99.

Cress, D., McPherson, J. and Rotolo, T (1997) 'Competition and commitment in voluntary memberships: The paradox of persistence and participation', *Sociological Perspectives*, 40(1): 61–79.

Crowe, D.M. and Shryer, J. (1995) 'Eco-colonialism', *Wildlife Society Bulletin (1973–2006)*, 23(1): 26–30.

Crowther, J. and Scandrett, E. (2016) 'Making the connections between the academy and social movements', *Forschungsjournal Soziale Bewegungen*, 29(4): FSJB-plus. Available at: https://forschungsjournal.de/fjsb/wp-content/uploads/fjsb-plus_2016-4_scandrett_crowther.pdf last accessed 28 August 2023.

Cullen, P.P. (2005) 'Conflict and cooperation with the platform of European social NGOs', in J. Bandy and J. Smith (eds) *Coalitions across borders: Transnational protest and the neoliberal order*, Lanham, MD: Rowman and Littlefield, pp 71–94.

Cunningham, D. (2018) 'Differentiating hate: Threat and opportunity as drivers of organization vs action', *Sociological Research Online*, 23(2): 507–17.

Cunningham, I. (2011) 'Taking the strain? The psychological contract of voluntary sector employees following transfers of employment', in I. Cunningham and P. James (eds) *Voluntary organisations and public service delivery*, Abingdon: Routledge, pp 136-152.

D'Anjou, L. (1996) *Social movements and cultural change: The first abolition campaign revisited*, Hawthorne, NY: Aldine de Gruyter.

Dale, S. (1996) *McLuhan's children: The Greenpeace message and the media*, Ontario: Between The Lines.

Dalton, R. (1994) *The green rainbow. Environmental groups in Western Europe*, New Haven, CT: Yale University Press.

Damman, M., Heyse, L. and Mills, M. (2014) 'Gender, occupation, and promotion to management in the nonprofit sector', *Nonprofit Management and Leadership*, 25(2): 97–111.

Daniel, M. and de Leon, C. (2020) 'Leadership succession in intersectional mobilization: An analysis of the Chicago abortion fund, 1985–2015', *Mobilization: An International Quarterly*, 25(4): 461–74.

Dauvergne, P. and LeBaron, G. (2014) *Protest, Inc. The corporatization of activism*, Cambridge: Polity Press.

Davey, E. (2015) *Idealism beyond borders: The French revolutionary left and the rise of humanitarianism, 1954–1988*, Cambridge: Cambridge University Press.

De Jong, S. (2017) *Complicit sisters: Gender and women's issues across north-south divides*, New York: Oxford University Press.

De Moor, J. and Wahlström, M. (2019) 'Narrating political opportunities: explaining strategic adaptation in the climate movement', *Theory and Society*, 48(3): 419–51.

Dean, J. (2020) *The good glow: Charity and the symbolic power of doing good*, Bristol: Policy Press.

Dean, J, and Maiguashca, B. (2018) 'Gender, power and left politics: From feminisation to "feministisation"', *Politics & Gender*, 4(3): 376–406.

Deckman, M. (2017) 'How the Resist Trump movement could transform into the Tea Party of the Left', *USApp – American Politics and Policy Blog. (03 Mar 2017)*. Available at: https://blogs.lse.ac.uk/usappblog/2017/03/03/how-the-resist-trump-movement-could-transform-into-the-tea-party-of-the-left/ last accessed 22 August 2023.

Deegan, J. (1988) *Jane Addams and the men of the Chicago School: 1892–1918*, New Brunswick, NJ: Transaction Press.

della Porta, D. (1992) 'Political socialization in left-wing underground organizations: Biographies of Italian and German militants', *International Social Movement Research*, 4(1): 259–90.

della Porta, D. (1999) 'Protest, protests, and protest policing: Public discourses in Italy and Germany from the 1960s to the 1980s', in M. Giugni, D. McAdam and C. Tilly (eds) *How social movements matter*, Minneapolis, MN: University of Minnesota Press, pp 66–96.

della Porta, D. (2007) *The global justice movement in Western Europe*, London: Paradigm Press.

della Porta, D. (2009) *Democracy in movement*, London: Palgrave.

della Porta (2017) *Movement parties against austerity*, Cambridge: Polity Press.

della Porta, D. (2020) 'Building bridges: Social movements and civil society in times of crisis', *VOLUNTAS: International Journal of Voluntary and NonProfit Organizations*, 31: 938–48.

della Porta, D. and Diani, M. (2006) *Social movements: An introduction*, Oxford: Blackwell Publishers.

della Porta, D. and Mosca, L. (2005) 'Global-net for global movements? A network of network for a movement of movements?', *Journal of Public Policy*, 25(1): 165–90.

Demirel-Pegg, T. and Pegg, S. (2015) 'Razed, repressed and bought off: The demobilization of the Ogoni protest campaign in the Niger Delta', *The Extractive Industries and Society*, 2(4): 654–63.

Dempsey, S.E. and Saunders, M.L. (2010) 'Meaningful work? Nonprofit marketization and work/life imbalance in popular autobiographies of social entrepreneurship', *Organization*, 17(4): 437–59.

Diamond, S. (1995) *Roads to dominion: Right-wing movements and political power in the United States*, New York: Guilford Press.

Diani, M. (1992) 'The concept of social movement', *The Sociological Review*, 40(1): 1–25.

Diani, M. (1995) *Green networks: A structural analysis of the Italian environmental movement*, Edinburgh: Edinburgh University Press.

Diani, M. (2000) 'Social movement networks virtual and real', *Information, Communication & Society*, 3(3): 386–401.

Diani, M. (2011) 'Social movements, networks and recruitment', in G. Ritzer and M. Ryan (eds) *The Blackwell Encyclopedia of Sociology*, Oxford: Blackwell, pp 566–67.

Diani, M. (2015) *The cement of civil society: Studying networks in localities*, Cambridge: Cambridge University Press.

Diani, M. and Donati, P.R. (1999) 'Organisational change in Western European environmental groups: a framework for analysis', *Environmental Politics*, 8(1): 13–34.

Dickson, L. and McCulloch, A. (1996) 'Shell, the Brent Spar and Greenpeace: A doomed tryst?', *Environmental Politics*, 5(1): 122–9.

Dickson, K. (2023) 'False consciousness and the phenomenology of white saviorism', in T. Khan, K. Dickson and M. Sondarjee (eds) *White saviorism in international development: theories, practices and lived experiences*, Wakefield, Quebec: Daraja Press, pp 98–115.

DiMaggio, P.J. and Powell, W.W. (1983) 'The iron cage revisited: Institutional isomorphism and collective rationality in organisational fields', *American Sociological Review*, 48(2): 147–60.

Dodd, N., Lamont, M. and Savage, M. (2017) 'Introduction to BJS special issue', *The British Journal of Sociology*, 68: S3–S10.

Doherty, B. and Saunders, C. (2021) 'Global climate strike protesters and media coverage of the protests in Truro and Manchester', in J. Bessant, A.M. Mesinas and S. Pickard (eds) *When students protest: Universities in the Global North*, Lanham, MD: Rowman and Littlefield, pp 251–68.

Dolan, P., Peasgood, T. and White, M. (2008) 'Do we really know what makes us happy? A review of the economic literature on the factors associated with subjective well-being', *Journal of Economic Psychology*, 29(1): 94–122.

Domínguez, L. and Luoma, C. (2020) 'Decolonising conservation policy: How colonial land and conservation ideologies persist and perpetuate Indigenous injustices at the expense of the environment', *Land*, 9(3): 65.

Donegani, C.P., McKay, S. and Moro, D. (2012) 'A dimming of the "warm glow"? Are non-profit workers in the UK still more satisfied with their jobs than other workers?', Third Sector Research Centre Working Paper 74. Available at: http://epapers.bham.ac.uk/1773/1/WP74_A_dimming_of_the_%E2%80%98warm_glow%E2%80%99_-_Donegani,_McKay_and_Moro,_April_2012.pdf, last accessed 1 April 2023.

Donini, A. (1995) 'The bureaucracy and the free spirits: Stagnation and innovation in the relationship between the UN and NGOs', *Third World Quarterly*, 16(3): 421–40.

Downton, J. and Wehr, P. (1998) 'Persistent pacifism: How activist commitment is developed and sustained', *Journal of Peace Research*, 35(5): 531–50.

Doyle, T. and McEarchen D. (1998) *Environment and politics*, London: Routledge.

Driscoll, D. (2020) 'When ignoring the news and going hiking can help you save the world: Environmental activist strategies for persistence', *Sociological Forum*, 35(1): 189–206.

Drury, J. and Reicher, S. (2000) 'Collective action and psychological change: The emergence of new social identities', *British Journal of Social Psychology*, 39: 579–604.

Drury, J., Reicher, S. and Stott, C. (2003) 'Transforming the boundaries of collective identity: From the 'local' anti-road campaign to 'global' resistance?', *Social Movement Studies*, 2: 191–212.

Duben, A. (1994) *Human rights and democratization: The role of local government and NGOs*, Istanbul: WALD.

Dufour, C., de Geoffroy, V., Maury, H. and Grünewald, F. (2004) 'Rights, standards and quality in a complex humanitarian space: Is Sphere the right tool?', *Disasters*, 28(2): 124–41.

Duncanson, C. (2015) 'Hegemonic masculinity and the possibility of change in gender relations', *Men and Masculinities*, 18(2): 231–48.

Duncanson, C. and Woodward, R. (2016) 'Regendering the military: theorizing women's military participation', *Security Dialogue*, 47(1): 3–21.

Dunham, C. and Bengtson, V. (1997) 'The long-term effects of political activism on intergenerational relations', *Youth and Society*, 24(1): 31–51.

Duyvendak, J.W. and Fillieule, O. (2015) 'Patterned fluidity: An interactionist perspective as a tool for exploring contentious politics', in J. Jasper and J.W. Duyvendak (eds) *Players and arenas: The interactive dynamics of protest*, Amsterdam: Amsterdam University Press, pp 295–318.

Earl, J. (2004) 'The cultural consequences of social movements', in D.A. Snow, S.A. Soule and H. Kriesi (eds) *The Blackwell companion to social movements*, Oxford: Blackwell Publishing, pp 508–30.

Earl, J. (2018) 'Technology and social media', in D.A. Snow, S.A. Soule, H. Kriesi and H.J. McCammon (eds) *The Wiley Blackwell companion to social movements*. Available at: https://doi.org/10.1002/9781119168577.ch16 Chichester, UK/Hoboken, NJ, USA Publisher: Wiley, pp: 289–305.

Earl, J. (2000) 'Methods, movement and outcomes: Methodological difficulties in the study of extra-movement outcomes', *Research in Social Movements, Conflicts and Change*, 22: 3–25.

Earl, J. and Garrett, R.K. (2016) 'The new information frontier: Toward a more nuanced view of social movement communication', *Social Movement Studies*, 16(4): 479–93.

Eaton, M. (2010) 'Manufacturing community in an online activist organization', *Information, Communication & Society*, 13(2): 174–92.

Edwards, B. and McCarthy, J. (2004) 'Resources and social movement mobilization', in D.A. Snow, S.A. Soule and H. Kriesi (eds) *The Blackwell companion to social movements*, Oxford: Blackwell, pp 116–53.

Edwards, B., McCarthy, J. and Mataic, D.R. (2018) 'The resource context of social movements', in D.A. Snow, S.A. Soule, H. Kriesi and H. McCammon (eds) *The Wiley Blackwell companion to social movements* (2nd edn), Oxford: Wiley Blackwell, pp 79–97.

Edwards, M. (1997) *NGOs, states and donors: Too close for comfort*, Basingstoke: Palgrave.

Einhorn, B. (1993) *Cinderella goes to market. Citizenship, gender, and women's movements in East Central Europe*, London: Verso.

Einhorn, B. (2006) *Citizenship in an enlarging Europe: From dream to awakening*, Basingstoke: Palgrave.

Einhorn, B. and Sever, C. (2003) 'Gender and civil society in Central and Eastern Europe', *International Feminist Journal of Politics*, 5(2): 163–90.

Einolf, C.J. and Philbrick, D. (2014) 'Generous or greedy marriage? A longitudinal study of volunteering and charitable giving', *Journal of Marriage and Family*, 76(3): 573–86.

Einwohner, R.L., Kelly-Thompson, K., Sinclair-Chapman, V., Tormos-Aponte, F., Weldon, S.L., Wright, J.M. and Wu, C. (2021) 'Active solidarity: Intersectional solidarity in action', *Social Politics: International Studies in Gender, State & Society*, 28(3): 704–29.

Eikhof, D.R., Warhurst, C. and Haunschild, A. (2007) 'Introduction: What work? What life? What balance?: Critical reflections on the work-life balance debate', *Employee Relations*, 29(4): 325–33.

Eisenstein, H. (1996) *Inside agitators. Australian femocrats and the state*, Philadelphia, PA: Temple University Press.

Eliasoph, N. (2011) *Making volunteers: Civic life after welfare's end*, Princeton, NJ: Princeton University Press.

Eliasoph, N. (2013) *The politics of volunteering*, Cambridge: Polity Press.

Eltanini, M. (2016) '"But it comes with a price": Employment in social movement organizations', PhD, University of Edinburgh.

Emejulu, A. (2022) *Fugitive feminism*, London: Silver Press.

Emejulu, A. and Bassel, L. (2015) 'Minority women, austerity and activism', *Race & Class*, 57(2): 86–95.

Emejulu, A. and Bassel, L. (2020) 'The politics of exhaustion', *City*, 24(1–2): 400–406.

Emejulu, A. and Bassel, L. (2023) 'The lonely activist: On being haunted', *The Sociological Review*, 0(0). https://doi.org/10.1177/00380261231179298

Emejulu, A. and Sobande, F. (eds) (2019) *To exist is to resist: Black feminism in Europe*, London: Pluto.

Eschle, C. (2017) 'Beyond Greenham woman? Gender identities and anti-nuclear activism in peace camps', *International Feminist Journal of Politics*, 19(4): 471–90.

Eschle, C. (2018) 'Troubling stories of the end of occupy: Feminist narratives of betrayal at Occupy Glasgow', *Social Movement Studies*, 17(5): 524–40.

Eschle, C. (2023) 'Protest camps as "homeplace"? Social reproduction in and against neoliberal capitalism', in C. Eschle and A. Bartlett (eds) *Feminism and protest camps*, Bristol: Bristol University Press, pp 157–75.

Eschle, C. and Bartlett, A. (2023) 'Introduction: Feminism/protest camps', in C. Eschle and A. Bartlett (eds) *Feminism and protest camps*, Bristol: Bristol University Press, pp 1–14.

Esping-Andersen, G. (1990) *The three worlds of welfare capitalism*, Cambridge: Polity Press.

Evans, E. and Kenny, M. (2020) 'Doing politics differently? Applying a feminist institutionalist lens to the UK Women's Equality Party', *Politics & Gender*, 16(1): 26–47.

Everill, B. (2020) *Not made by slaves: Ethical capitalism in the age of abolition*, Cambridge, MA: Harvard University Press.

Eyerman, R. and Barretta, S. (1996) 'From the 30s to the 60s: The folk music revival in the United States', *Theory and Society*, 25(4): 501–43.

Faludi, S. (2013) 'Death of a revolutionary. Shulamith Firestone's radical feminism', *The New Yorker*. Available at: https://www.newyorker.com/news/news-desk/a-note-on-the-new-york-radical-feminists - last accessed 22 August 2023.

Fast, L. (2014) *Aid in danger: The promises and perils of humanitarianism*, Philadelphia, PA: University of Pennsylvania Press.

Featherstone, D. and Hogsberg, C. (eds) (2021) *The Red and the Black: The Russian revolution and the Black Atlantic*, Manchester: Manchester University Press.

Fechter, A-M. (2012) 'The personal and the professional: Aid workers' relationships and values in the development process', *Third World Quarterly*, 33(8): 1387–404.

Feigenbaum, A. (2010) 'Now I'm a happy dyke! Creating collective identity and queer community in Greenham Women's songs', *Journal of Popular Music Studies*, 22(4): 367–88.

Feigenbaum, A., Frenzel, F. and McCurdy, P. (2013) *Protest camps*, London: Zed Books.

Feischmidt, M. and Zakarias, I. (2019) 'Politics of care and compassion: Civic help for refugees and its political implications in Hungary: A mixedmethods approach', in M. Feischmidt, L. Pries and C. Cantat (eds) *Refugee protection and civil society in Europe*, Cham: Palgrave Macmillan, pp 59–99.

Feixa, C., Pereira, I. and Juris, J.S. (2009) 'Global citizenship and the 'new, new' social movements: Iberian connections', *Young*, 17(4): 421–42.

Fendrich, J.M. and Tarleau, A.T. (1973) 'Marching to a different drummer: Occupational and political correlates of former student activists', *Social Forces*, 52: 245–53.

Ferber, A.L. (2018) '"Are you willing to die for this work?" Public targeted online harassment in higher education: SWS Presidential Address', *Gender & Society*, 32(3): 301–320.

Ferree, M.M. (2012) *Varieties of feminism: German gender politics in global perspective*, Stanford, CA: Stanford University Press.

Ferree, M.M. (2020) 'The crisis of masculinity for gendered democracies: Before, during, and after Trump', *Sociological Forum*, 35(S1): 898–917.

Ferree, M.M., Gamson, W.A., Gerhards, J. and Rucht, D. (2002) *Shaping abortion discourse: Democracy and the public sphere in Germany and the United States*, Cambridge, UK and New York: Cambridge University Press.

Ferree, M.M. and Hess, B.B. (2004) *Controversy and coalition: The new feminist movement across four decades of change* (3rd edn), New York: Routledge.

Ferree, M.M. and Martin, P.Y. (1995) *Feminist organizations: Harvest of the new women's movement*, Philadelphia, PA: Temple University Press.

Ferree, M.M. and Miller, F.D. (1985) 'Mobilization and meaning: Toward an integration of social psychological and resource perspectives on social movements', *Sociological Inquiry*, 55(1): 38–61.

Ferree, M.M. and Roth, S. (1998) 'Gender, class, and the interaction between social movements: A strike of West Berlin day care workers', *Gender & Society*, 12(6): 626–48.

Fielker, L. (2020) '*How did Third Sector Organisations in the UK adapt their operational models and use of technology during the first wave of the COVID-19 Pandemic*', MSc Social Research Methods Masters Dissertation: University of Southampton.

Fielker, L. (2021) 'Data protection, the third sector and resources', paper presented at the Voluntary Sector and Volunteering Research Conference – New Researchers Stream, Aston University, Birmingham, UK, 6–7 September 2021.

Fietze, B. (1997) '1968 als Symbol der ersten globalen Generation [1968: Symbol for the first global generation]', *Berliner Journal für Soziologie*, 7(3): 365–376.

Fillieule, O. (2015) 'Demobilization and disengagement in a life course perspective', in D. della Porta and M. Diani (eds) *The Oxford handbook of social movements*, Oxford: Oxford University Press, pp 277–88.

Fillieule, O. and Broqua, C. (2020) 'Sexual and reproductive rights movements and counter-movements from an interactionist perspective', *Social Movement Studies*, 19(1): 1–20.

Fillieule, O. and Neveu, E. (2019) 'Activists' trajectories in space and time', in O. Fillieule and E. Neveu (eds) *'Activists forever? Long-term impacts of political activism*, Cambridge: Cambridge University Press.

Fisher, C. (1996) *The Rise of National Socialism and the working classes in Weimar Germany*, Providence/Oxford: Berghahn Books.

Fisher, D. (2006) *Activism Inc: How the outsourcing of grassroots campaigns is strangling progressive politics in America*, Stanford, CA: Stanford University Press.

Fisher, D.R. (2019) *American resistance: From the Women's March to the Blue Wave,* New York: Columbia University Press.

Flesher Fominaya, C. (2020) *Democracy reloaded: Inside Spain's political laboratory from 15-M to Podemos.* Oxford: Oxford University Press.

Fligstein, N. and McAdam, D. (2012) *A theory of fields*, Oxford: Oxford University Press.

Foran, J. (2005) *Taking power: On the origins of third world revolutions*, New York: Cambridge University Press.

Fox, R. (2014) *Doctors without Borders: Humanitarian quests, impossible dreams of Médecins Sans Frontières*, Baltimore, MD: Johns Hopkins University Press.

Frantz, C. (2005) *Karriere in NGOs: Politik als Beruf jenseits der Parteien*, Wiesbaden: VS Verlag.

Franz, C. and McClelland, D. (1994) 'Lives of women and men active in the social protests of the 1960s: A longitudinal study', *Journal of Personality and Social Psychology*, 66(1): 196–205.

Fraser, N. (2009) 'Feminism, capitalism and the cunning of history', *New Left Review*, 56(March–April): 97–117.

Freeman, J. (1972) 'The tyranny of structurelessness', *Berkeley Journal of Sociology*, 17(1972–3): 151–64.

Freeman, J. (1975) *The politics of women's liberation: A case study of an emerging social movement and its relation to the policy process*, New York: D. McKay Publications.

Freeman, J. (1995) 'From seed to harvest: Transformations of feminist organizations and scholarship', in M.M. Ferree and Y.M. Martin (eds) *Feminist organizations: Harvest of the new women's movement*, Philadelphia, PA: Temple University Press, pp 397–410.

Friends of the Earth (nd) 'The Big Ask: How you helped make climate change history'. Available at: https://friendsoftheearth.uk/climate/big-ask-how-you-helped-make-climate-change-history, last accessed 1 April 2023.

Fukuyama, F. (1989) 'The end of history?', *The National Interest*, 16: 3–18.

Fuentes, E. (2013) 'Political mothering: Latina and African American mothers in the struggle for educational justice', *Anthropology & Education*, 44(3): 304–19.

Funk, N. (2007) 'Fifteen years of East-West Women's dialogue', in E. Jonson and J. C. Robinson (eds) *Living gender after Communism*, Bloomington and Indianapolis, IN: Indiana University Press, pp 203–26.

Gal, S. and Kligman, G. (2000) *The politics of gender after socialism*, Princeton, NJ: Princeton University Press.

Gallagher, Z. (2023) 'Will the real eco-terrorists please stand up?', *Hastings Environmental Law Journal*, 29(1): 27–46.

Gamson, W. (1975) *The strategy of social protest*, Homewood, IL: Dorsey.

Gamson, W. (1990) *The strategy of social protest* (2nd edn), Belmont, CA: Wadsworth.

Gamson, W. and Meyer, D. (1996) 'Framing of political opportunity', in D. McAdam, J.D. McCarthy and M.N. Zald (eds) *Comparative perspectives on social movements: Political opportunities, mobilizing structures, and cultural framing*, Cambridge: Cambridge University Press, pp 275–290.

Ganesh, S. and McAllum, K. (2012) 'Volunteering and professionalization: Trends in tension?', *Management Communication Quarterly*, 26(1): 152–58.

Garland, J., Saunders, C., Olcese, C. and Tedesco, D. (2023) 'Anti-fracking campaigns in the United Kingdom: The influence of local opportunity structures on protest', *Social Movement Studies*, 22(2): 211–31.

Garrett, R.K. (2006) 'Protest in an information society: A review of literature on social movements and new ICTs', *Information, Communication & Society*, 9(2): 202–24.

Geels, F.W. (2019) 'Socio-technical transitions to sustainability: A review of criticisms and elaborations of the Multi-Level Perspective', *Current Opinion in Environmental Sustainability*, 39: 187–201.

Gelb, J. and Hart, V. (1999) 'Feminist politics in a hostile environment: Obstacles and opportunities', in M. Giugni, D. McAdam and C. Tilly (eds) *How social movements matter*, Minneapolis, MN: University of Minnesota Press, pp 149–81.

Gerhards, J. and Rucht, D. (1992) 'Mesomobilization: Organizing and framing in two protest campaigns in West Germany', *American Journal of Sociology*, 98(3): 555–96.

Gerson, J.M. and Peiss, K. (1985) 'Boundaries, negotiation, consciousness: Reconceptualizing gender relations', *Social Problems*, 32(4): 317–31.

Ghaziani, A. and Kretschmer, K. (2018) 'Infighting and insurrection', in D.A. Snow, S.A. Soule, H. Kriesi and H.J. McCammon (eds) *The Wiley Blackwell companion to social movements*, Chichester, UK/Hoboken, NJ: Wiley, pp 220–35. Available at: https://doi.org/10.1002/9781119168577.ch12

Ghodsee, K. (2004) 'Feminism-by-design: Emerging capitalism, cultural feminism, and women's nongovernmental organizations in post-socialist Eastern Europe', *Signs: Journal of Women in Culture and Society*, 29(3): 727–53.

Ghodsee, K. (2005) 'Russia and the newly independent states: Nongovernmental ogres: How feminist NGOs undermine women in postsocialist Eastern Europe', *International Journal of Not-For-Profit Law*, 8(3): 44–59.

Giddens, A. (1984) *The constitution of society: Outline of the theory of structuration*, Berkeley, CA: University of California Press.

Gillham, P.F. and Edwards, B. (2011) 'Legitimacy management, preservation of exchange relationships, and the dissolution of the mobilization for global justice coalition', *Social Problems*, 58(3): 433–60.

Gilio-Whitaker, D. (2019) *As long as the grass grows: The Indigenous fight for environmental justice from colonization to Long Rock*, Boston, MA: Beacon Press.

Gilroy, P. (1993) *The Black Atlantic: Modernity and double consciousness*, Cambridge, MA: Harvard University Press.

Giugni, M. (1999) 'How social movements matter: Past research, present problems, future developments', in M. Giugni, D. McAdam and C. Tilly (eds) *How social movements matter*, Minneapolis, MN: University of Minnesota Press, pp xii–xxxiii.

Glasius, M. and Ishkanian, A. (2014) 'Surreptitious symbiosis: Engagement between activists and NGOs', *VOLUNTAS: International Journal of Voluntary and Nonprofit Organizations*, 26(6): 2620–44.

Gleeson, J. (2016) '"(Not) working 9–5": The consequences of contemporary Australian-based online feminist campaigns as digital labour', *Media International Australia*, 16(1): 77–85.

Gnaerig, B. and MacCormack, C.F. (1999) 'The challenges of globalization: Save the Children', *Nonprofit and Voluntary Sector Quarterly*, 28(1_suppl): 140–6.

Go, J. (2013) 'For a postcolonial sociology', *Theory and Society*, 42(1): 25–55.

Gökarıksel, B. and Smith, S. (2017) 'Intersectional feminism beyond US flag hijab and pussy hats in Trump's America', *Gender, Place & Culture*, 24(5): 628–44.

Goodfellow, M. (2019) *Hostile environment: How immigrants became scapegoats*, London: Verso.

Goodwin, J. and Jasper J.M. (1999) 'Caught in a winding, snarling vine: The structural bias of political process theory', *Sociological Forum*, 14(1): 27–54.

Gopal, P. (2019) *Insurgent empire: Anticolonial resistance and British dissent*, London: Verso Books.

Gorringe, H. and Rosie, M. (2006). '"Pants to poverty"? Making poverty history, Edinburgh 2005', *Sociological Research Online*, 11(1): 130–44.

Gorski, P.C. (2015) 'Relieving burnout and the "martyr syndrome" among social justice education activists: The implications and effects of mindfulness', *The Urban Review*, 47(4): 696–716.

Gorski, P.C. (2019) 'Fighting racism, battling burnout: Causes of activist burnout in US racial justice activists', *Ethnic and Racial Studies*, 42(5): 667–87.

Gorski, P.C. and Chen, C. (2015) '"Frayed all over": The causes and consequences of activist burnout among social justice education activists', *Educational Studies*, 51(5): 385–405.

Gould, R.V. (2005) 'Historical sociology and collective action', in J. Adams, E.S. Clemens and A.S. Orloff (eds) *Remaking modernity: Politics, history, and sociology*, Durham, NC and London: Duke University Press, pp 286–99.

Graff, A. and Korolczuk, E. (2021) *Anti-gender politics in the populist moment*, London: Routledge.

Grant, M. (2018) 'The Windrush generation have been treated appallingly: EU Migrants May expect an even worse deal', LSE Brexit. Available at: https://eprints.lse.ac.uk/89426/, last accessed 18 July 2023.

Grasso, M.T., Farrall, S., Gray, E, Hay, C. and Jennings, W. (2019) 'Thatcher's children, Blair's babies, political socialization and trickle-down value change: An age, period and cohort analysis', *British Journal of Political Science*, 49(1): 17–36.

Green, B. (1981) *Countryside conservation*, London: Allen and Unwin.

Green, J. and Jennings, W. (2017) *The politics of competence: Parties, public opinion and voters*, Cambridge: Cambridge University Press.

Greenfield, E.A. and Marks, N.F. (2004) 'Formal volunteering as a protective factor for older adults' psychological well-being', *The Journals of Gerontology Series B: Psychological Sciences and Social Sciences*, 59(5): S258–64.

Greenpeace International (2020) *Annual report*, Available at: https://www.greenpeace.org/international/publication/43852/annual-report-2019/, last accessed 8 December 2020.

Griffen, G. (1995) *Feminist activism in the 1990s*, London: Taylor and Francis.

Griffiths, M. and O'Callaghan, T. (2002) *International relations: The key concepts*, Abingdon: Routledge.

Grønbjerg, K.A., McAvoy, E., and Habecker, K. (2021) 'Indiana non-profit organisations and COVID-19: Impact on services, finances and staffing', *Voluntary Sector Review*, 12(1): 123–27.

Gross, E. and Etzioni, A. (1985) *Organizations in society*, Hoboken, NJ: Prentice-Hall: Gueterbock.

Grosser, K. and McCarthy, L. (2019) 'Imagining new feminist futures: How feminist social movements contest the neoliberalization of feminism in an increasingly corporate-dominated world', *Gender, Work & Organization*, 26(8): 1100–16.

Habermas, J. (1989) *The structural transformation of the public sphere. An inquiry into a category of bourgeois society*, Cambridge, MA: MIT Press.

Hager, M.A. and Brudney, J.L. (2008) 'Management capacity and retention of volunteers', in L. Troth (ed) *Challenges in volunteer management*, Charlotte, NC: Information Age Publishing, pp 9–27.

Hager, M.A. and Brudney, J.L. (2011) 'Problems recruiting volunteers: Nature versus nurture', *Nonprofit Management and Leadership*, 22(2): 137–57.

Haines, H.H. (1984) 'Black radicalism and the funding of civil rights: 1957–1970', *Social Problems*, 32(1): 31–43.

Hall, C., Draper, N., McClelland, K., Donington, K. and Lang, R. (2014) *Legacies of British slave-ownership: Colonial slavery and the formation of Victorian Britain*, Cambridge: Cambridge University Press.

Halford, S. and Savage, M. (2010) 'Reconceptualizing digital social inequality', *Information, Communication & Society*, 13(7): 937–55.

Hallgrimsdottir, H.K. and Benoit, C. (2007) 'From wage slaves to wage workers: Cultural opportunity structures and the evolution of the wage demands of the Knights of Labor and the American Federation of Labor, 1880–1900', *Social Forces*, 85(3): 1393–411.

Hamilton, M.C., Anderson, D. Broaddus, M. and Young, K. (2006) 'Gender stereotyping and under-representation of female characters in 200 popular children's picture books: A twenty-first century update', *Sex Roles*, 55(11): 757–65.

Hampele Ulrich, A. (2000) *Der Unabhängige Frauenverband. Ein frauenpolitisches Experiment im deutschen Vereinigungsprozess*, Berlin: Berliner Debatte.

Hannan, M.T. and Freeman, J. (1977) *Organizational ecology*, Cambridge, MA: Harvard University Press.

Hannan, M.T. and Freeman, J. (1989) 'Setting the record straight on organizational ecology: Rebuttal to Young', *American Journal of Sociology*, 95(2): 425–39.

Harflett, N. (2014) *For ever, for everyone? Patterns of volunteering: the case of the National Trust*. University of Southampton, School of Social Sciences, Doctoral Thesis.

Harflett, N. (2015) '"Bringing them with personal interests": The role of cultural capital in explaining who volunteers', *Voluntary Sector Review*, 6(1): 3–19.

Harlow, S. and Harp, D. (2012) 'Collective action on the web: A cross-cultural study of social networking sites and online and offline activism in the United States and Latin America', *Information, Communication & Society*, 15(2): 196–216.

Harman, S. (2016) 'The Bill and Melinda Gates Foundation and legitimacy in global health governance', *Global Governance: A Review of Multilateralism and International Organizations*, 22(3): 349–68.

Harrow, J. and Mole, V. (2005) '"I want to move once I have got things straight": Voluntary sector chief executives' career accounts', *Nonprofit Management and Leadership*, 16(1): 79–100.

Harris, B. and Bridgen, P. (2007) 'Introduction: The "mixed economy of welfare" and the historiography of welfare provision', in B. Harris and P. Bridgen (eds) *Charity and mutual aid in Europe and North America since 1800*, Abingdon and New York: Routledge, pp 1–18.

Harrison, E. (2013) 'Beyond the looking glass? "Aidland" reconsidered', *Critique of Anthropology*, 33(3): 263–79.

Hartley, L. (2019) 'From the local to the colonial: Toynbee Hall and the politics of poverty', *Victorian Studies*, 61(2): 278–88.

Harvey, D. (1999) 'Time-space compression and the postmodern condition', In M. Waters (ed) *Modernity: critical concepts*, London: Routledge, pp 98–118.

Haskell, T. (1985a) 'Capitalism and the origins of the humanitarian sensibility, Part 1', *American Historical Review*, 90(2): 339–61.

Haskell, T. (1985b) 'Capitalism and the origins of the humanitarian sensibility, Part 2', *American Historical Review*, 90(3): 547–66.

Hayes, G. and MacGregor, S. (2023) 'Taking political time: Thinking past the emergency timescapes of the new climate movements', *South Atlantic Quarterly*, 122(1): 181–91.

Havelkova, H. (1997) 'Transitory and persistent differences: Feminism East and West', in J.W. Scott, C. Kaplan and D. Keates (eds) *Transitions, environments, translations: feminism in international politics*, London and New York: Routledge, pp 56–62.

Heater, D. and Berridge, G.R. (1998) *Introduction to international relations*, Contemporary Political Studies Series, Basingstoke: Palgrave Macmillan.

Hendricks, C.M., Ercan, S.A. and Boswell, J. (2020) *Mending democracy: Democratic repair in disconnected times*, Oxford: Oxford University Press.

Hensby, A., Sibthorpe, J. and Driver, S. (2012) 'Resisting the "protest business": Bureaucracy, post-bureaucracy and active membership in social movement organizations', *Organization*, 19(6): 809–23.

Hildreth, A. (1994) 'The importance of purposes in "purposive" groups: Incentives and participation in the sanctuary movement', *American Journal of Political Science*, 38(2): 447–63.

Hilhorst, D. (2002) 'Being good at doing good? Quality and accountability of humanitarian NGOs', *Disasters*, 26(3): 193–212.

Hilhorst, D. (2005) 'Dead or alive? Ten years of the Code of Conduct for disaster relief', *Humanitarian Practice Network Humanitarian Exchange*, 29: 1–52.

Hilhorst, D. and Schmiemann, N. (2002) 'Humanitarian principles and organisational culture: Everyday practice in Médecins Sans Frontières-Holland', *Development in Practice*, 12(3–4): 490–500.

Hills, J., Le Grant, J. and Piachaud, D. (2002) *Understanding social exclusion*, Oxford: Oxford University Press.

Himmelfarb, G. (1990) 'Victorian philanthropy: The case of Toynbee Hall', *American Scholar*, 59(3): 373–84.

Hines, S. (2010) 'Introduction', in S. Hines and T. Sanger (eds) *Transgender identities: Towards a social analysis of gender diversity*, London: Routledge, 1–22.

Hochschild, A.R. (2016) *Strangers in their own land: Anger and mourning on the American right*, New York: The New Press.

Hodkinson, S. and Chatterton, P. (2006) 'Autonomy in the city? Reflections on the social centres movement in the UK', *City*, 10(3): 305–15.

Hoggett, P., Mayo. M. and Miller, C. (2009) *The dilemmas of development work: Ethical challenges in regeneration*, Bristol: Policy Press.

Hooghe, M. (2008) 'The political opportunity structure for civil society organisations in a multilevel context: Social movement organisations and the European Union', in W.A. Maloney and J.W. Van Deth (eds) *Civil society and governance in Europe: From national to international linkages*, Cheltenham: Edward Elgar, pp 71–90.

Hopgood, S. (2006) *Keepers of the flame: Understanding Amnesty International*, Ithaca, NY: Cornell University Press.

Horn, G.R. (2017) '1968: A social movement sui generis', in Berger, S., and Nehring, H. (eds) *The history of social movements in global perspective*, London: Palgrave Macmillan, pp 515–41.

Hoskins, B., Leonard, P. and Wilde, R. (2020) 'How effective is youth volunteering as an employment strategy? A mixed methods study of England', *Sociology*, 54(4): 763–81.

Houldey, G. (2022). *The vulnerable humanitarian: Ending burnout culture in the aid sector*, London: Routledge.

House, J. (1995) Americans' Changing Lives: Waves 1-11, University of Michigan, Institute for Social Research. Survey Research Centre. https://doi.org/10.3886/ICPSR04690.v9, last accessed 24 July 2023.

Howes, M. (1997) 'NGOs and the development of local institutions', *Journal of Modern African Studies*, 35: 17–35.

Human Dignity Trust (2023) Map of countries that criminalise LGBT People. Available at: https://www.humandignitytrust.org/lgbt-the-law/map-of-criminalisation/, last accessed 1 April 2023.

Hutter, S., Kriesi, H. and Lorenzini, J. (2018) 'Social movements in interaction with political parties', in D.A. Snow, S.A. Soule, H.P. Kriesi and H. McCammon (eds) *The Wiley Blackwell companion to social movements*, Chichester, UK/Hoboken, NJ: Wiley, pp 322–37.

INCITE! (eds) (2017) *The revolution will not be funded: Beyond the non-profit industrial complex*, Durham, NC and London: Duke University Press.

James, C.L.R. (2001) [1938] *The Black Jacobins: Toussaint L'Ouverture and the San Domingo Revolution*, London: Penguin UK.

Jasper, J.M. (1999) *The art of moral protest: Culture, biography and creativity in social movements*, Chicago, IL: University of Chicago Press.

Jasper, J.M. (2011) 'Emotion and social movements: Twenty years of theory and research', *Annual Review of Sociology*, 37: 285–303.

Jasper, J.M. (2013) 'Strategy', in D.A. Snow, D. della Porta, B. Klandermans and D. McAdam (eds), *The Wiley-Blackwell encyclopedia of social and political movements*: Volume III Pe-Z, Chichester: Blackwell Publishing, pp 1262–267.

Jasper, J. M. (2015) 'Playing the game', in J. Jasper and J.W. Duyvendak (eds) *Players and arenas: The interactive dynamics of protest*, Amsterdam: Amsterdam University Press, pp 9–32.

Jasper, J.M. (2021) 'Linking arenas: structuring concepts in the study of politics and protest', *Social Movement Studies*, 20(2): 243–57.

Jasper, J. and Duyvendak, J.W. (eds) (2015) *Players and arenas: The interactive dynamics of protest*, Amsterdam: Amsterdam University Press.

Jasper, J.M. and Poulsen, J.D. (1995) 'Recruiting strangers and friends: Moral shocks and social networks in animal rights and anti-nuclear protests', *Social Problems*, 42(4): 493–512.

Joas, H. (1990) 'The democratization of differentiation: On the creativity of collective action', in J. Alexander and P. Sztompka (eds) *Rethinking progress*, Boston, MA: Unwin Hyman, pp 182–201.

Johnston, H. (2015) 'Theory, method and mechanisms of framing: Reflections on the Syrian Civil War and Palestinian Intifada', *Civil Wars*, 17(2): 266–89.

Jordan, J. and Maloney, W. (1997) *The protest business*, Manchester: Manchester University Press.

Jordan, G. and Maloney, W.A. (1998) 'Manipulating membership: Supply-side influences on group size', *British Journal of Political Science*, 28(2): 389–409.

Joseph-Salisbury, R. and Connelly, L. (2021) *Anti-racist scholar-activism*, Manchester: Manchester University Press.

Joseph–Salisbury, R., Connelly, L. and Wangari-Jones, P. (2021) '"The UK is not innocent": Black Lives Matter, policing and abolition in the UK', *Equality, Diversity and Inclusion: An International Journal*, 40(1): 21–8.

Jupp, E. (2022) *Care, crisis and activism: The politics of everyday life*, Bristol: Bristol University Press.

Juris, J.S. (2012) 'Reflections on #Occupy Everywhere: Social media, public space, and emerging logics of aggregation', *American Ethnologist*, 39(2): 259–79.

Juska, A. and Edwards, B. (2005) 'Refusing the Trojan pig: The US-Poland coalition against corporate pork production', in J. Bandy and J. Smith (eds) *Coalitions Across Borders: Transnational Protest and the Neoliberal Order*, Lanham, MD: Rowman and Littlefield, pp 189–208.

Kakucs, N. and Pető, A. (2008) 'The impact of EU accession on gender equality in Hungary', in S. Roth (ed) *Gender politics in the expanding European Union: Mobilization, inclusion, exclusion*, Oxford and New York: Berghahn Books, pp 174–91.

Kalleberg, A.L. (2011) *Good jobs, bad jobs: The rise of polarized and precarious employment systems in the United States: 1970s–2000s*, New York: Russell Sage Foundation.

Kamat, S. (2004) 'The privatization of public interest: Theorizing NGO discourse in a neoliberal era', *Review of International Political Economy*, 11(1): 155–76.

Kantola, J. (2010) 'Shifting institutional and ideational terrains: The impact of Europeanisation and neoliberalism on women's policy agencies', *Policy & Politics*, 38(3): 353–68.

Kantola, J. and Squires, J. (2012) 'From state feminism to market feminism?', *International Political Science Review*, 33(4): 382–400.

Kaplan, L. (1997) *The story of Jane: The legendary underground feminist abortion service*, Chicago, IL: University of Chicago Press.

Karpf, D. (2016) *Analytic activism: Digital listening and the new political strategy*, Oxford: Oxford University Press.

Katzenstein, M.F. (1990) 'Feminism within American institutions: Unobtrusive mobilization in the 1980s', *Signs*, 16(1): 27–54.

Katzenstein, M.F. (1998). *Faithful and fearless: Moving feminist protest inside the church and military*, Princeton, NJ: Princeton University Press.

Kaufer, R. and Albrecht, A. (2022) 'Aufstand der letzten Generation', Aktionsformen und Legitimationsargumente. *Forschungjournal Soziale Bewegungen*. Available at: https://forschungsjournal.de/fjsb/wp-content/uploads/fjsb-plus_2022-4_albrecht_kaufer.pdf, last accessed 18 July 2023

Kavada, A. (2023) 'Project democracy in protest camps: Caring, the commons and feminist democratic theory', in C. Eschle and A. Bartlett (eds) *Feminism and protest camps*, Bristol: Bristol University Press, pp 176–94.

Keck, M. and Sikkink, K. (1998) *Activists beyond borders: Advocacy networks in international politics*, Ithaca, NY: Cornell University Press.

Kendall, J. and Knapp. M. (2000) 'Measuring the performance of voluntary organizations', *Public Management*, 2(1): 105–33.

Kerrow, K., Mordan, R., Pini, V., Raymond, J., Bartlett, A. and Eschle, C. (2023) 'Greenham women everywhere: A feminist experiment in recreating experience and shaping collective memory', in C. Eschle and A. Bartlett (eds) *Feminism and protest camps*, Bristol: Bristol University Press, pp 273–93.

Khan, T., Dickson, K. and Sondarjee, M. (eds) (2023) *White saviorism in international development: Theories, practices and lived experiences*, Wakefield, Quebec: Daraja Press.

Khondker, H.H. (2011) 'Role of the new media in the Arab Spring', *Globalizations*, 8(5): 675–79.

Kilby, P. (2006) 'Accountability for empowerment: Dilemmas facing non-governmental organizations', *World Development*, 34(6): 951–63.

Kirton, G. and Healy, G. (2012) '"Lift as you rise": Union women's leadership talk', *Human Relations*, 65(8): 979–99.

Klandermans, B. (2012) 'Between rituals and riots: The dynamics of street demonstrations', *Mobilization: An International Quarterly*, 17(3): 233–34.

Knutsen, W. (2016) 'The non-profit sector is dead: Long live the non-profit sector!', *VOLUNTAS: The International Journal of Voluntary and Non-profit Organizations*, 27: 1562–84.

Koddenbrock, K. (2016). 'More than morals: Making sense of the rise of humanitarian aid organisations', in V.M. Heins, K. Koddenbrock and C. Unrau (eds) *Humanitarianism and challenges of cooperation*, London: Routledge, pp 84–96.

Kollman, K. and Waites, M. (2009) 'The global politics of lesbian, gay, bisexual and transgender human rights: An introduction', *Contemporary Politics*, 15(1): 1–17.

Koopmans, R. (1999) 'Political. Opportunity. Structure. Some splitting to balance the lumping', *Sociological Forum*, 14(1): 93–105.

Korff, V.P., Balbo, N., Mills, M., Heyse, L. and Wittek, R. (2015) 'The impact of humanitarian context conditions and individual characteristics on aid worker retention', *Disasters*, 39(3): 522–45.

Korpi, W. (1978) *The working class in welfare capitalism: Work, unions and politics in Sweden*, London: Routledge & Kegan Paul.

Kothari, U. (2006) 'From colonialism to development: Continuities and divergences', *Journal of Commonwealth and Comparative Politics*, 44(1): 118–36.

Kováts, E. (2018) 'Questioning consensuses: Right-wing populism, anti-populism, and the threat of 'gender ideology', *Sociological Research Online*, 23(2). Available at: http://journals.sagepub.com/doi/full/10.1177/13607 80418764735 last accessed 18 July 2023.

Krause, M. (2014) *The good project: Humanitarian relief NGOs and the fragmentation of reason*, Chicago, IL: University of Chicago Press.

Kriesi, H., Koopmans, R., Duyvendak, J.W. and Giugin, M. (1995) *New social movements in Western Europe: A comparative analysis*, Minneapolis, MN: University of Minnesota Press.

Krinksy, J. and Reese, E. (2006) 'Forging and sustaining labor-community coalitions: The workfare justice movement in three cities', *Sociological Forum*, 21(4): 623–58.

Kubik, J. (1994) *The power of symbols against the symbols of power: The rise of Solidarity and the fall of state socialism in Poland*, University Park, PA: Pennsylvania State University Press.

Kuhar, R. and Paternotte, D. (2017) *Anti-gender campaigns in Europe: Mobilizing against equality*, London: Rowman & Littlefield.

Kyle, R.G., Milligan, C., Kearns, R.A., Larner, W., Fyfe, N.R. and Bondi, L. (2011) 'The tertiary turn. Locating "the academy" in autobiographical accounts of activism in Manchester, UK and Auckland, Aotearoa New Zealand', *Antipode*, 43(4): 1181–214.

Lang, S. (2013) *NGOs, civil society and the public sphere*, Cambridge: Cambridge University Press.

Larana, E., Johnston, H. and Gusfield, J.R. (1994) *New social movements: From ideology to identity*, Philadelphia, PA: Temple University Press.

Lavalette, M. (2011) *Radical social work today: Social work at the crossroads*, Bristol: Policy Press.

Leach, D.K. (2013) 'Culture and the structure of tyrannylessness', *The Sociological Quarterly*, 54(2): 181–91.

Leete, L. (2001) 'Whither the non-profit wage differential? Estimates from the 1990s Census', *Journal of Labour Economics*, 19(1): 136–70.

Leete, L. (2006) 'Work in the non-profit sector', in W.W. Powell and R. Steinberg. (eds) *The non profit sector: A research handbook*, New Haven, CT: Yale University Press, pp 159–79.

Lewis, D. (2008) 'Using life histories in social policy research: The case of third sector/public sector boundary crossing', *Journal of Social Policy*, 37(04): 559–78.

Lewis, D. (2015) 'Contesting parallel worlds: Time to abandon the distinction between the "international" and "domestic" contexts of third sector scholarship?', *VOLUNTAS: International Journal of Voluntary and Nonprofit Organizations*, 26(5): 2084–103.

Li, Y., Savage, M. and Warde, A. (2008) 'Social mobility and social capital in contemporary Britain', *The British Journal of Sociology*, 59(3): 391–411.

Lindsay, J. (2023) 'Male default: When images of neutral characters from picture books are not so neutral', *Gender Issues*, 40(1): 119–43.

Littler, J. (2023) *Left feminisms: Conversations on the personal and political*, London: Lawrence Wishart.

Lloyd, H.R. (2018) 'The myth of giving as good: Charitable giving represented as an end in itself', *Discourse, Context & Media*, 25: 122–31.

Lofland, J. (1996) *Social movement organizations. Guide to research on insurgent realities*, New York: Aldine de Gryter.

Lonetree, A. (2021) 'Decolonizing museums, memorials, and monuments', *The Public Historian*, 43(4): 21–7.

Loquercio, D., Hammersley, M. and Emmens, B. (2006) 'Understanding and addressing staff turnover in humanitarian agencies', Network Paper. H.P. Network. London Overseas Development Institute. 55.

Lorenzoni, I. and Benson, D. (2014) 'Radical institutional change in environmental governance: Explaining the origins of the UK Climate Change Act 2008 through discursive and streams perspectives', *Global Environmental Change*, 29: 10–21.

Lovenduski, J. and Randall, V. (1993) *Contemporary feminist politics*, Oxford: Oxford University Press.

Lowe, P. (1983) 'Values and institutions in the history of British nature conservation', in A. Warren and F.B. Goldsmith (eds) *Conservation in perspective*, Chichester: Wiley, pp 329–52.

Luetchford, M. and Burns, P. (2003) *Waging the War on Want: 50 years of campaigning against world poverty: An authorised history*, London: War on Want.

Luna, Z.T. (2010) 'Marching toward reproductive justice: Coalitional (re) framing of the March for Women's Lives', *Sociological Inquiry*, 80(4): 554–78.

Lynch, S. and Smith, K. (2010) 'The dilemma of judging unpaid workers', *Personnel Review*, 39(1): 80–95.

Lyons, K., Hanley, J., Wearing, S. and Neil, J. (2012) 'Gap year volunteer tourism: Myths of global citizenship?', *Annals of Tourism Research*, 39(1): 361–78.

MacSheoin, T. (2016) 'The world according to social movement journals: A preliminary mapping.' *Interface: A Journal for and about Social Movements*, 8(1): 181–204.

Mackay, F. (2015) 'Political not generational: Getting real about contemporary UK radical feminism', *Social Movement Studies*, 14(4): 427–42.

Mackay, F. (2021) *Female masculinities and the gender wars: The politics of sex*, London: Bloomsbury.

Mackay, F. (2023) '"You can't kill the spirit" (but you can try): Gendered contestations and contradictions at Menwith Hill Women's Peace Camp', in C. Eschle and A. Bartlett (eds) *Feminism and protest camps*, Bristol: Bristol University Press, pp 61–77.

Maier, F. and Meyer, M. (2016) 'Nonprofit organizations becoming business-like: A systematic review', *Nonprofit and Voluntary Sector Quarterly*, 45(1): 64–86.

Maier, S.L. (2008) 'Are rape crisis centers feminist organizations?', *Feminist Criminology*, 3(2): 82–100.

Malm, A. (2021) *How to blow up a pipeline*, London: Verso.

Mansbach, R. and Rafferty, K.L. (2008) *Introduction to global politics*, New York: Routledge.

Mannheim, K. (1952) 'The problem of generations', in P. Kecskemeti (ed) *Essays on the sociology of knowledge*, New York: Oxford University Press, pp 276–322.

Mansbridge, J. (1986) *Why we lost the ERA*, Chicago, IL: University of Chicago Press.

Mansbridge, J. (1995) 'What is the feminist movement?', in M.M. Ferree and Y.M. Martin (eds) *Feminist organizations: Harvest of the new women's movement*, Philadelphia, PA: Temple University Press, pp 27–34.

Marsh, A. (1974) 'Explorations in unorthodox political behaviour: A scale to measure "protest potential"', *European Journal of Political Research*, 2(2): 107–29.

Martens, K. (2005) *NGOs and the United Nations: Institutionalization, professionalization and adaptation*, Cham: Springer.

Martin de Almagro, M. (2018) 'Hybrid clubs: A feminist approach to peacebuilding in the Democratic Republic of Congo', *Journal of Intervention and Statebuilding*, 12(3): 319–34.

Martin, M. and Islar, M. (2021) 'The "end of the world" vs the "end of the month": Understanding social resistance to sustainability transition agendas, a lesson from the Yellow Vests in France', *Sustainability Science*, 16: 601–14.

Martin, P.Y. (1990) 'Rethinking feminist organizations', *Gender and Society*, 4(2): 182–206.

Marx, J.D. (1999) 'Motivational characteristics associated with health and human service volunteers', *Administration in Social Work*, 23(1): 51–66.

Masilela, T.C., Foster, R. and Chetty, M. (2013) 'The eHealth strategy for South Africa 2012–2016: How far are we?', *South African Health Review*, 2013/14(1): 15–24.

Maslach, C. and Gomes M.E. (2006) 'Overcoming burnout', in R.M. MacNair (ed) *Working for peace: A handbook of practical psychology and other tools*, Atascadero: Impact Publishers, pp 43–49.

Matthews, N. (1995) 'Feminist clashes with the state: Tactical choices by state-funded rape crisis centers', in M.M. Ferree and P.Y. Martin (eds) *Feminist organizations: Harvest of the new women's movement*, Philadelphia, PA: Temple University Press, pp 291–305.

Maxwell, D. (2005) 'Decolonialization', in N. Etherington (ed) *Missions and empire*, Oxford: Oxford University Press, pp 285–306.

Mayer, B., Brown, P. and Morello-Frosch, R. (2010) 'Labor-environmental coalition formation: Framing and the right to know', *Sociological Forum*, 25(4): 746–68.

Mayer, M. (2020) 'What does it mean to be a (radical) urban scholar-activist, or activist scholar, today?', *City*, 24(1–2): 35–51.

McAdam, D. (1982) *Political process and the development of black insurgency, 1930–1970*, Chicago, IL: University of Chicago Press.

McAdam, D. (1986) 'Recruitment to high risk activism', *American Journal of Sociology*, 92: 64–90.

McAdam, D. (1989) 'The biographical consequences of activism', *American Sociological Review*, 48: 735–54.

McAdam, D. (1999) 'The biographical impact of activism', in M. Giugni, D. McAdam and C. Tilly (eds) *How social movements matter*, Minneapolis, MN: University of Minnesota Press, pp 119–48.

McAdam, D. and Sewell, W.H. (2001) 'It's about time: Temporality in the study of social movements and revolutions', *Silence and Voice in the Study of Contentious Politics*, 1: 89–125.

McAdam, D., Tarrow, S. and Tilly, C. (2001) *Dynamics of contention*, Cambridge: Cambridge University Press.

McCall, L. and Orloff, A.S. (2017) 'The multidimensional politics of inequality: Taking stock of identity politics in the US Presidential Election of 2016', *The British Journal of Sociology*, 68: S34–S56.

McCammon, H.J. and Campbell, K.E. (2002) 'Allies on the road to victory: Coalition formation between the suffragists and the woman's Christian temperance union', *Mobilization: An International Quarterly*, 7: 231–51.

McCarthy, J.D. and Zald, M.N. (1973) 'The trend of social movements in America: Professionalization and resource mobilization', in J.D. McCarthy and M.N. Zald (eds) *Social movements in an organizational society: Collected essays*, New Brunswick: Transaction Books, pp 337–89.

McCarthy, J.D. and Zald, M.N. (1977) 'Resource mobilization and social movements: A partial theory', *American Journal of Sociology*, 82(6): 1212–41.

McDonald, C. and Charlesworth, S. (2011) 'Outsourcing and the Austrialian nonprofit sector', in I. Cunningham and P. James (eds) *Voluntary organisations and public service delivery*, Abingdon: Routledge.

McGoey, L. (2012) 'Philanthrocapitalism and its critics', *Poetics*, 40(2): 185–99.

McMullin, C. (2021) 'Migrant integration services and coping with the digital divide: challenges and opportunities of the COVID-19 pandemic', *Voluntary Sector Review*, 12(1): 129–36.

McPherson, M. (1983) 'An ecology of affiliation', *American Sociology Review*, 48(4): 519–32.

McVeigh, R. and Estep, K. (2019). *The politics of losing: Trump, the Klan and the mainstreaming of resentment*, New York: Columbia University Press.

Mead, G.H. (1977) *On social psychology* [Selected papers, edited and with a revised introduction by Anselm Strauss], Chicago, IL: University of Chicago Press.

Meadows, D.H. (1972) *Club of Rome's project on the predicament of mankind: The limits to growth*, New York: New American Library.

Meer, N. (2022) *The cruel optimism of racial justice*, Bristol: Policy Press.

Meier, S. and Stutzer, A. (2008) 'Is volunteering rewarding in itself?', *Economica*, 75(297): 39–59.

Melucci, A. (1989) *Nomads of the present: Social movements and individual needs in contemporary society*, Philadelphia, PA: Temple University Press.

Melucci, A. (1996) *Challenging codes*, Cambridge: Cambridge University Press.

Memou, A. (2017) 'Art, activism and the Tate', *Third Text*, 31(5–6): 619–631.

Mercea, D. (2012) 'Digital prefigurative participation: The entwinement of online communication and offline participation in protest events', *New Media & Society*, 14(1): 153–69.

Meyer, D.S. (1999) 'How the cold war was really won: The effects of the anti-nuclear movements of the 1980s', in M. Giugni, D. McAdam and C. Tilly (eds) *How social movements matter*, Minneapolis, MN: University of Minnesota Press, pp 182–203.

Meyer, D.S. (2003) 'Political opportunity and nested institutions', *Social Movement Studies*, 2(2): 17–35.

Meyer, D. (2021) *How social movements sometimes matter*, Cambridge: Polity Press.

Meyer, D.S. and Gamson, W. (1995) 'The challenge of cultural elites: celebrities and social movements', *Sociological Inquiry*, 65(2): 181–206.

Meyer, D.S. and Minkoff, D.C. (2004) 'Conceptualizing political opportunity', *Social Forces*, 82(4): 1457–92.

Meyer, D.S. and Staggenborg, S. (2012) 'Thinking about strategy', in G.M. Maney, V. Kutz-Flamenbaum, D.A. Rohlinger and J. Goodwin (eds) *Strategies for social change*, Minneapolis, MN: University of Minnesota Press, pp 3–22.

Meyer, D.S. and Tarrow, S. (eds) (2018) *The resistance: The dawn of the anti-Trump opposition movement*, Oxford: Oxford University Press.

Meyer, D.S. and Whittier, N. (1994) 'Social movement spillover', *Social Problems*, 41(2): 277–98.

Michels, R. ([1911] 1962) *Political parties: A sociological study of the oligarchical tendencies of modern democracy*, New York: Free Press.

Miethe, I. (1999) *Frauen in der DDR-Opposition: Lebensgeschichtliche und kollektivgeschichtliche Verläufe in einer Frauenfriedensgruppe*, Opladen: Leske + Budrich.

Miethe, I. (2000) 'Changes in spaces of political activism: Transforming East Germany', in R. Breckner, D. Kalekin-Fischman and I. Miethe (eds) *Biographies and the division of Europe: Experiences, action, and change on the 'Eastern Side*, Opladen: Leske & Budrich, pp 315–34.

Miethe, I. and Roth, S. (2005) 'Zum Verhältnis von Biographie- und Bewegungsforschung', in B. Voelter, B. Dausien, H. Lutz and G. Rosenthal, (eds) *Biographieforschung im Diskurs*, Wiesbaden: VS Verlag, pp 103–18.

Milbourne, L. (2013) *Voluntary sector in transition: Hard times or new opportunities*, Bristol: Policy Press.

Milkman, R. (1990) 'Gender and trade unionism in historical perspective', in L.A. Tilly and P. Gurin (eds) *Women, politics, and change*, New York: Russell Sage Foundation, pp 87–107.

Milkman, R. (2017) 'A new political generation: Millennials and the post-2008 wave of protest', *American Sociological Review*, 82(1): 1–31.

Mirvis, P.H. (1992) 'The quality of employment in the nonprofit sector: An update on employee attitudes in nonprofits versus business and government', *Nonprofit Management and Leadership*, 3(1): 23–41.

Mitchell, K. and Pallister-Wilkens, P. (eds) (2023) *The Routledge international handbook of critical philanthropy and humanitarianism*, London: Routledge.

Mitlin, D., Kickey, S. and Bebbington, A. (2007) 'Reclaiming development? NGOs and the challenge of alternatives', *World Development*, 35(10): 1699–720.

Mohan, J. (2011) 'Mapping the Big Society: Perspectives from the third sector research centre', *Third Sector Research Centre*, Working Paper 62. Available at: https://www.birmingham.ac.uk/documents/college-social-sciences/social-policy/tsrc/working-papers/working-paper-62.pdf, last accessed 28 August 2023.

Molloy, S. (2009) 'Strategic management of not-for-profit organizations', in D.J. Newlands, and M.J. Hopper (eds) *The global business handbook: The eight dimensions of international management*, Farnham: Gower Publishing Limited, pp 337–49.

Moody, J. (2021) 'Off the pedestal: The fall of Edward Colston', *Public History Review*, 28: 1–5.

Moore, K. (1999) 'Political protest and institutional change: The anti-Vietnam war movement and American science', in M. Giugni, D. McAdam and C. Tilly (eds) *How social movements matter*, Minneapolis, MN: University of Minnesota Press, pp 97–118.

Moore, S.E.H. (2008) *Ribbon culture*, Basingstoke: Palgrave MacMillan.

Morgen, S. (1995) '"It was the best of times, it was the worst of times": emotional discourse in the work cultures of feminist health clinics', in M.M. Ferree and P.Y. Martin (eds) *Feminist organizations: Harvest of the new women's movement*, Philadelphia, PA: Temple University Press, pp 137–44.

Morgensen, S.L. (2011) 'The biopolitics of settler colonialism: Right here, right now', *Settler Colonial Studies*, 1(1): 52–76.

Morris, A.D. (1984) *Origins of the civil rights movement: Black communities organising for change*, New York: The Free Press.

Morris, A.D. (1992) 'Political consciousness and collective action', in A. Morris and P. Oliver (eds) *Frontiers of social movement theory*, New Haven, CT: Yale University Press, pp 351–373.

Morris, A.D. and Staggenborg, S. (2007) 'Leadership in social movements', in D.A. Snow, S.A. Soule and H. Kriesi (eds) *The Blackwell companion to social movements*, Oxford: Blackwell, pp 171–96.

Mouffe, C. (2014) 'Democratic politics and conflict: An agonistic approach', in M. Lakitsch (ed) *Political power reconsidered: State power and civic activism between legitimacy and violence*, Münster: LIT Verlag, pp 17–29.

Mudde, C. and Kaltwasser, C.R. (2017) *Populism: A very short introduction*, New York: Oxford University Press.

Musick, M. and Wilson, J. (2008) *Volunteers: A social profile*, Bloomington, IN: Indiana University Press.

Nakabuye, H.F., Nirere, S. and Oladosu, A.T. (2020) 'The Fridays For Future movement in Uganda and Nigeria', in C. Henry, J Rockström and N. Stern (eds) *Standing up for a sustainable world*, Cheltenham: Edward Elgar, pp 212–18.

Naples, N. (1998) *Community activism and feminist politics. Organizing across race, class, and gender*, New York: Routledge.

Narayan, J. (2017) 'The wages of whiteness in the absence of wages: Racial capitalism, reactionary intercommunalism and the rise of Trumpism', *Third World Quarterly*, 38(11): 2482–2500.

National Trust (2020) Addressing our histories of colonialism and historic slavery. Available at: https://www.nationaltrust.org.uk/features/address ing-the-histories-of-slavery-and-colonialism-at-the-national-trust, last accessed 1 April 2023.

NCVO (2014) 'UK Civil Society Almanac 2014'. Available at: https://ncvo-app-wagtail-mediaa721a567-uwkfinin077j.s3.amazonaws.com/documents/ncvo-uk-civil-society-almanac-2014-small.pdf, last accessed 28 August 2023.

NCVO (2015) 'UK Civil Society Almanac 2015'. Available at: https://ncvo-app-wagtail-mediaa721a567-uwkfinin077j.s3.amazonaws.com/documents/ncvo-uk-civil-society-almanac-2015.pdf, last accessed 28 August 2023.

NCVO (2016) 'UK Civil Society Almanac 2016'. Available at: https://ncvo-app-wagtail-mediaa721a567-uwkfinin077j.s3.amazonaws.com/documents/ncvo-uk-civil-society-almanac-2016.pdf, last accessed 28 August 2023.

Nepstad, S.E. and Smith, C.S. (1999) 'Rethinking recruitment to high-risk activism: The case of Nicaragua Exchange', *Mobilization: An International Quarterly*, 4: 40–51.

Nepstad, S.E. (2004) 'Persistent resistance: Commitment and community in the Plowshares movement', *Social Problems*, 51(1): 43–60.

Nesbit, R. (2017) 'Advocacy recruits: Demographic predictors of volunteering for advocacy-related organizations;', *VOLUNTAS: International Journal of Voluntary and Nonprofit Organizations*, 28: 958–87.

Newman, J. (2012) *Working the spaces of power: Activism, neoliberalism and gendered labour*, London: Bloomsbury Academic.

Nielsen, H.P. (2013) 'Joint purpose? Intersectionality in the hands of anti-racist and gender equality activists in Europe', *Ethnicities*, 13(3): 276–94.

Njoku, A., Ahmed, Y. and Bolaji, B. (2021) 'Police brutality against Blacks in the United States and ensuing protests: Implications for social distancing and Black health during COVID-19', *Journal of Human Behavior in the Social Environment*, 31(1–4): 262–70.

Nulman, E. (2016) *Climate change and social movements: Civil society and the development of national climate change policy*, Basingstoke: Palgrave Macmillan.

Oberschall, A. (1973) *Social conflict and social movements*, Englewood Cliffs, NJ: Prentice-Hall.

Obi, C.I. (1997) 'Globalisation and local resistance: The case of the Ogoni versus Shell', *New Political Economy*, 2(1): 137–48.

Olcese, C. (2014) 'Social media and political activism: Breaking the offline and online division', in E. Avril and J.N. Neem (eds) *Democracy, participation and contestation*, London: Routledge, pp 270–84.

Oliver, C. (1991) 'Network relations and loss of organizational autonomy', *Human Relations*, 44(9): 943–61.

Olson, M. (1965) *The logic of collective action*, Cambridge, MA: Harvard University Press.

Onyx, J. and Maclean, M. (1996) 'Careers in the third sector', *Nonprofit Management and Leadership*, 6(4): 331–45.

Ospina, S. and Foldy, E. (2010) 'Building bridges from the margins: The work of leadership in social change organisations', *The Leadership Quarterly*, 21: 292–307.

Ostrander, S.A. (2010) 'Social change organizations', in H. Anheier and S. Toepler, (eds) *International encyclopedia of civil Society*, Cham: Springer Science, pp 1396–1400.

Osunyomi, B.D. and Grobbelaar, S.S. (2015) 'Integrating eHealth in HIV/AIDS intervention programmes in South Africa: Original research', *South African Journal of Information Management*, (17)1: 1–10.

Otu, A., Ahinkorah, B.O., Ameyaw, E.K., Seidu, A.A. and Yaya, S. (2020) 'One country, two crises: What Covid-19 reveals about health inequalities among BAME communities in the United Kingdom and the sustainability of its health system?', *International Journal for Equity in Health*, 19, 189. https://doi.org/10.1186/s12939-020-01307-z, last accessed 28 August 2023.

Owen, C. (2020) 'Participatory authoritarianism: From bureaucratic transformation to civic participation in Russia and China', *Review of International Studies*, 46(4): 415–34.

Palacious-Valladares, I. (2016) 'Protest communities and activist enthusiasm: Student occupations in contemporary Argentina, Chile and Uruguay', *Interface: A Journal on Social Movements*, 8(2): 150–70.

Pardo, M. (1995) 'Doing it for the kids: Mexican American community activists, border feminists?', in M.M. Ferree and P.Y. Martin (eds) *Feminist organizations: Harvest of the New Women's movement*, Philadelphia, PA: Temple University Press, pp 356–71.

Parekh, B. (1997) *Gandhi: A very short introduction*, Oxford: Oxford University Press.

Parker, C.S. (2021) 'Status threat: Moving the right further to the right?', *Daedalus*, 150(2): 56–75.

Parry, J., Brookfield, K. and Bolton, V. (2021) 'The long arm of the household: Gendered struggles in combining paid work with social and civil participation over the lifecourse', *Gender, Work & Organization*, 28(1): 361–78.

Passmore, K. (2017) 'Fascism as a social movement in a transnational context', in S. Berger and H. Nehring (eds) *The History of social movements in global perspective*, London: Palgrave MacMillan, pp 579–617.

Passy, F. and Giugni, M. (2000) 'Life-spheres, networks, and sustained participation in social movements: A phenomenological approach to political commitment', *Sociological Forum*, 15(1): 117–44.

Pavan, E. (2014) 'Embedding digital communications within collective action networks: A multidimensional network approach', *Mobilization: An International Quarterly*, 19(4): 441–55.

Pavan, E. (2020) '"We are family." The conflict between conservative movements and feminists', *Contemporary Italian Politics*, 12(2): 243–57.

Paxton, P., Hughes, M.M. and Green, J.L. (2006) 'The international women's movement and women's political representation, 1893–2003', *American Sociological Review*, 71(6): 898–920.

Payne, J.L. (2006) 'Did the United States create democracy in Germany?', *The Independent Review*, 11(2): 209–21.

Pearce, R., Erikainen, S. and Vincent, B. (2020) 'TERF wars: An introduction', *The Sociological Review*, 68(4): 677–98.

Perelli-Harris, B., Berrington, A., Sánchez Gassen, N., Galezewska, P. and Holland, J. A. (2017) 'The rise in divorce and cohabitation: Is there a link?', *Population and Development Review*, 43(2): 303–29.

Pescosolida, B.A., Grauerhoz, E. and Milkie, M.A. (1997) 'Culture and conflict: The portrayal of Blacks in US children's picture books through the mid- and late-twentieth Century', *American Sociological Review*, 62(3): 443–64.

Peterson, A. and Reiter, H. (2016) *The ritual of May Day in Western Europe: Past, present and future*, London: Routledge.

Petersen, M.J. (2012) 'Trajectories of transnational Muslim NGOs', *Development in Practice*, 22(5–6): 763–78.

Petras, J. (1999) 'NGOs in the service of imperialism', *Journal of Contemporary Asia*, 29(4): 429–40.

Pettinicchio, D. (2012) 'Institutional activism: Reconsidering the insider/outsider dichotomy', *Sociology Compass*, 6(6): 499–510.

Pickard, S. (2019) 'Young environmental activists are doing it themselves', *Political Insight*, 10(4): 4–7.

Pickerill, J. and Krinsky, J. (2012) 'Why does Occupy matter?', *Social Movement Studies*, 11(3–4): 279–87.

Pieck, S.K. (2013) 'Transnational activist networks: Mobilization between emotion and bureaucracy', *Social Movement Studies*, 12(2): 121–37.

Pilkington, H. (2016) *Loud and proud. Passion and politics in the English Defence League*, Manchester: Manchester University Press.

Pinquart, M. and Sorensen, S. (2001) 'Influences on loneliness in older adults: A meta-analysis', *Basic and Applied Social Psychology*, 23(4): 245–66.

Piven, F.F. and Cloward, R.A. (1979) [1977] *Poor people's movements: Why the succeed, how they fail*, New York: Vintage.

Plagnol, A.C. and Huppert, F.A. (2010) 'Happy to help? Exploring the factors associated with variations in rates of volunteering across Europe', *Social Indicators Research*, 97(2): 157–76.

Poguntke, T. (2002) 'Green parties in national governments: From protest to acquiescence?', *Environmental Politics*, 11(1): 133–45.

Polletta, F. (1999) '"Free spaces" in collective action', *Theory and Society*, 28(1): 1–38.

Polletta, F. (2006) 'Awkward movements: An introduction', *Mobilization: An International Quarterly*, 11(4): 475–78.

Potorti, M. (2017) '"Feeding the revolution": The Black Panther Party, hunger, and community survival', *Journal of African American Studies*, 21: 85–110.

Powell, C. (2001) Remarks to the National Foreign Policy Conference for Leaders of Nongovernmental Organizations. US Department of State. Available at: https://2001-2009.state.gov/secretary/former/powell/remarks/2001/5762.htm, last accessed 1 April 2023.

Pugh, M. (2000) *Women and the women's movement in Britain*, Basingstoke: MacMillan Press.

Quaranta, M. (2014) 'The "normalisation" of the protester: Changes in political action in Italy (1981–2009)', *South European Society and Politics*, 19(1): 25–50.

Quaranta, M. (2017) 'Protest and contentious action: Contentious politics and political violence, political behaviour', *Oxford Research Encyclopedias*. DOI: 10.1093/acrefore/9780190228637.013.225.

Raeburn, N.C. (2004) *Changing corporate America from the inside out: lesbian and lay workplace rights*, Minneapolis, MN: University of Minnesota Press.

Ramanth, R. (2009) 'Limits to institutional isomorphism: Examining internal processes in NGO-government interactions', *Nonprofit and Voluntary Sector Quarterly*, 38(1): 51–76.

Ray, R. (1999) *Fields of protest: Women's movements in India*, Minneapolis, MN: University of Minnesota Press.

Reese, E., Kerkenrath, M., Chase-Dunn, C., Giem, R., Guttierrez, E., Kim, L. and Petit, C. (2006) 'Alliances and Divisions within "the Movement of Movements": Survey Findings from the 2005 World Social Forum', paper presented at the 2006 annual meeting of the American Sociological Association, Montreal.

Rees, J., Mullins, D. and Bovaird, T. (2012) 'Third sector partnerships for public service delivery: An evidence review', Working Paper 88, Birmingham: Third Sector Research Centre, Available at: https://www. birmingham.ac.uk/documents/college-social-sciences/social-policy/tsrc/ working-papers/working-paper-88.pdf, last accessed 24 July 2023.

Reinelt, C. (1995) 'Moving onto the terrain of the state. The battered women's movement and the politics of engagement', in M.M. Ferree and P.Y. Martin (eds) *Feminist organizations: Harvest of the new women's movement*, Philadelphia, PA: Temple University Press, pp 84–104.

Redfield, P. (2008) 'Doctors without Borders and the moral economy of pharmaceuticals', in A. Bullard (ed) *Human rights in crisis*, Aldershot: Ashgate Press, pp 129–44.

Redfield, P. and Bornstein, E. (2011) 'An introduction to the anthropology of humanitarianism', in E. Bornstein and P. Redfield (eds) *The forces of compassion: Humanitarianism between ethics and politics*, Santa Fe, NM: School of Advanced Research, pp 3–30.

Reger, Jo. (2007) 'New dimensions in the study of social movement leadership', *American Behavioral Scientist*, 50(10): 1303–5.

Reich, R. (2016) 'Repugnant to the whole idea of democracy? On the role of foundations in democratic societies', *PS: Political Science & Politics*, 49(3): 466–72.

Reich, R. (2018) *Just giving: Why philanthropy is failing democracy and how it can do better*, Princeton, NJ: Princeton University Press.

Richardson, F. (2006) 'Meeting the demand for skilled and experienced humanitarian workers', *Development in Practice*, 16(3): 334–41.

Rickard, K. (2010) 'Memorializing the White Rose resistance group in post-war Germany', in B. Niven and C. Paver (eds) *Memorialization in Germany since 1945*, Basingstoke: Palgrave Macmillan, pp 157–67.

Richey, L.A. and Brockington, D. (2020) 'Celebrity humanitarianism: Using tropes of engagement to understand north/south relations', *Perspectives on Politics*, 18(1): 43–59.

Rieff, D. (2002) *A bed for the night: Humanitarianism in crisis*, New York: Simon and Schuster.

Roberts, J.M. and Devine, F. (2004) 'Some everyday experiences of voluntarism: Social capital, pleasure, and the contingency of participation', *Social Politics: International Studies in Gender, State & Society*, 11(2): 280–96.

Roberts, K. (2007) 'Work-life balance – the sources of the contemporary problem and the probable outcomes: A review and interpretation of the evidence', *Employee Relations*, 29(4): 334–51.

Robinson, N. (2000) 'The politics of the car: The limits of actor-centred models of agenda setting', in B. Seel, M. Paterson. and B. Doherty (eds) *Direct action in British environmentalism*, London: Routledge, pp 199–218.

Robnett, B. (1996) 'African-American women in the Civil Rights movement, 1954–1965: Gender, leadership, and micromobilization', *American Journal of Sociology*, 101(6): 1661–93.

Rodgers, K. (2010) '"Anger is why we're all here": Mobilizing and managing emotions in a professional activist organization', *Social Movement Studies*, 9(3): 273–91.

Rojas, F. and King, B.G. (2018) 'How social movements interact with organizations and fields', in D.A. Snow, S.A. Soule, H. Kriesi and H.J. McCammon (eds) *The Wiley Blackwell companion to social movements*, Chichester, UK/Hoboken, NJ: Wiley, pp 203–19 https://doi.org/10.1002/9781119168577.ch11.

Rootes, C. (2003) *Environmental movements in Western Europe*, Cambridge: Cambridge University Press.

Rootes, C. (2006) 'Facing south? British environmental movement organisations and the challenge of globalisation', *Environmental Politics*, 15(5): 768–86.

Rootes. C. and Saunders, C. (2005) 'Social movements in Britain since the 1960s', DEMOS Working Paper No. 1/2005.

Rootes, C. and Saunders, C. (2007) 'The global justice movement in Great Britain', in D. della Porta (ed) *The global justice movement: Cross-national and transnational perspectives*, Boulder, CO: Paradigm Publishers, pp 128–56.

Rose, F. (2000) *Coalitions across the class divide: Lessons from the labor, peace and environmental movements*, Ithaca, NY: Cornell University Press.

Roseneil, S. (1995) *Disarming patriarchy: Feminism and political action at Greenham*, Buckingham: Open University Press.

Roseneil, S. (2000) *Common women, uncommon practices: The queer feminisms of Greenham*, London and New York: Cassell.

Roseneil, S., Halsaa, B. and Sümer, S. (eds) (2012) *Remaking citizenship in multicultural Europe*, Basingstoke: Palgrave Macmillan.

Rossdale, C. (2019) *Resisting militarism. Direct action and the politics of subversion*, Edinburgh: Edinburgh University Press.

Rosso, B.D., Dekas, K.H. and Wrzesniewski, A. (2010) 'On the meaning of work: A theoretical integration and review', *Research in Organizational Behavior*, 30: 91–127.

Roth, B. (2010) '"Organizing one's own" as good politics: Second wave feminists and the meaning of coalition', in N. Van Dyke and H.J. McCammon (eds) *Strategic alliances, coalition building and social movements*, Minneapolis, MN: University of Minnesota Press, pp 99–118.

Roth, B. (2017) *The life and death of ACT UP/LA: Anti-AIDS activism in Los Angeles from the 1980s to the 2000s*, Cambridge: Cambridge University Press.

Roth, B. (2018) 'Learning from the Tea Party: The US Indivisible Movement as countermovement in the era of Trump', *Sociological Research Online*, first published 21 March 2018. http://journals.sagepub.com/doi/full/10.1177/1360780418764733

Roth, S. (2000) 'Developing working-class feminism: A biographical approach to social movement participation', in S. Stryker, T.J. Owens and R.W. White (eds) *Self, identity and social movements*, Minneapolis, MN: University of Minnesota Press, pp 300–23.

Roth, S. (2003) *Building movement bridges: The coalition of Labor union women*, Westport, CT: Praeger.

Roth, S. (2007) 'Sisterhood and solidarity? Women's organizations in the expanded European Union', *Social Politics*, 14(4): 460–87.

Roth, S. (2008) *Gender politics in the expanding European Union. Mobilization, inclusion, exclusion*, Oxford and New York: Berghahn Books.

Roth, S. (2012) 'Professionalisation trends and inequality: Experiences and practices in aid relationships', *Third World Quarterly*, 33(8): 1459–74.

Roth, S. (2015) *The paradoxes of aid work: Passionate professionals*, London: Routledge.

Roth, S. (2016) 'Professionalisation and precariousness: Perspectives on the sustainability of activism in everyday life', *Interface: A Journal for and about Social Movements*, 8(2): 29–58.

Roth, S. (2017) 'Varieties of European women's movements', in A. Basu (ed) *Women's movements in the global era: The power of local feminisms*, Boulder, CO: Westview Press, pp 185–212.

Roth, S. (2018) 'Introduction to rapid response contemporary counter-movements in the age of Brexit and Trump', *Sociological Research Online*, 23(2): 496–506.

Roth, S. (2021) 'Intersectionality and coalitions in social movement research: A survey and outlook', *Sociology Compass*, 15(7): e12885.

Roth, S. and Saunders, C. (2019) 'Gender differences in political participation: Comparing street demonstrators in Sweden and the United Kingdom', *Sociology*, 53(3): 571–89.

Roth, S. and Saunders, C. (2020) 'Do gender regimes matter? Gender differences in involvement in anti-austerity protests: A comparison of Spain, Sweden and the United Kingdom', *Social Movement Studies*, 19(3): 303–324.

Roth, S. and Saunders, C. (2022) 'Micro-level effects of political participation', in M, Giugni and M. Grasso (eds) *The Oxford handbook of political participation*, Oxford: Oxford University Press, pp 797–814.

Roth, S. and Saunders, C. (forthcoming) 'Studying social change makers: Self-transformation processes and the biographical consequences of participation in social change organizations', in B. Bunk and S. Maurer (eds) *Protest und Selbstverhältnisse*, Weinheim and Munich: Beltz/Juventa.

Roth, S., Purkayastha, B. and Denskus, T. (eds) (2024) Handbook of *humanitarianism and inequality*, Cheltenham: Edward Elgar.

Roth, S., Saunders, C. and Fox, S. (2023) Persistence, Precarity and Professionalisation – a Critical Evaluation of 'Biographical Availability' and 'Biographical Consequences'. Presentation at the Annual Conference of the British Sociological Association, Manchester, University of Manchester, 14 April 2023.

Roth, S., Saunders, C. and Olcese, C. (2014) 'Occupy as a free space: Mobilization processes and outcomes', *Sociological Research Online*, 19(1). Available at: http://www.socresonline.org.uk/19/1/1.html last accessed 22 August 2023.

Rowell, A. (2017) *Green backlash: Global subversion of the environment movement*. Abingdon: Routledge.

Rucht, D. (1999) 'The impact of environmental movements in Western societies', in M. Giugni, D. McAdam and C. Tilly (eds) *How social movements matter*, Minneapolis, MN: University of Minnesota Press, pp 204–24.

Rucht, D. (2013) 'Schlüsselfiguren statt Führer: Zur (Selbst-)Steuerung sozialer Bewegungen', *Forschungsjournal Soziale Bewegungen*, 26(4): 32–43.

Rupp, L.J. (1994) 'Constructing internationalism: The case of transnational women's organizations, 1888–1945', *The American Historical Review*, 99(5): 1571–1600.

Rutherford, A.C. (2015) 'Rising wages in the expanding UK nonprofit sector from 1997 to 2007', *Nonprofit and Voluntary Sector Quarterly*, 44(1): 123–45.

Ryan, S. and Cole, K.R. (2009) 'From advocate to activist? Mapping the experiences of mothers of children on the autism spectrum', *Journal of Applied Research in Intellectual Disabilities*, 22(1): 43–53.

Ryfmann, P. (2011) 'Crises of maturity and transformation in French NGOs', in K. Blanchet and B. Martin (eds) *Many reasons to intervene: French and British Approaches to Humanitarian Action*, London: Hurst, pp 9–25.

Salamon, L.M. and Anheier, H.K. (1996) *The emerging nonprofit sector: An overview* (Vol. 1), Manchester: Manchester University Press.

Salamon, L.M. and Sokolowski, S.W. (2016) 'Beyond nonprofits: Re-conceptualizing the third sector', *VOLUNTAS: International Journal of Voluntary and Nonprofit Organizations*, 27(4): 1515–45.

Salamon, L.M., Sokolowski, W.S. and Haddock, M.A. (2011) 'Measuring the economic value of volunteer work globally: Concepts, estimates, and a roadmap to the future', *Annals of Public and Cooperative Economics*, 82(3): 217–52.

Salt, C. and Layzell, J. (1985) *Here we go! Women's memories of the 1984/5 Miners Strike*, London Political Committee: Co-operative Retail Services Limited.

Santos, B.D.S. (2013) *The rise of the global left: The World Social Forum and beyond*, London: Zed Books Ltd.

Saunders, C. (2008a) 'The Stop Climate Chaos Coalition: Climate change as a development issue', *Third World Quarterly*, 29(8): 1509–26.

Saunders, C. (2008b) 'Double edged swords: Collective identity and solidarity in the environment movement', *British Journal of Sociology*, 59(2): 227–53.

Saunders, C. (2009a) 'It's not just structural: Social movements are not homogenous responses to structural features, but networks shaped by organisational strategies and status', *Sociological Research Online*, 14(1): 4, http://www.socresonline.org.uk/14/1/4.html.

Saunders, C. (2009b) 'Organizational size and democratic practices: Can large be beautiful?', in D. della Porta (ed) *Democracy in Social Movements*, Basingstoke: Palgrave Macmillan, pp 150–70.

Saunders, C. (2009c) 'International aid and development', in N. Crowson, M. Hilton and J. McKay (eds) *NGOs in contemporary Britain*, London, Palgrave, pp 38–58.

Saunders, C. (2012) 'Reformism and radicalism in the Climate Camp in Britain: Benign coexistence, tensions and prospects for bridging', *Environmental Politics*, 21(5): 829–46.

Saunders, C. (2013) *Environmental networks and social movement theory*, London: Bloomsbury Academic.

Saunders, C. (2014) 'Insiders, thresholders and outsiders in West European global justice networks: Network positions and modes of coordination', *European Political Science Review*, 2(6): 167–89.

Saunders, C. and Andretta. M. (2009) 'NGOs: The effect of organizational formality, voice and influence on mobilization and participation in the global justice movement', in D. Della Porta (ed) *Another Europe is possible: Conceptions and practices of democracy in the European social forum*, London: Europe, pp 148–168.

Saunders, C. and Papadimitriou, T. (2012) 'Dropping the debt? British anti-debt campaigns and international development policy', in P. Utting, M. Piant and A. Ellersiek (eds) *Global justice activism and policy reform in Europe: Understanding when change happens*, Abbingdon: Routledge: pp 213–34.

Saunders, C. and Price, S. (2009) 'One person's eu-topia, another's hell: Climate camp as a heterotopia', *Environmental Politics*, 18(1): 117–22.

Saunders, C. and Roth, S. (2019) 'NGOs and social movement theory', in T. Davies (ed) *Routledge handbook of NGOs and international relations*, London: Routledge, pp 138–51.

Saunders, C., Doherty, B. and Hayes, G. (2020) 'A new climate movement?: Extinction Rebellion's activists in profile', Centre for Understanding Sustainable Prosperity Working Paper 25. Available at: https://cusp.ac.uk/themes/p/xr-study/, last accessed 20 July 2023.

Saunders, C., Grasso, M. and Hedges, C. (2018) 'Attention to climate change in British newspapers in three attention cycles (1997–2017)', *Geoforum*, 94: 94–102.

Saunders, C., Roth, S. and Olcese, C. (2016) 'Are we really "all in it together?": Anti-austerity protests in Britain', in M. Guigni and M. Grasso (eds) *Austerity and protest: Popular contention in times of economic crisis*, Abingdon: Routledge, pp 171–91.

Saunders, C., Grasso, M., Olcese, C., Rainsford, E. and Rootes, C. (2012) 'Explaining differential protest participation: Novices, returners, repeaters, and stalwarts', *Mobilization: An International Quarterly*, 17(3): 263–80.

Save the Children (2019) *Annual report*. Available at: https://www.savethechildren.org.uk/content/dam/gb/reports/annual-report-2019-save-the-children.pdf, last accessed 19 July 2023.

Sbicca, J., Hale, J. and Roeser, K. (2019) 'Collaborative concession in food movement networks: The uneven relations of resource mobilization', *Sustainability*, 11(10): 2881. Available at https://www.mdpi.com/2071-1050/11/10/2881, last accessed 28 August 2023.

Schade, J. (2007) 'Neutralität humanitärer NGOs in Kriegs- und Nachkriegssituationen. Ein frommer Wunsch?', in A. Klein and S. Roth (eds) *NGOs im Spannungsfeld von Krisenprävention und Sicherheitspolitik*, Wiesbaden: VS Verlag, pp 179–89.

Schelsky, H. (1974) 'The new strategy of revolution: The 'long march' through the institutions', *Modern Age*, 18(4): 345–55.

Schierup, C.U., Ålund, A. and Neergaard, A. (2018) '"Race" and the upsurge of antagonistic popular movements in Sweden', *Ethnic and Racial Studies*, 41(10): 1837–54.

Schierup, C.U. and Ålund, A. (2011) 'The end of Swedish exceptionalism? Citizenship, neoliberalism and the politics of exclusion', *Race & Class*, 53(1): 45–64.

Schradie, J. (2018) 'The digital activism gap: How class and cost shape online activism', *Social Problems*, 65(1): 51–74.

Schradie, J. (2019) *The revolution that wasn't: How digital activism favors conservatives*, Cambridge, MA: Harvard University Press.

Schumacher, E.F. (1973) *Small is beautiful: Economics as if people mattered*, London: Blond and Briggs.

Scrinzi, F. (2015) 'Righteous patriots, corrupted elites, undeserving poors: The construction of multiple social boundaries in the National Front', *Etnografia e Ricerca Qualitativa*, (1): 55–74.

Seibert, K., Williamson, A. and Moran, M. (2021) 'Voluntary sector peak bodies during the COVID-19 crisis: a case study of Philanthropy Australia', *Voluntary Sector Review*, 12(1): 143–54.

Shah, B.V. (2011) *Laotian daughters: Working toward community, belonging and environmental justice*, Philadelphia, PA: Temple University Press.

Shahin, S., Nakahara, J. and Sánchez, M. (2021) 'Black Lives Matter goes global: Connective action meets cultural hybridity in Brazil, India, and Japan', *New Media & Society*: 14614448211057106.

Shaiko, R.G. (1993) 'Greenpeace USA: Something old, new, borrowed', *The ANNALS of the American Academy of Political and Social Science*, 528(1): 88–100.

Shepherd, L.J. (2011) 'Sex, security and superhero(in)es: From 1325 to 1820 and beyond', *International Feminist Journal of Politics*, 13(4): 504–21.

Shepherd, L.J. (2018) 'Activism in/and the academy: Reflections on "social engagement"', *Journal of Narrative Politics*, 5(1): 45–56.

Sherkat, D E. and Blocker, T.J. (1997) 'Explaining the political and personal consequences of protest', *Social Forces*, 75(3): 1049–70.

Shirky, C. (2008) *Here comes everybody: The power of organizing without organizations*, London: Penguin.

Shriver, T.E., Miller, A.C. and Cable, S. (2003) 'Women's work: Women's involvement in the gulf war illness movement', *The Sociological Quarterly*, 44(4): 639–58.

Shutt, C. (2012) 'A moral economy? Social interpretations of money in aidland', *Third World Quarterly*, 33(8): 1527–43.

Siklova, J. (1997) 'McDonalds, Terminator's, Coca Cola ads and feminism? Imports from the West', in A. Renne (ed) *Ana's land. Sisterhood in Eastern Europe*, Boulder, CO: Westview Press, pp 76–81.

Simeant, J. (2005) 'What is going global? The Internationalization of French NGOs "without borders"', *Review of International Political Economy*, 12(5): 851–83.

Sisk, S.M., and Duncan, L.G. (2006) 'Parenting in the peaceful home. Working for peace', in MacNair, R. (ed) *A Handbook of Practical Psychology and Other Tool*, Atascadero: Impact Publishers, pp 55–62.

Siurua, H. (2006) 'Nature above people: Rolston and "fortress" conservation in the South', *Ethics and the Environment*, 11(1): 71–96.

Skeggs, B. and Yuill, S. (2016) 'Capital experimentation with person/a formation: how Facebook's monetization refigures the relationship between property, personhood and protest', *Information, Communication & Society*, 19(3): 380–96.

Skocpol, T. (1979) *States and social revolutions: A comparative analysis of France, Russia, and China*, New York: Cambridge University Press.

Skocpol, T. (1992) *Protecting soldiers and mothers. The political origins of social policy in the United States*, Cambridge: Cambridge University Press.

Skocpol, T. and Williamson, V. (2012) *The Tea Party and the remaking of Republican Conservativism*, New York: Oxford University Press.

Slate, N. (2012) *Black power beyond borders*, New York: Palgrave Macmillan.

Slate, N. (2015) 'From colored cosmopolitanism to human rights: A historical overview of the transnational Black freedom struggle', *Journal of Civil and Human Rights*, 1(1): 3–24.

Slavova, K. (2006) 'Looking at western feminisms through the double lens of Eastern Europe and the Third World', in J. Lukic, J. Regulska and Z. Darja (eds) *Women and citizenship in Central and Eastern Europe*, Aldershot, UK and Burlington, VT: Ashgate, pp 245–64.

Slim, H. (2011) 'Establishment radicals: An historical overview of British NGOs', in K. Blanchet and B. Martin, (eds) *Many reasons to intervene: French and British approaches to humanitarian action*, London: Hurst, pp 27–39.

Sloat, A. (2005) 'The rebirth of civil society: The growth of women's NGOs in Central and Eastern Europe', *European Journal of Women's Studies*, 12(4): 437–52.

Smith, C. (1991) *The emergence of liberation theology: Radical religion and social movement theory*, Chicago, IL: University of Chicago Press.

Smith, J. (2015) 'Social movements and the multilateral arena', in D. della Porta and M. Diani (eds) *The Oxford handbook of social movements*, Oxford: Oxford University Press, pp 607–18.

Smith, J., and Bandy, J. (2005) 'Introduction: Cooperation and conflict in transnational protest', in J. Bandy and J. Smith (eds) *Coalitions across borders: Transnational protest and the neoliberal order*, Lanham, MD: Rowman and Littlefield, pp 1–18.

Sommers-Flanagan, R., and Sommers-Flanagan, J. (2006) 'Parenting for peace. Working for peace', in MacNair, R. M. (ed) *A Handbook of practical psychology and other Tools*, Atascadero: Impact Publishers, pp 220–229.

Spalter-Roth, R. and Schreiber, R. (1995) 'Outsider issues and insider tactics. Strategic tensions in the women's policy network in the 1980s', in M. Ferree, and P. Y. Martin (eds) *Feminist organisations: Harvest of the new women's movement*, Philadelphia, PA: Temple University Press, pp 105–27.

Stafford, E.R. and Polonsky, M.J. (2000) 'Environmental NGO-business collaboration and strategic bridging: A case analysis of the Greenpeace-Foron alliance', *Business Strategy and the Environment*, 9(2): 122–35.

Staggenborg, S. (1986) 'Coalition work in the pro-choice movement: Organizational and environmental opportunities and obstacles', *Social Problems*, 33: 374–90.

Staggenborg, S. (1988) 'The consequences of professionalization and formalization in the pro-choice movement', *American Sociological Review*, 53(4): 585–605.

Staggenborg, S. (1989) 'Stability and innovation in the women's movement: A comparison of two movement organizations', *Social Problems*, 36(1): 75–92.

Staggenborg, S. (1995) 'Can feminist organizations be effective?, in M.M. Ferree and P.Y. Martin (eds) *Feminist organizations: Harvest of the new women's movement*, Philadelphia, PA: Temple University Press, pp 339–55.

Staggenborg, S. (2020) *Grassroots environmentalism*, Cambridge: Cambridge University Press.

Stamatov, P. (2010) 'Activist religion, empire and the emergence of modern long-distance advocacy networks', *American Sociological Review*, 75(4): 607–28.

Stamps, D.L. (2020) 'B(l)ack by popular demand: an analysis of positive black male characters in television and audiences' community cultural wealth', *Journal of Communication Inquiry*, 45(2): 97–118.

Standing, G. (2011) *The Precariat: The new dangerous class*, London and New York: Bloomsbury.

Steinmetz, G. (ed) (2013) *Sociology and empire: The imperial entanglements of a discipline*, Durham, NC and London: Duke University Press.

Stephenson, H. and Zeldes, K. (2008) '"Write a chapter and change the world" How the Women's Health Book Collective transformed women's health then – and now', *American Journal of Public Health*, 98: 1741–5.

Stetson, D.M. and Mazur, A. (1995) *Comparative state feminism*, London: Sage.

Stoker, L. and Jennings, M.K. (1995) 'Life-cycle transitions and political participation: The case of marriage', *American Political Science Review*, 89(2): 421–33.

Strolovitch, D.Z. (2007) *Affirmative advocacy: Race, class, and gender in interest group politics*, Chicago, IL: University of Chicago Press.

Stroup, S.S. (2012) *Borders among activists: International NGOs, in the United States, Britain, and France*, Ithaca, NY: Cornell University Press.

Stroup, S.S. (2019) 'NGOs' interactions with states', in T. Davies (ed) *Routledge Handbook of NGOs and international relations*, London: Routledge, pp 32–45.

Stroup, S.S. and Wong, W.H. (2017) *The authority trap: Strategic choices of international NGOs*, Ithaca, NY and London: Cornell.

Sugarman, B. (1967) 'Involvement in youth culture, academic achievement and conformity in school: An empirical study of London schoolboys', *The British Journal of Sociology*, 18: 151–317.

Sultana, F. (2022) 'The unbearable heaviness of climate coloniality', *Political Geography* 99. Available at: https://doi.org/10.1016/j.polgeo.2022.102638

Swidler, A. and Watkins, S.C. (2017) *A fraught embrace: The romance and reality of AIDS altruism in Africa*, Princeton, NJ: Princeton University Press.

Tang, F. (2006) 'What resources are needed for volunteerism? A life course perspective', *Journal of Applied Gerontology*, 25(5): 375–90.

Tarrow, S.G. (1994) *Power in movement*, Cambridge: Cambridge University Press.

Tarrow, S.G. (1998) *Power in movement* (2nd edn), Cambridge: Cambridge University Press.

Tarrow, S.G. (2005) *The new transnational activism*, Cambridge: Cambridge University Press.

Tarrow, S.G. (2021) *Movements and parties: Critical connections in American political development*, Cambridge: Cambridge University Press.

Tarrow, S.G. (2022) *Power in movement: Social movements and contentious politics updated and revised third edition*, Cambridge: Cambridge University Press.

Tavarez, J. (2022) '"There's people out there doing more than me ...": Activist burnout among bisexual college students within LGBTQ campus spaces', *Journal of Diversity in Higher Education*. Advance online publication. https://doi.org/10.1037/dhe0000442.

Taylor, R. (2004) 'Extending conceptual boundaries: Work, voluntary work and employment', *Work, Employment & Society*, 18(1): 29–49.

Taylor, R. (2005) 'Rethinking voluntary work', *The Sociological Review*, 53(2): 117–35.

Taylor, R. (2015) 'Volunteering and unpaid work', in S. Edgell, H. Gottfried and E. Granter (eds) *The SAGE handbook of the sociology of work and employment*, London: Sage, pp 485–501.

Taylor, R. and Roth, S. (2019) 'Exploring meaningful work in the third sector', in R. Yeoman, C. Bailey, A. Maddern and M. Thompson (eds) *The Oxford handbook of meaningful work*, Oxford: Oxford University Press, pp 257–73.

Taylor, V. (1989) 'Social movement continuity: The women's movement in abeyance', *American Sociological Review*, 54(5): 761–75.

Taylor, V. and Leitz, L. (2010) 'From infanticide to activism: The transformation of emotions and identity in self-help movements', in J.C. Banaszak-Holl, S.R. Levitsky and M.N. Zald (eds) *Social movements and the transformation of American health care*, Oxford: Oxford University Press, pp 266–83.

Taylor, V. and Raeburn, N.C. (1995) 'Identity politics as high risk activism: Career consequences for lesbian, gay and bisexual sociologists', *Social Problems*, 42(2): 252–73.

Taylor, V. and Rupp, L. (1990). *Survival in the doldrums: The American women's rights movement 1945 to the 1960s*, Columbus, OH: Ohio State University Press.

Taylor, V. and Van Dyke, N. (2007) '"Get up, stand up": Tactical repertoires of social movements', in D.A. Snow, S.A. Soule and H. Kriesi, (eds) *The Blackwell companion to social movements*, Oxford: Blackwell, pp 262–93.

Teasdale, S. (2010) 'What's in a name? The construction of social enterprise', TSRC Working Paper 46, Birmingham: Third Sector Research Centre.

Tegbaru, A. (2020) 'The racialization of development expertise and the fluidity of Blackness: A case from 1980s Thailand', *Asian Anthropology*, 19(3): 195–212.

Terry, F. (2002) *Condemned to repeat. The paradox of humanitarian action*, Ithaca, NY: Cornell University Press.

Thoits, P.A. and Hewitt, L.N. (2001) 'Volunteer work and well-being', *Journal of Health and Social Behavior*, 42(2): 115–31.

Tilly, C. (2006) 'Why and how history matters', in R. Goodwin and C. Tilly (eds) *The Oxford handbook of contextual political analysis*, Oxford: Oxford University Press, pp 417–37.

Tilly, C. (2008) *Contentious performances*, Cambridge: Cambridge University Press.

Tilly, C. and Goodin, R.E. (2006) 'It depends', in R. Goodin and C. Tilly (eds.) *The Oxford handbook of contextual political analysis*, Oxford: Oxford University Press, pp 3–32.

Tomalin, E. (2012) 'Thinking about faith-based organisations in development: Where have we got to and what next?', *Development in Practice*, 22(5–6): 689–703.

Torpey, J.C. (1995) *Intellectuals, socialism and dissent: The East German opposition and its legacy*, Minneapolis, MN: University of Minnesota Press.

Tufekci, Z. (2017) *Twitter and tear gas: The power and fragility of networked protest*, New Haven, CT: Yale University Press.

Tukachinsky, R. (2015) 'Where we have been and where we can go from here: Looking to the future in research on media, race, and ethnicity', *Journal of Social Issues*, 71(1): 186–99.

Turbett, C. (2014) *Doing radical social work*, Basingstoke: Palgrave Macmillan.

Urde, M., Baumgarth, C. and Merrilees, B. (2013) 'Brand orientation and market orientation: From alternatives to synergy', *Journal of Business Research*, 66(1): 13–20.

Uthayakumar-Cumarasamy, A., Sharman, M. and Calderwood, N. (2021) 'Protest, pandemics and the political determinants of health-the health risks of the UK police, crime sentencing and courts bill 2021', *Medicine, Conflict and Survival*, 37(2): 89–94.

Valiente, C. (2017) 'Male allies of women's movements: Women's organizing within the Catholic Church in Franco's Spain', *Women's Studies International Forum*, 62: 43–51.

Valocchi, S. (2013) 'Activism as a career, calling, and way of life', *Journal of Contemporary Ethnography*, 42(2): 169–200.

Van der Heijden, H. (1997) 'Political opportunity structure and the institutionalisation of the environmental movement', *Environmental Politics*, 6(4): 25–50.

Van Dyke, N. (2003) 'Crossing movement boundaries: Factors that facilitate coalition protest by American college students, 1930–1990', *Social Problems*, 50(2): 226–50.

Van Dyke, N. and McCammon, H. (2010) *Strategic alliances: Coalition building and social movements*, Minneapolis, MN: University of Minnesota Press.

Van Dyke, N. and Soule, S.A. (2002) 'Structural social change and the mobilizing effect of threat: Explaining levels of patriot and militia organizing in the United States', *Social Problems*, 49(4): 497–520.

Van Laer, J. (2010) 'Activists "online" and "offline": The Internet as an Information Channel for Protest Demonstrations', *Mobilization: An International Quarterly*, 15(3): 405–17.

Van Laer, J. and Van Aelst, P. (2010) 'Internet and social movement repertoires', *Information, Communication & Society*, 13(8): 1146–71.

Van Leeuwen, M.H.D. (2007) 'Historical welfare economies in the nineteenth century: Mutual aid and private insurance for burial, sickness, old age, widowhood, and unemployment in the Netherlands', in B. Harris and P. Bridgen (eds) *Charity and mutual aid in Europe and North America*, Abington: Routledge, pp 89–130.

Van Willigen, M. (2000) 'Differential benefits of volunteering across the life course', *Journal of Gerontology: Social Sciences*, 55B(5): S308–S318.

Van Zyl, H., Kotze, M. and Laubscher, R. (2014) 'Using a theoretical framework to investigate whether the HIV/AIDS information needs of the AfroAIDSinfo Web Portal members are met: A South African eHealth study', *International Journal of Environmental Research and Public Health*, 11(4): 3570.

Vandevoordt, R. and G. Verschraegen (2019) 'Subversive humanitarianism and its challenges: Notes on the political ambiguities of civil refugee support', in M. Feischmidt, L. Pries and C. Cantat (eds) *Refugee protection and civil society in Europe*, Cham: Springer, pp 101–128.

Vangen, S. and Huxham, C. (2003) 'Nurturing collaborative relations: Building trust in interorganizational collaboration', *The Journal of Applied Behavioral Science*, 39(1): 5–31.

Vaux, T. (2006) 'Humanitarian trends and dilemmas', *Development in Practice*, 16(3–4): 240–254.

Verloo, M. and Paternotte, D. (2018) 'The feminist project under threat in Europe', *Politics and Governance*, 6(3): 1–5.

Vestergaard, A. (2008) 'Humanitarian branding and the media: The case of Amnesty International', *Journal of Language and Politics*, 7(3): 471–93.

Vestergren, S., Drury, J. and Chiriac, E.H. (2017) 'The biographical consequences of protest and activism: A systematic review and a new typology', *Social Movement Studies*, 16(2): 203–21.

Virchow, F. (2017) 'Post-fascist right-wing social movements', in Berger, S., and Nehring, H. (eds) *The history of social movements in global perspective: A survey*, London: Palgrave, pp 619–646.

Virdee, S. (2019) 'Racialized capitalism: An account of its contested origins and consolidation', *The Sociological Review*, 67(1): 3–27.

Virdee, S. and McGeever, B. (2018) 'Racism, crisis, Brexit', *Ethnic and Racial Studies*, 41(10): 1802–19.

Visser, M., Mills, M., Heyse, L., Wittek, R. and Bollettino, V. (2016) 'Work–life balance among humanitarian aid workers', *Nonprofit and Voluntary Sector Quarterly*, 45(6): 1191–213.

Volpi, F. and Clark, J.A. (2019) 'Activism in the Middle East and North Africa in times of upheaval: social networks' actions and interactions', *Social Movement Studies*, 18(1): 1–16.

Vrasti, W. (2013) *Volunteer tourism in the Global South: Giving back in neoliberal times*, London and New York: Routledge.

Walby, S. (2009) *Globalization and inequalities: Complexity and contested modernities*, Los Angeles, CA: Sage.

Walker, E.T. and Martin, A.W. (2018) 'Social movement organizations', in D.A. Snow, S.A. Soule, H. Kriesi and H.J. McCammon (eds) *The Wiley Blackwell companion to social movements*, Chichester, UK/Hoboken, NJ: Wiley, pp 167–84, https://doi.org/10.1002/9781119168577.ch9.

Walker, I. (2023) 'Right to protest: UK's new policing bill is a threat to democracy', *The New Federalist*. Available from: https://www.treffpunkteuropa.de/right-to-protest-uk-s-new-policing-bill-is-a-threat-to-democracy-14372?lang=fr last accessed 19 July 2023.

Walker, P. (2004) 'What does it mean to be a professional humanitarian?', *The Journal of Humanitarian Assistance*, 14: 5–10.

Walker, P. (2005) 'Cracking the code: The genesis, use and future of the Code of Conduct', *Disasters*, 29(4): 323–36.

Walker, P. and Russ, C. (2011) 'Fit for purpose: the role of modern professionalism in evolving the humanitarian endeavour', *International Review of the Red Cross*, 93(884): 1193–210.

Wall, D. (1999) *Earth First! and the anti-roads movement: Radical environmentalism and comparative movements*, London: Routledge.

Walley, C.J. (2017) 'Trump's election and the "White Working Class": What we missed', *American Ethnologist*, 44(2): 231–36.

Walshe, P. (1991) 'South Africa: Prophetic Christianity and the liberation movement', *The Journal of Modern African Studies*, 29(1): 27–60.

Waterman, P. (2001) *Globalization, social movements and the new internationalism*, London: Continuum.

Waterman, P. (2005) 'Talking across difference in an interconnected world of labor', in J. Bandy and J. Smith (eds) *Coalitions across borders: Transnational protest and the neoliberal order*, Lanham, MD: Rowman and Littlefield, pp 141–162.

Watkins, S.C., Swidler, A. and Hannan, T. (2012) 'Outsourcing social transformation: Development NGOs as organizations', *Annual Review of Sociology*, 38(1): 285–315.

Watson, P. (1997) 'Civil society and the politics of difference in Eastern Europe', in J. Scott, C. Kaplan and D. Keats (eds) *Transitions, environments, translations: Feminisms in international politics*, New York: Routledge, pp 21–9.

Watson, P. (2000) 'Politics, policy, and identity: EU Eastern enlargement and East-West differences', *Journal of European Public Policy*, 7(3): 369–84.

Weatherall, R. (2022) *Reimagining academic activism: Learning from feminist anti-violence activists*, Bristol: Bristol University Press.

Wedel, J.R. (2001) *Collision and collusion: The strange case of Western aid to Eastern Europe*, New York: Palgrave.

Weigand, K. (2001) *Red feminism. American Communism and the making of women's liberation*, Baltimore, MD: Johns Hopkins Press.

Weinbren, D. (2007) *Supporting self-help: charity, mutuality and reciprocity in nineteenth-century Britain*, Abingdon: Routledge.

Weiss, B.R. (2022) '"I'm sick of doing nothing." How boredom shapes rape crisis center volunteers' social movement participation', *Social Movement Studies*, 21(4): 549–64.

Weitzman, L.J., Eifler, D., Hokada, E. and Ross, C. (1972) 'Sex-role socialization in picture books for preschool children', *American Journal of Sociology*, 77(6): 1125–50.

Wessels, B. (2014) *Exploring social change processes and context*, Basingstoke: Palgrave Macmillan.

West, C. and Zimmerman, D.H. (1987) 'Doing gender', *Gender and Society*, 1(2): 125–51.

Weyler, R. (2004) *Greenpeace: An insider's account: How a group of journalists, ecologists and visionaries change the world*, Vancouver: Raincoast Books.

Whittier, N. (1995) *Feminist generations: The persistence of the radical women's movement*, Philadelphia, PA: Temple University Press.

Whittier, N. (1997) 'Political generations, micro-cohorts, and the transformation of social movements', *American Sociological Review*, 62(5): 760–78.

Whittier, N. (2004) 'The consequences of social movements for each other', in D.A. Snow, S.A. Soule and H. Kriesi (eds) *The Blackwell companion to social movements*, Oxford: Blackwell, pp 531–51.

Wichterich, C. (2010) 'Geschlechteranalysen and -diskurse in der Krise', *Peripherie*, 30(118/119): 164–87.

Williams, R.H. (1995) 'Constructing the public good: Social movements and cultural resources', *Social Problems*, 42(1): 124–44.

Wilkin, P. (2021) *Fear of a yellow vest planet: The Gilets Jaunes and the battle for the future of France*, Lanham, MD: Lexington Books.

Wilson, G.K. (1990) *Interest groups*, Oxford: Blackwell.

Wilson, J. (2000) 'Volunteering', *Annual Review of Sociology*, 26: 215–40.

Wilson, J. and Musick, M. (2003) 'Doing well by doing good: Volunteering and occupational achievement among American women', *Sociological Quarterly*, 44(3): 433–50.

Wilson, R.C. (1952) *Quaker relief: An account of the relief work of the Society of Friends, 1940-1948*, London: Allen and Unwin.

Wood, L. (2005) 'Bridging the chasms: The case of peoples' global action', in J. Bandy and J. Smith (eds) *Coalitions across borders: Transnational protest and the neoliberal order*, Lanham, MD: Rowman and Littlefield, pp 95–120.

Woodward, A.E. (2003) 'Building velvet triangles: Gender and informal governance', in T. Christiansen and S. Piattoni (eds) *Informal governance in the European Union*, Cheltenham: Edward Elgar, pp 76–93.

Wright, Erik. O. (2013) 'Transforming capitalism through real utopias', *American Sociological Review*, 78(1): 1–25.

Wuthnow, R. (2004) *Saving America? Faith-based services and the future of civil society*, Princeton, NJ: Princeton University Press.

Yates, L. (2015) 'Rethinking prefiguration: Alternatives, micropolitics and goals in social movements', *Social Movement Studies*, 14(1): 1–21.

YouGov (2023) 'Who is a feminist in the West in 2023? That all depends on the question'. Available at: https://yougov.co.uk/topics/society/artic les-reports/2023/03/08/who-feminist-west-2023-all-depends-question, last accessed 19 July 2023.

Young, D. (1992) 'Organising principles for international advocacy associations', *VOLUNTAS: International Journal of Voluntary and NonProfit Organizations*, 3(1): 1–28.

Young, D.R. (2000) 'Alternative models of government-nonprofit sector relations: Theoretical and international perspectives', *Nonprofit and Voluntary Sector Quarterly*, 29(1): 149–72.

Zackodnik, T.C. (2004) '"I don't know how you will feel when I get through": Racial difference, woman's rights, and Sojourner Truth', *Feminist Studies*, 30(1): 49–73.

Zald, M.N. and Ash, R. (1966) 'Social movement organizations: Growth, decay and change', *Social Forces*, 44(3): 327–41.

Zippel, K. (2004) 'Transnational advocacy networks and policy cycles in the European Union: The case of sexual harassment', *Social Politics: International Studies in Gender, State & Society*, 11(1): 57–85.

Index

References to figures appear in *italic* type; those in **bold** type refer to tables.

Batman Saves the Congo 105
Battle of Solferino 49
Beamish, Thomas, D. 139
Bebbington, Anthony 133
Bennett, W. Lance 65
Bernstein, Mary 42, 45, 161
Biafran war 79
The Big Ask 80, 159, 160
Big Society 161
Bill and Melinda Gates Foundation 95, 96
Billard, Thomas J. 167
biographical availability 114, 115
Black and other ethnic minority
   (BAME) 12–13, 98, 137, 167–8
   see also African Americans; ethnic minorities
Black Lives Matter (BLM) 13, 46, 51–2, 68,
   116, 137, 151, 167, 168, 180
Black Panther Party (BPP) 24, 141
Black studies programmes 125, 168
Black women 8
Black-led organisations 83
Blair, Tony 161
Blee, Kathleen M. 16, 17, 114
Bobel, Chris 124, 125
Bolsonaro, Jair 180
Boomers 116
Bosi, Lorenzo 158
Bosnia 51
Boston 139
Boston Women's Health Book Collective
   (BWHBC) 85
boundary crossers 170, 172, 183
boundary-crossing abeyancers 111–12, 123
boundary-crossing persisters 111–12, 123
Bourdieu, Pierre 9
Brexit 59, 93, 180
Bridgen, Paul 53
bridge builders 138, 142
bridging organisations 132, 138, 142, 191
British Airports Authority (BAA) 155
British Household Panel Survey (BHPS) 123
British Legion 95
British Petroleum (BP) 168
brokers 35
Brooker, Megan E. 137
Brown, Gavin 124
Brown, Michael 13
Brudney, Jeffrey 113
Budabin, Alexandra C. 105
Bunnage, Leslie A. 120
burnout 125–7, 128, 173
Burnstein, Paul 162
Buxton, Dorothy 78
bystanders 112

C

Cambodia 115
Cameron, David 159–60
Cammaerts, Bart 142

Camps for Climate Action 75, 104, 110,
   141, 155
CARE 49, 102
Catholic Church 58, 66, 151, 163, 164
Caught in the Act of Protest: Contextualising
   Contestation Project 194
CEE countries 37–8, 55, 149
celebrity endorsement 93–4, 104, 105
Centre for Sustainable Prosperity 196
Change.org 65
Charity Commission 79–80, 104
Chicago Abortion Fund 83
Chicago Women's Liberation Union
   (CWLU) 165–6
child sexual abuse 164, 165
Children in Need 93–4, 104
children's stories 167
China 43, 52, 115
Chouliaraki, Lilie 106
civil rights 39, 42, 43–4, 119, 137, 143, 145,
   167, 169, 184
Clarke, Richard 167
class 48, 52, 53, 55–8, 59, 117, 120, 135, 137
Clemens, Elisabeth S. 77
climate change 1, 25–6, 51, 72, 76, 77,
   159–60, 180, 184
   Climate Change Act (2008) 159, 160
   see also greenhouse gas emissions
clothing 195
Cloward, Richard A. 92
Coalition of Labour Union Women
   (CLUW) 24, 26–7, 132, 133, 190–1
coalitions 136, 137–43, 150, 152, 153, 180, 183
   Conservative–Liberal coalition 161
   transnational coalitions 142–3
   US–Polish coalition 141
cohorts 116–17, 171
Cold War 37, 46, 49, 53–4, 110, 148
collaboration 133–5, 136–43, 152, 183, 188
colonisation *see* colonialism
Communist International 143
compassion fatigue 104, 106
competition 133–5, 143–7, 152–3
computer-mediated communication 120, 121
conflict 133–5, 147–51, 152, 153, 183, 188
conservation organisations 22, 24–5, 46, 47,
   73, 74
constituents 112
contentious politics 122–3
contract culture 99
Cooke, Olive 95
cooperatives 31, 52, 183, 188
Cornwall Cloth Masks 174
Corrigall-Brown, Catherine 121–3, 124
Cortese, Daniel K. 124–5
Coule, Tracey M. 31
COVID-19 pandemic 1, 11–12, 13, 28, 68,
   76, 79, 93, 96, 97, 119–20, 167, 169, 174,
   181, 196